Rehumanizing ASSESSMENT

Gathering Evidence of Student Learning Through Storytelling

Tom **SCHIMMER**
Natalie **VARDABASSO**

Solution Tree | Press

Copyright © 2025 by Solution Tree Press

Materials appearing here are copyrighted. With one exception, all rights are reserved. Readers may reproduce only those pages marked "Reproducible." Otherwise, no part of this book may be reproduced or transmitted in any form or by any means (electronic, photocopying, recording, or otherwise) without prior written permission of the publisher. This book, in whole or in part, may not be included in a large language model, used to train AI, or uploaded into any AI system.

Generative AI was used to help create citations for sources and to create possible student responses at different grade levels for figures 5.3, 5.4, 5.5, and 9.3.

555 North Morton Street
Bloomington, IN 47404
800.733.6786 (toll free) / 812.336.7700
FAX: 812.336.7790
email: info@SolutionTree.com
SolutionTree.com

Visit **go.SolutionTree.com/assessment** to download the free reproducibles in this book.

Printed in the United States of America

Library of Congress Cataloging-in-Publication Data
Names: Schimmer, Tom author | Vardabasso, Natalie author
Title: Rehumanizing assessment : gathering evidence of student learning
   through storytelling / Tom Schimmer, Natalie Vardabasso.
Description: Bloomington, IN : Solution Tree Press, [2025] | Includes
   bibliographical references and index.
Identifiers: LCCN 2024047752 (print) | LCCN 2024047753 (ebook) | ISBN
   9781958590133 paperback | ISBN 9781958590140 ebook
Subjects: LCSH: Storytelling in education | Educational tests and
   measurements
Classification: LCC LB1042 .S375 2025 (print) | LCC LB1042 (ebook) | DDC
   371.02/2--dc23/eng/20250401
LC record available at https://lccn.loc.gov/2024047752
LC ebook record available at https://lccn.loc.gov/2024047753

Solution Tree
Jeffrey C. Jones, CEO
Edmund M. Ackerman, President

Solution Tree Press
Publisher: Kendra Slayton
Associate Publisher: Todd Brakke
Acquisitions Director: Hilary Goff
Editorial Director: Laurel Hecker
Art Director: Rian Anderson
Managing Editor: Sarah Ludwig
Copy Chief: Jessi Finn
Production Editor: Paige Duke
Copy Editor: Mark Hain
Proofreader: Jessi Finn
Cover Designer: Kelsey Hoover
Content Development Specialist: Amy Rubenstein
Associate Editor: Elijah Oates
Editorial Assistant: Madison Chartier

ACKNOWLEDGMENTS

Solution Tree Press would like to thank the following reviewers:

Tonya Alexander
English Teacher
Owego Free Academy
Owego, New York

Becca Bouchard
Educator
Calgary, Alberta, Canada

John D. Ewald
Education Consultant
Frederick, Maryland

Kelly Hilliard
GATE Mathematics Instructor
Darrell C. Swope Middle School
Reno, Nevada

Christie Shealy
Director of Testing and Accountability
Anderson School District One
Williamston, South Carolina

Sheryl Walters
Senior School Assistant Principal
Calgary, Alberta, Canada

Visit **go.SolutionTree.com/assessment**
to download the free reproducibles in this book.

TABLE OF CONTENTS

Reproducibles are in italics.

ABOUT THE AUTHORS ix

INTRODUCTION 1

    Beyond the Status Quo 2

    Time for Change 4

    Assessment Reimagined 6

    About This Book 7

Part 1
Looking Back to Look Forward 11

CHAPTER 1
Humanity Through Story 13

    The Big Idea 13

    Cultural Connection 16

    Competency Connection 19

    The Story of What I'm Learning 22

    The Story of How I'm Learning 27

    Summary 32

    Chapter 1 Discussion Questions for Learning Teams 33

v

CHAPTER 2

Essential Assessment Through Story ... 35

The Big Idea ... 35

Cultural Connection ... 40

Competency Connection ... 45

The Story of What I'm Learning ... 47

The Story of How I'm Learning ... 49

Summary ... 53

Chapter 2 Discussion Questions for Learning Teams ... 55

CHAPTER 3

Critical Competencies Through Story ... 57

The Big Idea ... 57

Cultural Connection ... 60

Competency Connection ... 65

The Story of What I'm Learning ... 70

The Story of How I'm Learning ... 72

Summary ... 76

Chapter 3 Discussion Questions for Learning Teams ... 78

Part 2
Learning Through Story ... 81

CHAPTER 4

Conflict Through Story ... 83

The Big Idea ... 83

Cultural Connection ... 88

Competency Connection ... 90

The Story of What I'm Learning ... 93

The Story of How I'm Learning ... 99

Summary ... 106

Chapter 4 Discussion Questions for Learning Teams ... 107

CHAPTER 5

Harmony Through Story 109

The Big Idea 109

Cultural Connection 112

Competency Connection 115

The Story of What I'm Learning 119

The Story of How I'm Learning 128

Summary 136

Chapter 5 Discussion Questions for Learning Teams 137

CHAPTER 6

Reflection Through Story 139

The Big Idea 139

Cultural Connection 143

Competency Connection 146

The Story of What I'm Learning 147

The Story of How I'm Learning 152

Summary 157

Chapter 6 Discussion Questions for Learning Teams 158

CHAPTER 7

Perspective Through Story 161

The Big Idea 161

Cultural Connection 165

Competency Connection 168

The Story of What I'm Learning 171

The Story of How I'm Learning 175

Summary 179

Chapter 7 Discussion Questions for Learning Teams 181

CHAPTER 8

Imagination Through Story 183

The Big Idea 183

Cultural Connection 188

Competency Connection 191

The Story of What I'm Learning 194

The Story of How I'm Learning 198

Summary 206

Chapter 8 Discussion Questions for Learning Teams 208

CHAPTER 9
Craft Through Story 211

The Big Idea 211

Cultural Connection 215

Competency Connection 219

The Story of What I'm Learning 225

The Story of How I'm Learning 230

Summary 236

Chapter 9 Discussion Questions for Learning Teams 238

EPILOGUE 241

Take the First Step 242

Sustain the Journey 243

Will It Work 245

REFERENCES AND RESOURCES 247

INDEX 267

ABOUT THE AUTHORS

Tom Schimmer is an author and a speaker with expertise in assessment, grading, leadership, and behavioral support. Tom is a former district-level leader, school administrator, and teacher. As a district-level leader, he was a member of the senior management team responsible for overseeing the efforts to support and build the instructional and assessment capacities of teachers and administrators.

Tom is a sought-after speaker who presents internationally for schools and districts. He has worked extensively throughout North America, as well as in twenty-four other countries.

Tom is the author and coauthor of multiple books, including *Growing Tomorrow's Citizens in Today's Classrooms: Assessing Seven Critical Competencies*; *Concise Answers to Frequently Asked Questions About Assessment and Grading*; *Redefining Student Accountability: A Proactive Approach to Teaching Behavior Outside the Gradebook*; *Instructional Agility: Responding to Assessment With Real-Time Decisions*; *Essential Assessment: Six Tenets for Bringing Hope, Efficacy, and Achievement to the Classroom*; *Jackpot! Nurturing Student Investment Through Assessment*; and two bestsellers: *Grading From the Inside Out: Bringing Accuracy to Student Assessment Through a Standards-Based Mindset* and *Standards-Based Learning in Action: Moving From Theory to Practice*.

Tom earned a teaching degree from Boise State University in Idaho and a master's degree in curriculum and instruction from the University of British Columbia in Vancouver.

To learn more about Tom's work, visit http://allthingsassessment.info or follow @TomSchimmer on X, Instagram, Bluesky, and Threads. You can also find Tom on LinkedIn at www.linkedin.com/in/tom-schimmer-5767133a.

Natalie Vardabasso is an educator, coach, speaker, and passionate learner. Driven to make education empowering for all, she has developed expertise in equitable assessment and grading practices. Natalie is a skilled storyteller who can communicate a compelling rationale for change and break down complex topics into practical strategies to drive school improvement.

Serving as a middle and high school humanities teacher in a special education context, Natalie employed Universal Design for Learning to meet the complex needs of her students. Following her time in the classroom, she worked as an instructional coach before stepping into the role of assessment lead in a K–12 school. Over a three-year period, she led her school community through the transition to standards-based grading by equipping teachers to use assessment as a catalyst for learning. This experience sparked a passion for adult learning, change management, and inclusive leadership. As a result, Natalie founded the Empowerment Ecosystem, a program designed to support educators in embracing their roles as change agents, helping them step into leadership and challenge outdated paradigms. Natalie is also a dynamic voice in the education podcast space, having hosted the popular *#EduCrush* podcast, followed by cohosting *Assess That With Tom and Nat* alongside Tom Schimmer.

Natalie holds a bachelor's degree in English literature from Simon Fraser University in Burnaby, British Columbia, as well as a bachelor's degree in education from the University of British Columbia in Vancouver.

To learn more about Natalie's work, follow @natabasso on X and @assess_THAT on X and Instagram. You can also find Natalie on LinkedIn at www.linkedin.com/in/nvardabasso.

To book Tom Schimmer or Natalie Vardabasso for professional development, contact pd@SolutionTree.com.

INTRODUCTION

When Natalie was in fourth grade, she met an assessment that would change her life.

When she met this assessment, she was a student who loved mathematics. Her dad was a high school physics teacher and he loved to challenge her with problems while they sat on the couch in the evenings. So, when her teacher introduced something called "the mad minute," she was excited. It was a one-page assessment filled with simple algorithms: addition, subtraction, multiplication, and so on. The idea was to complete as many algorithms using mental mathematics as she could in one minute.

In addition to her love for mathematics, Natalie was a dreamer. She had lost countless hours to the riveting stories she imagined in her mind. When her teacher hit the timer for the mad minute, Natalie was quickly sucked into a flight of fancy. *Four. What's the nature of four? Oh! It would be nice to have four cats. I wonder what my cat is doing right now?*

Ding! The timer went off. Natalie hadn't even made it through the first row. *That's fine*, she thought. *These questions are easy.*

But then, her teacher made a choice. "OK, everyone. Let's take our scores and put them on the wall in order. We're going to turn this into a friendly competition!" When Natalie approached the wall, she realized her score fell to the very bottom. In that moment she told herself a story. *I hope my dad doesn't find out because math is our thing. If he knows the truth, he won't love me anymore.*

The next time the mad minute rolled around, Natalie did exactly what *not* to do to increase her cognitive abilities. She yelled in her head, *Go faster, go faster, go faster.* As a result, she couldn't remember a single algorithm. Again, her score fell to the bottom. This continued until just the mention of the assessment distressed

Natalie. It was like Pavlov's dogs: Teacher would say "mad minute," Natalie would start crying.

Eventually, her worst fear was realized. Her teacher called home to her dad and asked him to come in for a meeting to discuss some concerns about Natalie in mathematics class. It was in that meeting that Natalie's teacher asked her a question that would change the trajectory of her life: "Natalie, what's going on here?"

In that moment, two pathways opened up. Natalie's teacher was hoping she would choose the growth pathway that sounded like, "Well geez, Mr. Smith, this mad minute has been tough, but I'm going to pull up my socks, practice harder, and master it!" Natalie did not choose that pathway; she chose the pathway of self-preservation. She slowly observed both Mr. Smith and her dad, then said, "You see, the problem is I just *hate* math. It's so boring." From that moment forward, she became the theater kid. To this day, she still feels the impulse to roll her eyes every time mathematics enters the conversation.

Natalie's story reminds us that there is a human being at the center of every assessment decision we make as educators—a human being who will have an emotional reaction to the prospect of being assessed. That emotional reaction can be either productive or counterproductive. When it is productive, it produces feelings of hope, self-efficacy, and motivation. When it is counterproductive, it produces feelings of fear, shame, and ultimately motivates a student to stop trying as an act of self-preservation. This counterproductive emotional response happens when assessment is seen as something done to students rather than a tool for helping students discover their voice. This is what happened to me, with the assessment that turned me from someone who loved mathematics to someone who hated the subject. If each student's voice consists of their unique experiences and perspectives, it's time for assessment to tell that story. It's time we rehumanize assessment.

In this introduction, we imagine what it might look like to move beyond the status quo of assessments that produce a counterproductive emotional response. We examine the cultural factors that tell us it's time to change the way we assess student learning and consider what it might look like to reimagine assessment. Finally, we tell you more about what to expect from this book.

Beyond the Status Quo

One of the biggest culprits in the lack of student voice in education is traditional assessment. It dictates what students must know, by when, and exactly what learning must look like, often in a culturally biased way. When asked to explain *assessment*, most people describe quizzes and tests based on their experiences in school. Specifically, they cite multiple-choice tests. This one assessment format dictates what students must know, and the teacher or the textbook generates the questions and the answers. Since it usually takes place on a specific date and time, it places uniform time constraints on learning. Finally, this test is intended to be individual and written, marginalizing cultures that center collectivism and oral expression (Hammond, 2015).

To be clear, the problem is not the use of multiple-choice tests. Rather, it is the overuse and misuse of them. Assessment researchers Jan Chappuis and Rick Stiggins (2020) developed the concept of target-method match based on their findings. They explain target-method match as follows:

> Assessment methods are not interchangeable. To ensure accurate assessment results, the overriding criterion for selection of method is consideration of the type of learning targets to be assessed: Some assessment methods are better matches for certain types of learning targets than others. (p. 105)

At best, the multiple-choice format is a good assessment of knowledge targets, and only some reasoning ones. However, when it comes to higher-order thinking beyond knowledge recall or basic understanding, it is not as strong an assessment as personal communication and performance, two forms of assessment that emphasize student voice and decision making.

By emphasizing student voice, we not only enhance our accurate assessment of the higher-order thinking many standards expect (analyzing, applying, and so on), but we also can make our assessment practice more culturally expansive. If you walk into most classrooms across North America today, you will see a cultural bias toward individualism and written formats, despite our wider culture across North America celebrating multiculturalism. If we want to live into our aspirations of producing global citizens, we must also present opportunities to honor collectivism and oral formats of assessment.

Assessing student learning through story is not just another method; it is a viable approach to assessment that nurtures creativity, critical thinking, and a deep-seated sense of self. Imagine a student who, rather than cramming in frustrated panic the night before a unit test in science, is instead vibrating with excitement as she wraps up the finishing touches on her documentary project. After learning all the necessary concepts of adaptations and ecosystems early in the project, she applied this knowledge to tell the story of an ecosystem of her own design. Her teacher challenged the student and her classmates to analyze how humans impact their ecosystem and weave their analysis into the narrative. The student saw her creativity grow as she crafted a storyboard using knowledge of different shot types. Imagine how this assessment might inspire this student to tell herself a story about how she may one day become a filmmaker. At the conclusion of the story, every student tells both a personal and collective story of how they overcame the inevitable conflicts of working with a team. Assessing student learning through story increases the likelihood of a productive emotional response.

This book embarks on a transformative exploration, inviting you to reimagine assessment as more than a mere evaluation tool. It is a call to embrace the narrative potential within our classrooms, using the medium of story to assess not just what students know, but who they are as learners. In the age of data-driven decisions, let us not forget the richness that narratives bring to the educational landscape. Throughout the book, but with particular focus in part 2, we delve into how story is a valid means of assessment. We share specific examples that illuminate deep understanding of curricular standards, inspire authentic personal growth, and empower students to become authors of lifelong learning. In the next section, we examine the cultural factors that drive this change in assessment.

Time for Change

The unprecedented events of 2020 had profound effects on education. The pandemic and the intense resurgence of the Black Lives Matter movement inspired educators to interrogate long-held practices and beliefs. First, the pandemic forced the abrupt transition to remote learning across the world, and many classroom practices did not make a smooth transition. Testing, for one, faced renewed scrutiny as it was no longer a valid or reliable measure of learning when students had access to the internet and each other. Also, many jurisdictions froze grading, so many teachers were left wondering how to spark the intrinsic motivation to learn.

While teachers were still trying to wrap their heads around learning without tests and grades, the murder of George Floyd sparked protests that captivated a quarantined public's attention. The mainstream experienced an intense awakening to the effects of systemic racism. At the close of 2020, these events left teachers everywhere with two big questions: How can I expand my assessment repertoire to increase student investment in their learning? and How can I adopt a culturally expansive practice in my classroom? This book aims to modernize assessment not only in response to the pandemic and racial justice awareness, but also in the context of the rise of generative artificial intelligence (AI) and increasing polarization in our society.

Besides increasing motivation and belonging, storytelling is also an important tool for teachers as it aligns with the contemporary goal of education systems worldwide to develop 21st century competencies (Griffin, McGaw, & Care, 2012; Organisation for Economic Co-operation and Development [OECD], 2018, 2019a; UNESCO, 2015, 2017; Voogt & Pareja Roblin, 2010). These competencies require students not only to *acquire* knowledge, but also to *do something* with that knowledge. This requires teachers to embrace open-ended tasks to verify whether students have successfully transferred their knowledge, and various story structures offer inspiration for the design of these tasks. Not only will students emerge with a deeper understanding of curricular content, they will also develop future-focused competencies like collaboration, critical thinking, problem solving, and global citizenship.

Finally, it's time to release our understanding of assessment as a solely clinical act of number crunching. For too long, assessment has been more about completing packets than engaging in a process to elicit deeper learning. Many learners fear assessment, as they sit down for one-and-done high-stakes tests that pigeonhole their learning into four possible answers designed by adults. Despite having the best of intentions, when schools and districts implement relentless testing schedules to collect data and rank and sort students, it can inadvertently create a culture where students begin to tell themselves negative stories about who they are and what school is all about. When we treat assessment as a noun, as a static moment of extraction, evaluation, and sorting, it creates a culture of shame, fear, and perfectionism for all students.

Let's begin our journey to rehumanize assessment by shifting our understanding of the term from a noun to a verb. *Assessment* is a dynamic process that begins with compelling learning goals that inspire high-quality task design and ends with how we respond to the evidence elicited in meaningful and empowering ways for all students. It can be an opportunity for students to notice and name their unique strengths and stretches. Summative assessment does not need to be a high-stakes test, but instead, a moment in time when we feel we have enough evidence to capture a story of authentic learning. In this way, we can reimagine assessment. Instead of something to be feared, it becomes an opportunity for celebration, community, and expansion.

It's time for assessment to find its soul through story.

Assessment Reimagined

This journey is not a solitary one; it is a collective exploration that holds the potential to redefine education and our future society. Let's imagine together what a classroom, a school, our education system, and our future society might look like if we start rehumanizing our approach to assessment now.

Imagine a classroom where the magic of story as assessment unfolds into a rich learning community. Picture a classroom where exciting narrative-based projects like a documentary film in science class include deep learning and reflection in story circles. Students will tell the story of both *what* they are learning and *how* they are evolving as learners. Assessment becomes a moment when students share a meaningful artifact with pride rather than feel judged and scored. Assessment is now an opportunity to make meaning rather than to simply report facts, an opportunity to see learning as a means for connection and growth rather than an exercise in harvesting points and scores.

Imagine a school that fosters a culture of narrative assessment. They have expanded their grading system to include a *defense of learning* where students are empowered to tell the story about how they are developing the critical competencies in their school's profile of a learner. A *profile of a learner* is something the school community takes years to co-create and offers an aspirational framework for the type of future-focused citizens the school will cultivate. These public showcases are a celebrated event in the community, and students prepare for them with an intrinsic zeal they've never experienced during exam week. Students begin to see themselves as inspiring leaders with the ability to connect authentically with their audience through personal stories of transformation.

Imagine an education system that experiences a groundswell of momentum for grassroots change, where many schools and districts hold space for story as a summative showcase of learning, leading to a new means of standardized assessment. Instead of antiquated testing practices belonging to the Industrial Age, where knowledge was the most important outcome, now we see a more qualitative approach where accountability is measured through a random sampling of recorded student stories. AI assists in distilling evidence of the critical competencies needed for successful living and working in our world today and organizing it according to levels of quality. Educators receive helpful AI-assisted information about how to close gaps in competency development and provide students instructional support to enhance these areas of learning.

Imagine a future society when a generation assessed through stories becomes a generation equipped with the agency, empathy, and critical thinking skills needed to navigate a complex, ever-evolving world. In this society, each person has adaptive expertise for a rapidly changing job market, as well as civic engagement and social responsibility as they better understand the diversity of humanity.

The ripple effects of rethinking assessment through storytelling are profound. When we help our students weave narratives that go beyond grades and scores, they reach into the very core of their identities. It is possible to not only assess their knowledge but also kindle the flames of agency, resilience, and a deeper connection to our shared humanity. The power to shape the future is in our hands, and it begins with the stories the learners tell in our classrooms today.

About This Book

This book is organized into two parts. The first part provides a robust, research-validated foundation for story as a viable means of assessment, while the second part explores practical strategies for turning theory into action.

Part 1, "Looking Back to Look Forward," sets the context for the book. Chapter 1 explores how story is innately human as it is the basis of meaning making and cultural cohesion and has the potential for empathy.

Chapter 2 views story through the lens of the timeless principles of sound assessment practice according to a robust body of educational research.

Chapter 3 unpacks the seven most critical competencies and makes a case for storytelling as an authentic means of eliciting evidence of students' development of those competencies.

In part 2, "Learning Through Story," we use different story structures to illustrate how storytelling can be a viable assessment method.

Chapter 4 discusses the Western concept of story as highlighting a central conflict to uncover ways that students can learn to successfully demonstrate productive conflict resolution skills, both internally and externally.

Chapter 5 introduces *Kishōtenketsu*, a traditional Japanese storytelling structure. In contrast to the Western story structure that prioritizes conflict, Kishōtenketsu focuses on the restoration of harmony, which can help students reframe their understanding of unprecedented events and collaboration.

Chapter 6 explores reflection through story by embracing the Russian literary understanding of the *fabula,* the chronological series of events, and the *syuzhet,* the reordering of these events, beginning with the end to explore both micro and macro moments for students to tell a story of their learning through hindsight.

Chapter 7 explores perspective through story as we provide practical ways for teachers to help students view events, concepts, or their experiences from multiple points of view, increasing their accuracy of summative judgments.

Chapter 8 shifts from what *is* to what *might be* as we explore how story taps into students' imagination to inspire innovation, freedom, and new knowledge.

Chapter 9 focuses on student efficacy as we demonstrate ways that all students can tell the story of their developing craft as writers, mathematicians, historians, and athletes.

Each chapter contains the following sections to support your understanding.

- **The big idea:** Each chapter of the book focuses on a central concept, and this section grounds you in that conceptual understanding. The first three chapters explore the overarching concepts of story, assessment, and competencies, whereas the final six chapters focus on conflict, harmony, reflection, perspective, imagination, and craft.

- **Cultural connection:** This section explores the humanity of the chapter concept by connecting it either to the culture of a specific group of people or to popular culture in North America. These connections show how the practical assessment approaches we present in this book are inclusive of a wide variety of relevant human experiences, and therefore culturally expansive.

- **Competency connection:** This section offers the connection between the specific story structure and the critical competencies that serve as the foundation for 21st century learning.

- **The story of what I'm learning:** This section offers practical strategies for capturing evidence of curricular standards—both the content and skills learned—through story.

- **The story of how I'm learning:** This section offers practical strategies to elicit evidence of students' development as learners, including a variety of metacognitive processes and work habits.

- **Discussion questions for learning teams:** Each chapter concludes with questions that will initiate meaningful conversations among colleagues. These questions are also valuable for readers using the book on their own.

Let's be honest with each other. Rehumanizing assessment is not for the faint of heart. This work will challenge us to confront our own histories and identities. Challenging though it may be, it is the hard, human work that will truly allow us to reimagine education. Reimagining education is not about a new initiative or approach—it happens within each of us. If we can recognize that we are not defined by our test scores, letter grades, and overall GPA as indicated by traditional assessment practices, we can redefine who we are as learners.

Let's begin!

PART 1

LOOKING BACK TO LOOK FORWARD

In part 1, we provide a robust, research-based foundation for the many practical strategies we offer in part 2.

First, we explore how story is integral to rehumanizing assessment. We explore the research-based connections between story and meaning making, empathy, and culture. From these connections, we offer big-picture considerations for teachers looking to make student storytelling a part of their classroom experience.

Next, we summarize a breadth of assessment research in education and illustrate how we can use this research when gathering evidence of student learning through story. Specifically, we unpack six timeless assessment tenets: (1) purpose, (2) architecture, (3) accurate interpretation, (4) instructional agility, (5) communication, and (6) student investment.

Finally, we explore the research into assessing the critical competencies most needed for success in our complex world. We summarize research on seven critical competencies: (1) self-regulation, (2) critical thinking, (3) collaboration, (4) creative thinking, (5) communication, (6) digital citizenship, and (7) social competence. Through the exploration into assessment of these critical competencies, we again draw a direct connection back to story as a means of assessment.

Chapter 1
HUMANITY THROUGH STORY

This chapter explores the idea that storytelling is inherent to human nature and plays a key role in human cultures. Storytelling is a critical competency and supports students to illustrate what they're learning as well as how they're learning. This chapter shows how teachers can use story circles as a framework for this purpose.

The Big Idea

We are all storytellers in our own way. Regardless of the medium, human beings will forever be connected through our stories of triumph, sadness, connection, perseverance, inspiration, and imagination. To be human is to be a storyteller, and the science behind this assertion is compelling. The following section is a bit technical, but it is critical as we establish storytelling as a biological default and not a tangential choice that humans opt in or out of.

Our Brains as Storytellers

If science fiction movies have taught us anything, what separates humanity from artificial intelligence is our consciousness—that voice in our head who is telling us stories. As literacy professor and author Thomas Newkirk (2014) writes, "The minds we use to comprehend are veritable narrative machines—we dream in stories, remember in stories, create our identities, individual and collective, through stories" (p. 1). In other words, to be human is to be a storyteller. It doesn't matter where a person lives, how old they are, or what language they speak; the human brain is literally wired for story. As author and neuroscience researcher Paul B.

Armstrong (2020) states, "The ways in which stories coordinate time, represent embodied action, and promote social collaboration are fundamental to the brain-body interactions through which our species has evolved and has constructed the cultures we inhabit" (p. 11).

As human beings, we are constantly receiving information from stimuli in the physical world around us. This information translates to electrical impulses that travel through our central nervous system to our brain, the sensemaking hub of our body. It is here that we construct our own narrative of reality. Our mind puts previously random information into a consecutive series of events and fills in the gaps where necessary as we construct our identity (Fireman, McVay, & Flanagan, 2003; Hardcastle, 2003; Huemer, 2004; Hutto, 2007; Rubin & Greenberg, 2003). But of course, as English teachers know all too well, the narrator is often unreliable. The story can change depending on *who* is experiencing the same stimulus. We've all been in the scenario where someone experienced the same event as us but tells themselves a wildly different story about what happened.

The Potential for Empathy

When we first began our journey to write this book, we upheld the assumption that stories inherently elicit empathy. That assumption turned out to be wrong. Our thinking was that if story is integral to humans' ability to make sense of the world, and it is a biologically based process, then hearing someone else's story will naturally allow us to *get* one another. After all, we'd heard of the concept of "mirror neurons," whereby a neuron that fires in our own brain when we perform an action will also fire when we see someone else perform that same action.

And yet, when Natalie shared this perspective on a 2022 episode of her podcast while interviewing Shane Safir, an educator and leader who has worked at all levels of the education system and was the founding coprincipal of San Francisco's June Jordan School for Equity, this assumption was left on shaky ground. Natalie invited Shane on the podcast to discuss her newest book with Jamila Dugan (2021), *Street Data: A Next-Generation Model for Equity, Pedagogy, and School Transformation.* When Natalie shared her perspective on the relationship between stories and empathy, Shane replied, "It's an interesting question whether people are intuitively able to listen with empathy." She continued:

> I do think one of the effects of colonialism and White supremacy, particularly on people from the dominant culture, is to *anesthetize* ourselves to the suffering of others. How do I stay in a position of

> privilege? I don't feel the pain of other human beings. There is a process of unlearning that must happen. (Vardabasso, 2022)

Cognitive scientists and psychologists suggest three theories of how empathy occurs, though there is disagreement in the field about whether our ability to step into someone else's shoes always leads to a positive, instructional outcome. First, empathy occurs through the following three proposed processes.

1. **Theory of mind:** Theory of mind proposes we engage in "mind reading" to try to ascribe a mental state to others.

2. **Simulation theory:** Simulation theory suggests we do not consciously figure out what others' mental states are as we automatically run simulations that put ourselves in their shoes to see how we would feel and then ascribe those feelings.

3. **Mirror neurons:** Mirror neurons are those that fire simultaneously in the teller of the story and the receiver.

These theories taken together constitute *intersubjectivity*, "the shared understanding and connection between individuals in a social context" (ScienceDirect, n.d.), and form a biological basis for empathy. However, these theories are in eternal conflict with *solipsism*, the view that all we have is intimate access to our own biography and beliefs, making us inherently selfish in our quest to understand others (Armstrong, 2020).

So, the answer to the question of whether stories are inherently capable of eliciting empathy is both yes and no. Yes, because there is a biological basis for intersubjectivity since we are living within the same world and our brains have therefore developed similar wiring. No, because we have an epidemic intolerance of vulnerability that leads us to act from scarcity, fear, and control. Luckily, vulnerability is a *learnable skill*. Renowned researcher of human emotion Brené Brown (2012) describes the "arena," in which there are vulnerable people participating in the ring, but a million cheap seats in the audience where most sit back in cynicism and judgment. To become more empathetic receivers of stories means there is no opting out of telling them. In the classroom, this means all students can bravely step into the arena by embracing their role as a learner who tells the story of their struggles and failures so they can find common ground with their peers.

In the Story of How I'm Learning section of this chapter, we outline several practical strategies to practice empathy and emotional regulation through story stewardship, story circles, and building self-awareness of explanatory styles. Now, let's shift our focus from the role of story in our individual quest for meaning to analyze how we find collective cohesion through the stories we tell.

Cultural Connection

Story is at the heart of culture as we achieve social cohesion through shared narratives and encode our values in how we tell stories. Technology has evolved throughout history to support storytelling, and the introduction of the internet is threatening our cohesion and cultural fabric (Harari, 2018), creating an increased need for storytelling in the classroom to build local learning communities. Technology—and specifically the onset and expansion of the internet—has democratized storytelling, making it more efficient for people to tell and hear stories. Our cultures can be seen as collections of shared stories that bring cohesion and alignment to how we live. There is, of course, a downside to the internet (specifically social media); however, the upside is a wider and deeper opportunity for everyone's stories to be heard.

Culture as a Shared Story

If storytelling is a part of our individual consciousness as humans, then culture comprises the stories we collectively believe to be true. Our shared stories unleash a profound capacity for cooperation and have built religions, nations, and conglomerate corporations. They have motivated humans throughout history to construct architectural wonders and navigate the hardships of working life. They have inspired us to sacrifice our lives on the battlefield and compelled us to organize in protest in the face of injustice. The social cohesion we have achieved is so important that our cultural stories are passed from generation to generation. Our cultural stories shape our individual behavior, and our personal narratives shape our cultures. On a national level, "people are as healthy and confident as the stories they tell themselves. Sick storytellers can make their nations sick. And sick nations make for sick storytellers" (Okri, 2009).

Now, thanks to the internet, it is possible to become culturally bound to ever-emerging stories that threaten our wider cultural fabric. We are facing a crisis of culture because the stories that once connected us are becoming less plausible. The liberal story, for instance, which has been the political blueprint for the United States, is starting to unravel because "liberalism has no obvious answers to the biggest problems we face:

ecological collapse and technological disruption" (Harari, 2018), not to mention the ever-present threat of mutually assured destruction by nuclear war. It's become easy for an opportunistic leader, whether through politics or YouTube, to offer a new narrative for people to rally around. We believe in stories in our human quest to belong, even when they go against long-standing institutions.

By embracing storytelling in our classrooms and schools, we have a chance to build positive cultural cohesion by answering the age-old questions *Who am I?* and *Who are we?* In the bewilderment of our wider cultural upheaval, we can craft narratives in our classrooms that communicate values of vulnerability, integrity, kindness, and learning. Hopefully, our students will carry these stories forward to build a better future for us all. Imagine, for instance, the citizenship of a country that is able to take ownership of the things they can change within themselves rather than looking for someone else to blame for their suffering. A political rhetoric of hate would fall on deaf ears.

Values Create Storytelling Styles

Values are "freely chosen, verbally constructed consequences of ongoing, dynamic, evolving patterns of activity which establish predominant reinforcers for that activity that are intrinsic in engagement in the valued behavioral pattern itself" (Wilson & DuFrene, 2009, p. 64). Since our values are integral to our actions, it follows that the stories we tell will reflect our values. If we hope to explore the potential of storytelling in the classroom, we must attend to our own cultural bias when it comes to story. Stories communicate the values of a culture through the interplay between what they're about and the way they are told. This means if we want to expand our assessment strategies to include storytelling, then we need to be mindful of a variety of storytelling styles that speak to different cultural values.

In a 1997 study about the impact of cultural background on storytelling in school-aged children, psychology professor Allyssa McCabe finds that there are wide variations in style between and within cultures. Consider the following findings from McCabe's (1997) research.

- In North American culture, girls tend to feature more dialogue in their stories than boys do. Also, North American children generally adhere to a story structure closely resembling a fairy tale, meaning they focus on a main event that teaches an important lesson.

- Japanese children living in America often told concise narratives consisting of several different events. In style, these stories looked like haiku and demonstrated a cultural value of minimalism.

- African American children often told lengthy stories unified by a single theme with four lines per subtopic. Like jazz music, these stories did not have a linear pattern of organization and were heavy on linguistic devices like irony, rhyme, alliteration, and metaphor, demonstrating how valuable aesthetic is to the storytellers.

- Puerto Rican children emphasized familial relationships over events in their stories, centering their learning on the dynamics of these connections.

Taken together, these variations in style show that "cultural differences are valued, valuable, and deeply embedded" (McCabe, 1997, p. 467) in the stories we tell.

To rehumanize storytelling, therefore, we need to be mindful of stylistic variation as a manifestation of culture by building task-neutral criteria (that is, rubrics aligned with learning goals rather than task expectations). If we give our students a story structure with which to share their learning, we must honor their role as the narrator. If we misunderstand the values inherent in different styles and assess the product, rather than the learning, we might assess their stories as rambling, off topic, or unimaginative, and limit the potential of storytelling to deepen and demonstrate learning for *all* students. Our first step is to take the time to understand our students' values. Then, when we view storytelling through the lens of assessment, we must remember to build task-neutral rubrics that focus squarely on the learning outcome the story is meant to reveal rather than the specific story structure itself. In part 2 of this book (page 81), we offer an example of these types of rubrics in the Competency Connection section. By assessing a competency like collaboration or creative thinking rather than a product, we can remain both task neutral and culturally expansive when assessing through story.

The Evolution of Storytelling Technology

Story is so integral to our humanity and cultures, our technology has evolved throughout history in a quest to maintain social cohesion as population expands. The communities of our earliest ancestors verbally passed stories from person to person and generation to generation. As population expanded, the written word was invented and applied to religious texts that taught, through story, how humans were to behave as members of religions that reached across many geographical communities. This was the way of the world until 1440, when Johannes Gutenberg invented the printing press, a new technology that changed everything.

When we invent groundbreaking technology, we tend to first use it to replicate the status quo. This was true with the printing press; Gutenberg's first printed text was the Bible. Eventually, humans came to see the possibilities of the printing press, and this led to the creation of many new text-based media such as novels, newspapers, magazines, and pamphlets. After the printing press, our desire to see the stories we consumed led to the creation of film technology starting in the 1890s.

Throughout most of the 20th century in North America, storytelling via the media represented a limited, biased perspective on the world, reflecting the dominant culture of those in powerful positions in media companies and often portraying ethnic and racial minorities in stereotypical ways (Dixon, Weeks, & Smith, 2019; Larrazet & Rigoni, 2014; Thornton, 2013). The creation of the internet in the 1990s radically changed this power dynamic and storytelling as we know it.

The internet is the ultimate storytelling network. It provides an important redistribution of power and offers a haven for marginalized communities to gather and for creativity and collaboration to flourish. In fact, the authors of this book met through the social media platform X! However, as with all technologies, this powerful tool introduces unprecedented challenges. We are now able to construct our own stories through the click of a button; then algorithms funnel us into communities that echo our bias. This has led to political polarization, extremist perspectives, and a firehose of information causing widespread overwhelm and dizzying complexity. The internet has caused immense technological disruption to our wider social cohesion by hacking our biological need for story and splintering dominant culture into many subcultures (Harari, 2018). Now, those of us in education must reclaim storytelling as it once was: a tool for building local learning communities. Though our students are natural storytellers on the basis of their humanity, when we teach them how to develop this ability as a competency in and of itself, they can use storytelling as a tool to its full potential.

Competency Connection

Storytelling involves many critical 21st century competencies, which we explore more deeply in chapter 3 (page 57). However, it's important here to note the connection to humanity through story. The means by which we tell stories has modernized and will continue to do so.

Storytelling as Critical Competency

With the invention of the internet and the explosion of social media, modern culture is obsessed with storytelling. Though it might not seem like it on the surface, the apps that consume much of our day are largely spaces for us to construct and consume stories. We have all become creators as we strive to get the perfect image, paired with the perfect caption, to reflect some degree of aspirational truth about our lives. In fact, many social media platforms now have a story feature where users can produce a short series of videos, images, and animations to summarize the events of their day, share content that speaks to them, or offer a reflection.

It's tempting to write off our new storytelling media as shallow entertainment for younger generations. However, many major business publications are heralding the rise of the *creator economy*. A 2021 *Forbes* article describes how this new market exploded while we were all stuck inside during the pandemic:

> Companies began to build their businesses around these platforms, bringing a rise to a new type of solopreneur: the content creator. This includes social media influencers, bloggers and video makers who use software and finance tools that assist in their growth and monetization. This group is one of the fastest-growing economies today. (Bogliari, 2021)

The rise of the creator economy shows that storytelling has become a viable profession thanks to the introduction of social media. If we maintain that the purpose of education is to prepare students for future jobs, then helping them become expert storytellers has become a part of our job.

Leaders as Storytellers

Expert storytellers building empathetic communities through their stories wield a lot of influence. This ability extends not only to our social media platforms, but also to leadership and entrepreneurship. In fact, leaders who rely heavily on data and lists are becoming irrelevant to those who can speak to the minds and hearts of the humans they seek to impact. In her TED Talk, "How Your Brain Responds to Stories—And Why They Are Crucial for Leaders," Karen Eber (TED, 2021) explains that despite knowing better, too many leaders rely on dry lists of data points that allow people to fill in the gaps themselves. One example of this was the crisis that unfolded in North America as chief medical officers shared the most relevant evidence about the COVID-19 pandemic in their typical stoic fashion, leaving millions of citizens free to construct their own narratives about the data. This led to the rise of many subcultures, the most antisocial of which rejected the science altogether.

Though this lack of storytelling in leadership permeates all industries, it's especially worrisome when it comes to science. In a 2018 article in the *Journal of Neuroscience*, several leaders in the field conclude, "There is much more we have to learn about how we as scientists can incorporate storytelling into our professional lives as we strive to make science more understandable, more inclusive, and ultimately, more beneficial to the world" (Suzuki, Feliú-Mójer, Hasson, Yehuda, & Zarate, 2018).

For this reason, great leaders need to find harmony between data and story by putting the data in the context of a setting, characters, and conflict in a way that builds tension toward an outcome. A great leader can hook their audience as they ask, "Where is she going with this?" and engage their hearts between the data points. These types of leaders reflect deeply to craft a story by asking themselves, "What problem am I trying to solve? What do I want people to do differently?" If students are to succeed as leaders in any field, they must become skilled storytellers.

Stories as a Catalyst for Change

With the rise of social media, storytelling has become a learnable technique accessible to everyone. We are living through the democratization of storytelling.

There is a specific structure to a story that *moves* others. Marshall Ganz (2020), senior lecturer at Harvard University's Kennedy School of Government, suggests a specific structure that sparks action called the *public narrative*. It consists of the story of self, the story of us, and the story of now. Consider the following questions to understand how all of these three stories work together to form an overall public narrative (Ganz, 2020).

- **Story of self:** What personal story reveals how you were called to leadership? What was a dark moment you faced and what choices did you make to overcome hardship? How can you reveal who you are through vivid details in the story?
- **Story of us:** Who is your audience? What do they value and how do you share those values? How can you show that you've listened to and

understood what it is they really want? How do their values connect to your cause?

- **Story of now:** What is a tangible call to action for your audience? What is the price of inaction? What vision can they bring to life when they take action? What small step can they take to get started immediately?

Through the stories of self and us, the storyteller builds a connection with their audience that gives them a human imperative for the action they are being asked to take, increasing the likelihood they will accept the call to adventure. However, to craft a public narrative, it's important that the storyteller works in reverse, beginning with getting crystal clear on the story of now. Storytellers in our social media age who follow this structure are most successful at moving their audience to become subscribers, followers, and customers. Additionally, activists who use this structure grow their coalitions and movements for positive social change. It is undoubtedly a structure for story that we must share with students if we want to support them using their unique experiences as a springboard to make a positive impact on the world when they share a defense of learning, as discussed in chapter 6 (page 139).

The Story of What I'm Learning

Students can tell the story of the standards they are learning on both a small and a large scale. The scope of the stories that we invite students to share can vary between micro moments and macro tales of learning. On the micro end of the scale, for example, students may be invited to step inside the perspective of different people during a history lesson or to solve a problem within a story during mathematics class. They may make sense of a collaborative activity by describing a moment of conflict resolution. Alternatively, at the macro end of the scale, students may tell the story of a historical period in a project-based learning experience where they make a serial podcast. Or they may tell the story of how they are developing the competencies in their school's profile of a learner in a formal presentation to peers and parents. Keep in mind that the *micro* moments of storytelling in the classroom are the necessary practice for the *macro* moments of storytelling to an external audience.

Now that we've established the where and when, let's look at the how. Namely, we'll unpack timeless story elements and structures, then explore an array of storytelling media.

Five Essential Story Elements

There are five elements essential to every story: (1) character, (2) setting, (3) conflict, (4) plot, and (5) theme. Every story involves a person (or personified animal or object) that begins in status quo but eventually faces a challenge that moves them into new places and experiences where they can either rise to the challenge or succumb to it, emerging with a new insight about themselves and the world they inhabit. While the insights, or themes, that emerge from stories are as varied and diverse as the human beings discovering them, there are some predictable aspects to story elements. For instance, characters can be either static or dynamic, resistant to change or open to new learning and growth. Conflict can be either internal, within the character themselves, or external, in the form of the main character versus another character, nature, or society. When it comes to plot, many English language arts (ELA) teachers are quick to cite the *plot roller coaster* that includes an introduction, inciting incident, rising action, climax, falling action, and resolution (either positive or tragic).

We can see patterns throughout history in how these five story elements interact (Booker, 2004). These patterns can provide the scaffolding for a wide variety of student stories. We introduce more culturally expansive story structures for classroom application in part 2 (page 81). Consider the following tropes seen in stories throughout history, as Christopher Booker (2004) describes in his book *The Seven Basic Plots*.

- **Rags to riches:** This story involves a main character who begins in a humble, perhaps downtrodden, state but demonstrates potential for greatness. The story tells how they live up to their potential and reach a higher status of wealth, success, and importance.

- **Comedy:** This story moves beyond the common understanding of comedy as involving humor to describe how a deeper understanding and relationship emerged following interpersonal conflict.

- **Tragedy:** This story involves a main character with a tragic flaw that leads them to make a poor decision or grave mistake that leads to their downfall.

- **Quest:** As the name suggests, this story involves a main character who embarks on a quest to a faraway place to obtain a great prize.

- **Voyage and return:** In this story, the main character travels to a faraway land that at first seems strange but exciting. However, soon they feel trapped in the world and must make a thrilling escape back to the safety of their own world. The character may return home with new insights about themselves and the world, or the return may stunt their growth, as they leave the opportunity for growth and a better life behind and retreat to the shelter of their home.

- **Overcoming the monster:** The main character must overcome a "monster" (or villain) that is posing a threat to their community. They often defeat the monster in its own lair using some type of magical weapon and win a treasure, or a kingdom, as their reward.

- **Rebirth:** As one of the more passive stories, this one features the main character being rescued by someone else. In this story, they are trapped in a "living death" or the forces of a villain until they are freed through the loving act of someone else. While they gain freedom, they avoid having to resolve their own inner conflict.

To begin designing assessment experiences where students can tell the story of what they are learning, teachers can reflect on the following questions.

- **Character:** Are students the main character in their story, or is it an important person or concept from the curriculum?

- **Setting:** Does the story take place in the past, present, or future?

- **Conflict:** What challenge must characters overcome to learn and grow? Is it internal or external?

- **Plot:** What story structure might help students scaffold their storytelling?

- **Theme:** What learning does this story reveal about course standards and critical competencies?

For instance, a teacher may invite students into a reflective storytelling experience after a unit of study. In this way, the students are the main character of their story and the setting is the past. To scaffold their storytelling, students may choose from three structures: rags to riches, tragedy, or rebirth. Students are supported to define their ultimate conflict as internal (frustration, lack of motivation, fear, confusion, and so on) or external (content, peers, environment, and so on). With this support, some students tell a story of triumph, others of failure, and some of being rescued. This evidence is powerful formative information about what is working in instruction, what isn't, and who needs more targeted support. Feedback would look as simple as asking a question to prompt deeper reflection, perhaps even goal setting ahead of the next unit.

Formats

Three formats that each assessment method might take are written, oral, or visual, or a combination of some or all of these. In traditional school settings, the written word has reigned supreme. Formal and written assessment methods are (falsely) believed to be more valid than, for example, oral traditions valued by Indigenous cultures. In the assessment literature, validity means that an assessment *measures what it is intended to measure*, which means we must utilize *methods* (selected response versus constructed response) that are appropriately aligned to elicit the cognitive rigor of the standards (Chappuis & Stiggins, 2020). However, the format (oral, visual, written) is a choice teachers can make within the appropriate method. It's important to note that the written format is a potential barrier for students if they have a written expression disability or are learning English as an additional language, since oral communication develops faster than reading and writing skills (Almeida, 2007).

With this expansive view of assessment formats in mind, the possibilities for the media through which students can tell the story of their learning are endless. For instance, while students may tell the story of a historical period for social studies, the documentary medium through which they tell the story reveals their digital and visual literacy skills, thus meeting several ELA standards. On top of gathering more robust evidence of learning, the authenticity of storytelling media in our culture today means students will find more relevance in the assessment of their learning. In short, embracing a wide variety of storytelling media as assessment increases the complexity of the task, reveals more evidence of learning, and deepens engagement.

With the technological disruption of written text by generative software like ChatGPT, it is even fair to assume that we are going to see the scales tip toward oral and visual formats in the future. After all, artificial intelligence cannot replace a person telling their story, and writing could soon be seen as a low-level task better left to computers.

Consider the following creative structures students may use to tell the story of their learning.

- **Vignette:** A vignette is an incomplete story—an impressionistic scene that centers on one moment in time. It could help the reader to better understand a person, place, idea, or thing. These slow-motion moments focus on the senses rather than the sequence of events we might find in a plot.

- **List:** There are many creative ways to tell a story as a list. One way might be to break up scenes into a numbered list, and another might be to organize ideas or moments under a concept. This structure often involves a number in the title, such as "Ten Ways to Fail" or "Five Reasons to Study."

- **Epistle:** This story structure involves a series of letters. However, in our modern age, this might be any medium that we use for communication, including newspaper clippings, text messages, or online posts—there are limitless artifacts that capture the stories of our lives. These artifacts might tell the story of an evolving relationship, understanding, or identity.

- **Dialogue:** This story structure is the closest to how we experience stories in our lives—in conversation with others. In this format, setting, characters, and conflicts are all established through what is said rather than what happens. This format demonstrates how our stories are shaped largely through our interactions with others. Podcasts have exploded in popularity as they feature audio-only stories through dialogues between hosts and guests.

- **Second person:** In this story structure, the narrator talks directly to the audience, addressing them as "you." This point of view allows the author to put the reader in the present moment of the story as if it is happening to them.

- **Micro fiction:** This structure tells a story in the fewest words possible. Ernest Hemingway is said to have told a flash fiction story in six words: "For sale. Baby shoes. Never worn" (Nunez, 2022). This structure invites the teller to distill the most important elements of the story.

- **Unusual point of view (POV):** Typically, we tell a story from our own perspective or that of another human being. However, what if a story were told from the perspective of an object? Or an animal? A natural element? By doing this, the author can give the narrator, whatever form it takes, humanity and consciousness. Some might even say a soul. A story with an unusual point of view allows us to see ourselves in a new light.

The point is not that every structure would work with every standard or learning outcome. Rather, the collection of creative formats can be applied to the curricular standards. Students, along with their teacher, could agree on what an effective format would be for the specific learning at hand. For instance, a teacher may provide a choice board to their students with several different storytelling formats for conveying their understanding of a specific procedure they've just learned in mathematics. Some students write a series of letters between two important factors, while some craft a second-person narrative as though they are the procedure talking to the student. Some students write out their story, while others choose to audio record theirs. What matters most here is that all students are engaged in the constructed-response method of assessment, which maintains the same cognitive rigor, despite choosing different formats that play to their strengths.

Now that we've explored the building blocks of the many micro and macro stories that students might tell in the classroom, let's interrogate how we maintain a safe culture for nurturing student voice in our classrooms.

The Story of How I'm Learning

Stories are inherently personal, so it's important to care for the sanctity of not just the story but the storyteller as well. Telling the story of *how* one is learning is a vulnerable proposition for many students, so mindfulness matters.

Story Stewardship

To amplify student storytelling in the classroom, we must teach, develop, and maintain an expectation of *story stewardship*. This means honoring the personal and sacred nature of story by listening well, honoring privacy, believing the storyteller, and demonstrating genuine curiosity. There is always the chance that our story might make someone else uncomfortable, sparking a less-than-favorable response. It is likely this behavior will emerge in the classroom, so it is important that we build an expectation of story stewardship early on. That way, we can respond when we observe students who struggle to meet it.

As a researcher who has spent decades studying empathy, Brown (2021) points to three critical ways we fail to demonstrate story stewardship toward one another. To help students understand this expectation, we encourage you to share these pitfalls and lead a discussion about them.

- **Defaulting to being the knower, advice giver, or problem solver:** Rather than this performative act of connection that drives disconnection, Brown (2021) suggests we instead show curiosity by saying, "I'm grateful that you're sharing this with me. What does support look like? I can listen and be with you, I can help problem solve, or whatever else you need. You tell me."

- **Narrative tap-outs:** When a story makes us uncomfortable, there is potential for avoidant behavior on a spectrum from subtle to complete shutdown. This applies to not just receiving stories, but a fear of telling our own stories as well. As Brown (2021) writes, "Tapping out of stewarding someone's story can feel like betrayal, and tapping out of sharing our own story feels like betraying ourselves." An important discussion to have with students is to brainstorm strategies for how we can stay engaged and brave when we're feeling uncomfortable, such as through self-talk, deep breaths, and taking breaks when needed.

- **Narrative takeover:** This is the predominant way that we struggle to show story stewardship in our society today. Narrative takeover occurs when we discredit the truth of the storyteller and instead center our own truth by shifting the focus to our perspective and expressing disbelief toward the storyteller (Brown, 2021). Narrative takeover is the greatest threat to cultural cohesion and is therefore critical to address at the classroom level. Coach students to stay with the storyteller by asking questions out of genuine curiosity and to fight the natural urge to respond with, "Yeah, but . . ."

In the following section, we describe the story circle protocol, which teaches and reinforces the critical skill of deep listening and story stewardship.

Story Circles

Circles are symbolic of equality. When students sit in a circle and are invited to share their stories one by one, it communicates that all stories are important and deserve attention. Also, listening to the stories of others builds intercultural competence and inspires rethinking and creativity (Grant, 2021; UNESCO, 2021). Many teachers may be familiar with the concept of a circle meeting where students circle up to discuss topics that are pertinent at the time. Circle meetings are also the ideal setting for students to tell the story of how they are developing as a learner.

The story circle protocol is an act of decolonization, as it disrupts the value of a hierarchy and honors the oral tradition of Indigenous cultures. Scholars Larry Brendtro, Martin Brokenleg, and Steve Van Bockern (1990) explain that a "circle of courage" is rooted in a core value of belonging, which builds the foundation for other outcomes we value in the school space, such as independence, mastery, and generosity. Students will not rise to the challenge of learning if they don't feel their story belongs in the classroom.

For students to get the most out of the protocol, story circles must be consistent, safe, and facilitated. The frequency we suggest for a story circle is weekly (ideally at the end of the week), so students can look back and reflect on how they are learning; however, students can circle up as necessary. If students see that circles are becoming a predictable part of the classroom rhythm, they will become more comfortable with them. To increase psychological safety for students, we suggest establishing the following important norms and then asking the students if they have any others to propose.

- Everyone has the right to pass.
- What's said in the circle stays in the circle.
- Keep your hands, feet, and chair to yourself.
- Listen deeply without offering a reply.
- Be careful of negative nonverbal cues, such as facial expressions.

Set up the story circle by ensuring that everyone can see everyone else and no one is sitting on a chair that makes them higher or lower than the rest of the group. Explain the purpose of the circle, review the norms, then pose a first question to the group. To scaffold students' confidence to share, we suggest allowing students to answer with one word first, moving around the entire circle, before inviting them to share the story behind their word in a second round. If you have a large class, an alternative to the round-robin approach of students sharing the story behind their word is to open the floor to whoever feels called to share, maintaining the norm of not replying to others' stories. It can bring closure to the circle to have each student go around once more and share a final word that reflects their learning, be it a word that stuck with them from a story or a feeling they have.

Consider the following list of possible prompts to open a story circle.

- What was a challenge you faced in class this week? Did you overcome it? Why or why not?
- What one word would describe how you feel about class this week? Why?
- Which mistake has taught you the most important lesson?
- How would you describe your collaboration on this project?
- Where does learning come easiest to you? Why?

- If achieving flow means being completely absorbed by what you are doing, so much so that you lose track of time, when did you last feel you were in flow?
- What was the high this week? What did it teach you?
- What was the low of the week? What did it teach you?
- When did you last feel invisible? What was that like?
- When did you feel invincible? What was that like?

Consider this list a starting point, as many of the story structures we explore throughout the book would also make for great prompts. As you will see when you review the list, some prompts may require that students have individual think time prior to circling up.

Self-Awareness of Explanatory Style

If our mind is a storyteller, the stories we tell ourselves define our mindset. In general, all humans have a tendency toward being either the victim or an active agent in the stories they tell themselves. According to researchers, our *explanatory style* predicts depression, achievement, and overall health, with the pessimistic side of the ledger leading to decreased outcomes (Skinner, 2023; Zullow, Oettingen, Peterson, & Seligman, 1988). One of the prominent researchers in this area, Martin Seligman (Maier & Seligman, 2016), has a very specific name for this negative pattern of behavior: *learned helplessness*. In short, our habits of narration are a predictor of whether we will see our future through a pessimistic or optimistic lens. The tone of our narrator is the foundation of hope.

As teachers explore opportunities to amplify student storytelling in the classroom, explanatory style provides an important lens for assessment as it reveals a student's *fixed* mindset, making future learning unlikely, or a *growth* mindset, open to change (Dweck, 2006). One of the most important aspects of this theory to help students understand is that our thoughts dictate our emotions, not the other way around. For instance, a student who is often anxious likely has an explanatory style that puts them at the mercy of malicious peers and teachers, whereas one who is calm believes they did the best they could in any interaction and will take follow-up steps if someone has harmed them. Further, our emotional state is the basis of behavior. The stories we tell ourselves can take a neutral event in the external world and send us down two totally different emotional and behavioral pathways. This is Bernard Weiner's (2010) attributional theory. Figure 1.1 describes this pattern using the common school event of receiving feedback.

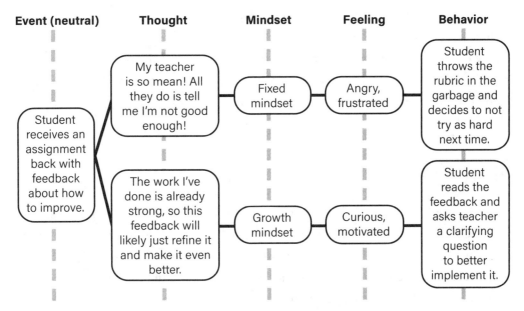

FIGURE 1.1: How a student's explanatory style impacts mindset and behavior.

One of the most important lessons every human can learn is that we have the power to change the story we tell ourselves. To support students telling the story of how they are learning, provide direct instruction on explanatory styles, teaching students what they are. Use figure 1.1 to explore different events students are likely to encounter and play with different thoughts to see how they might impact feelings and behavior. For example, invite students to explore different thoughts in response to the following events.

- A peer isn't looking at you as you talk to them.
- You play a game with friends and win.
- You receive a quiz back and see a failing grade.
- You have a project due in two weeks.
- A good friend says they can't hang out this weekend.
- You receive an award at the end of the year.

It's important to note that exploring explanatory styles is not simply an exercise in toxic positivity. There are events many students experience in school that are rooted in historical systems of oppression like racism and sexism. If a student experiences an overtly racist comment from a peer or teacher, we are not suggesting they change their internal narrative to let the other person off the hook for their behavior. Instead, this activity is a means to help students learn how to find self-compassion in moments of injustice so they can take appropriate action as a result.

For instance, if a student thinks, "There are probably a lot of people who also believe that racist comment," they are likely to feel shame and engage in self-protective behavior in the future. Instead, if that student learns to tell themselves, "No matter how I responded, I did the best I could in a threatening situation," they will feel calmer, more confident, and likely to take action to ensure their peer is accountable for their words.

Summary

Stories are fundamental to our consciousness as human beings and the basis of how we make meaning of the world. They offer the potential for deeper empathy if we can learn to tolerate uncomfortable emotions. Those of us working in education must seize the moment to embrace student storytelling as a means of assessment to foster deeper learning, demonstrate cultural responsiveness, and teach a future-ready skill. As teachers, we can't afford to view storytelling as a tangential "fun" activity to include as time permits. Rather, we invite you to view it as the most essential way of rehumanizing the assessment experience, making it more than just a clinical exercise in gathering data.

The possibilities for storytelling as assessment are endless, ranging from micro- to macro-opportunities to demonstrate learning. While there are many tropes and creative formats for teachers to draw from when gathering evidence of *what* students are learning (course standards), using story circles provides a consistent framework for students to tell the story of *how* they are learning.

Chapter 1 Discussion Questions for Learning Teams

Journal your response to the following prompts in the space provided. Share your thoughts during team discussion.

1. What quote or passage encapsulates your biggest takeaway from this chapter? What immediate action (small, medium, or large) will you take because of this takeaway? Explain both to your team.

2. Despite the research supporting stories as fundamental to meaning making, why do you think student storytelling is often limited to the primary years of school?

3. How are students currently using technology to tell their learning stories in your classroom or school?

Page 1 of 2

Rehumanizing Assessment © 2025 Solution Tree Press • SolutionTree.com
Visit **go.SolutionTree.com/assessment** to download this free reproducible.

4. How are you currently supporting students to tell stories on a microlevel in your classroom or school? What about a macrolevel?

5. Which of the major story tropes (see page 23) might students adapt to tell the story of *what* they are learning (course standards), or *how* they are learning (personal growth and development)?

6. Which of the creative structures (see page 25) for storytelling are you most curious to try in your context? How might you make it work?

7. To what degree are students' lived experiences shared in your context to build belonging? How might you make this practice more consistent, safe, and facilitated?

Chapter 2
ESSENTIAL ASSESSMENT THROUGH STORY

The humanity of storytelling allows us to rehumanize assessment by using story as a valid assessment method. For too long, *valid and reliable* assessments have been (wrongly) defined through the narrow and clinical lens of tests, assignments, and projects. The fundamentals of assessment are timeless and universally applicable, regardless of what's being assessed. In short, assessment is more of a process than a packet. Storytelling is not simply a peripheral relief from the rigors of *real learning*: it is a demonstration of real learning.

This chapter affirms that assessment is necessary for eliciting authentic evidence of learning and provides six foundational assessment tenets for doing so. Teachers must guide students to become self-regulatory with their learning, and storytelling is an effective approach for this due to its inherent personalization and ability to provide student agency. Storytelling is also culturally expansive in its capacity to embody diverse cultural archetypes and supportive of critical competencies. Using self-assessment, students can tell the story of what they're learning and practice metacognitive strategies to understand their own thinking and tell the story of how they're learning.

The Big Idea

Assessment is *essential*. Anything of substance in schools relies on an accurate assessment of evidence, whether it be to describe student learning or evaluate the success of an implementation plan—any implementation plan. Anything can be accurately assessed, even storytelling, provided we follow six timeless, research-based tenets, which we discuss in the following section. We follow that with a discussion about why assessment is essential and how students self-regulate their learning.

Six Assessment Tenets

After a thorough review of the academic literature on assessment, Tom, along with his colleagues Cassandra Erkens and Nicole Dimich (2017), determined that all classroom assessment should be based on the following six essential assessment tenets:

1. **Assessment purpose:** Understanding our assessment purpose means we have a clear picture of how we intend to use the emerging assessment results before the assessment. The formative purpose of assessment is about continual learning; the summative purpose is about the verification of learning. Though they serve a different purpose, formative and summative assessment can develop a seamless, mutually supportive relationship.

2. **Assessment architecture:** Assessment is most effective when it is planned, purposeful, and intentionally sequenced in advance of instruction by all of those responsible for the delivery. Assessment architecture is a blueprint that tightly sequences essential standards; teases out learning targets; identifies the assessments that reflect learning targets; and determines the use of assessments.

3. **Accurate interpretation:** The interpretation of assessment results must be accurate, accessible, and reliable. This means the items and tasks in our assessments must accurately reflect the standards we are gathering information on. Essential to the accurate interpretation [are] clear criteria, aligned inferences of what the criteria represent, and the continual calibration to avoid inconsistencies or tangential influences.

4. **Instructional agility:** Being instructionally agile means teachers have the capacity to use emerging evidence to make real-time modifications within the context of the expected learning. Whether at the classroom or school level, the true power of assessment comes when emerging results are used to determine what comes next in the learning.

5. **Communication of results:** The communication of assessment results must generate productive responses from learners and all stakeholders who support them. Whether through feedback or grades, the communication of proficiency must serve as a catalyst for continual learning.

6. **Student investment:** There is a symbiotic relationship between assessment and self-regulation. When learners understand this, they are able to track their progress, reflect on what they are learning and where they need to go next. (p. 5)

Whether assessing traditionally or through story, the fundamental tenets of assessment provided by these six tenets are non-negotiable for any assessment to yield accurate information about student performance. Assessment is the engine that drives effective teaching and is essential for moving from *content coverage* to *effective teaching*.

Assessment Drives Learning

Since everything of substance in any school relies on accurate assessment evidence, investing in one's assessment *literacy*—understanding these six timeless tenets of assessment—is the most efficient and effective professional investment any teacher can make. Certainly, those who wish to incorporate storytelling as a viable approach to assessment will need to be particularly competent (and savvy) about how they approach classroom assessment if the results of those assessments are to be accurate and reliable. Leveraging story as a viable means of assessment is not just about designing great prompts; it's more about having a clear plan to *respond* to this evidence.

Inaccurate formative assessment runs the risk of misinforming students about what's next. A literature review by education scholars Maria Araceli Ruiz-Primo and Min Li (2013) finds unanimous agreement in academia that effective feedback is the key to raising student achievement, yet its mere existence is insufficient. Feedback that is too task specific, for example, can lead to improved performance on that task but have no impact (or even a negative impact) on a student's long-term learning. Likewise, feedback could have little to no impact on students' acute performances, but over time have a positive impact on learning (Wiliam, 2018). So, while it is tempting to oversimplify the positive impact that feedback has on learning, those who are assessment literate and have a deep understanding of the research know that feedback sometimes doesn't work and can, in fact, have a negative impact. The quality of the feedback, and how students subsequently act on the feedback, are much more important than its existence. To be called effective, feedback must elicit a productive response from the recipient (Erkens et al., 2017; Kluger & DeNisi, 1996; Wiliam, 2011).

Inaccurate summative assessment runs the risk of misinforming students, families, and stakeholders about the degree to which a student has met the standards. Remembering that the distinction between the purpose of formative and summative assessments has everything to do with how the evidence is used (Black, 2013), the risk of being misinformed comes from the design of the assessment and the interpretation, not the purpose itself. Using storytelling as an assessment method requires teachers to be skilled at making inferences about quality since stories, for the most part, will be judged on quality rather than simply right or wrong. Quality is not a binary choice but a question of the degree to which the student has met the criteria.

We can't teach without assessment since teachers need to use evidence either to inform the next steps in learning or to verify that learning has occurred. Using storytelling as a viable assessment method doesn't require a new understanding of assessment; rather, it allows the assessment-literate teacher to broaden the opportunities for students to show what they know in a more inclusive and culturally expansive way. It is only through their assessment literacy that teachers can support students becoming self-regulated learners.

The Self-Regulation of Learning

Whether telling the story of *what* they're learning or *how* they're learning, students must be at the center of the assessment process if they are going to be fully invested in their own learning. While developing assessment literacy is necessary for teachers to gather accurate formative and summative evidence, the ultimate goal is to teach students how to assess their own learning. Student investment is a first among equals in the six tenets of assessment, serving as an outcome of the other five.

The big picture (and most desirable outcome) is to have students use the assessment process (that is, the before, during, and after an assessment) to become more self-regulatory about their learning. Student investment occurs when assessment and the self-regulation of learning engage in a symbiotic relationship (Erkens et al., 2017). The assessment cycle can serve as an input to the self-regulatory process; the self-regulatory process can improve achievement. While the desire among educators to have students self-regulate their learning is ubiquitous, the process for how to achieve that outcome is often less understood. The assessment process provides the substance from which students can engage in metacognitive, self-regulatory activities that have them reflect on *how* they learn. The three-step models developed by researchers D. Royce Sadler (on assessment) and Barry Zimmerman (on self-regulated learning) align seamlessly for this purpose.

Sadler's (1989) conceptualization of students monitoring their own learning posits that students must be clear on what they are supposed to learn and have the capacity to monitor and adjust their own work. Consider Sadler's (1989) three guidelines to ensure formative assessment enables new learning. Students must (1) have a shared understanding of quality work (Where am I going?), (2) be able to compare their work to the established criteria (Where am I now?), and (3) take action to address any shortcomings (How do I close the gap?). These have been integral to the development of subsequent assessment (and self-assessment) frameworks since the 1990s. Now consider Zimmerman's (2011) three-phase model of self-regulation: (1) forethought, (2) performance monitoring, and (3) reflection. Zimmerman's model aligns beautifully with Sadler's three questions as each phase can be simultaneously facilitated through the assessment process. When we hold space for students to self-regulate their learning, they build their assessment literacy.

Figure 2.1 highlights examples of what students would do within the two models. The relationship between the two is best understood through the lens of *while*. Students will engage in self-regulatory processes while moving through the assessment cycle; students will move through the three phases of self-regulation while experiencing the assessment cycle.

Three Assessment Questions (Sadler, 1989)	Three Phases of Self-Regulation (Zimmerman, 2011)
Where am I going? • Clear learning goals and success criteria • Examination of exemplars	**Forethought phase** • Task analysis (set goals and plans) • Self-motivation beliefs (self-efficacy, interest, goal orientation, and outcome expectancies)
Where am I now? • Self and peer assessment of learning • Making real-time adjustments	**Performance phase** • Self-control (using a variety of tasks, interest, and management strategies) • Self-observation (metacognitive monitoring and self-recording)
How do I close the gap? • Self-identification of necessary support • Seeking support from the teacher	**Reflection phase** • Self-judgment (self-evaluation and causal attribution) • Self-reaction (affect, satisfaction, and potentially adaptive or defensive responses)

FIGURE 2.1: Three assessment questions and three phases of self-regulation.

We can't lament that students aren't more invested in their own learning but then inadvertently (or intentionally) make them passive recipients to an entirely teacher-centered learning experience. They must be *taught* how to be more self-regulatory, and it's through the assessment cycle that teachers can accomplish this.

Student agency—students having authentic voice and choice within their learning—will only be strengthened through storytelling. Even when the content is factual and linear (for example, the causes of World War II), *telling the story* of that content (for example, relating the overarching story of World War II) requires students to see the content through a personal lens as they activate the self-regulatory process. Telling *their* story clearly requires students to metacognitively reflect on how they learn and under what conditions their learning is most effective. Rehumanizing assessment will only be possible when teachers use their assessment literacy to bring students inside the process and guide them to a deeper examination of both what they are learning and how they are learning it.

Cultural Connection

Storytelling is not only a viable assessment method that expands the opportunities for students to show what they know in a manner that is strength based and inclusive, it is also a way to bring more cultural responsivity to our classrooms. If we are going to be more culturally responsive and expansive, educators and stakeholders alike must accept that authentic demonstrations of learning may not always fit the decades-old traditional assessment formats.

Evidence Is Evidence

Storytelling as a viable assessment method first requires all educators and stakeholders to accept that evidence is evidence—there is no assessment method or format that is inherently superior or inferior to others. Assessment methods are not interchangeable. Certain assessment methods are a *better* fit for certain types of learning targets (Chappuis & Stiggins, 2020); the methods don't necessarily dictate the format. At its core, storytelling is a constructed response. As such, while storytelling will be most relevant when a constructed response is the most appropriate method, the format (written, oral, visual, and so on) can vary with that method. Not all assessments need to be a traditional stapled packet or an extended written response.

Advancements in technology have forced educators to rethink what constitutes quality evidence. Specifically, the focus on and interest in personalization and individualized instruction have been driven by advances in both technology and assessment (Chung et al., 2016). While the research on personalization dates to the early 1900s, "what differs today . . . is the availability of technology to make practical many of the ideas central to individualizing instruction" (Chung et al., 2016, p. 1). However, availability doesn't always equate to immediate implementation, as decades of advancements in information and communication technology (ICT) have not always led to significant changes in the field of assessment (Clarke-Midura & Dede, 2010). In fact, many edtech assessment platforms serve to replicate the status quo, reinforcing an overreliance on selected-response methods (multiple choice, matching, true or false, and so on), because they are easier to score faster via machine. Instead, we need to acknowledge the democratization of storytelling offered by the internet and social media and honor this cultural truth in our assessment practices.

Cultural Archetypes

The thought of being culturally responsive can be daunting. How can schools possibly be responsive to the vast number of cultures represented by their students? The answer is cultural archetypes. In her book *Culturally Responsive Teaching and the Brain*, educational researcher and author Zaretta Hammond (2015) recommends using cultural archetypes to create an inclusive environment without feeling overwhelmed by having to respond to the idiosyncrasies of every culture in the school. By balancing the cultural archetypes, teachers can create an authentically inclusive assessment context.

Cultural archetypes exist along two continuums. First, there are cultures that emphasize the importance of the *individual* (that is, the individual's achievements and independence are prioritized), and there are those more emphatic about the *collective* (that is, the collective achievement and relationships are prioritized). According to Hammond (2015), "The dominant culture [in North America] is individualistic, while the cultures of many African American, Latino, Pacific Islander, and Native American communities lean more toward collectivism" (p. 25). Common sense reveals that if schools are dominated by individualism, then whole cohorts of students are likely to be disenfranchised. This is not to suggest we swing the pendulum the other way; rather, it is about being culturally *expansive* to include both individualism and collectivism. Students can tell stories from the perspective of the individual and the collective.

The two other archetypes, according to Hammond (2015), are the *written tradition* and the *oral tradition*. Just as schools have traditionally emphasized individualism, they have also emphasized the written tradition, as most assessment evidence has been (and maybe still is) written or typed; this requires little to no interpersonal interaction. The oral tradition, by contrast, is how cultures have preserved knowledge through generations. Hammond (2015) explains it as follows:

> By telling stories and coding knowledge into songs, chants, proverbs, and poetry, groups with a strong oral tradition record and sustain their cultures and cultural identities by word of mouth. The oral tradition places a heavy emphasis on relationships because the process connects the speaker and listener in a communal experience. (p. 28)

Again, the point of emphasis is not to swing the pendulum to the other side but to expand the opportunities to be most inclusive and responsive. Students can tell stories in both written and oral formats.

By intentionally putting these four archetypes together and then distributing storytelling as a viable assessment format across the four quadrants, as figure 2.2 demonstrates, teachers will be culturally responsive in their approach to assessment.

	Written Tradition	**Oral Tradition**
Individual	Storytelling by the individual through writing *For example, students write a written reflection on how they overcame various obstacles during an inquiry-based learning experience.*	Storytelling by the individual through oral or physical expression *For example, students present "My Journey to Better Learning Habits" to a small group of peers that describes the ways they've improved their approach to learning.*
Collective	Storytelling by the collective through writing *For example, groups collectively write "Our Turning Point as a Team," where the small groups coauthor a reflection (maybe a blog or social media post) that articulates a specific breakthrough their team had and how it came about.*	Storytelling by the collective through oral or physical expression *For example, small groups present "Our Growth as a Learning Team," where they collectively present to their classmates their strengths and areas they would like to grow as a collective.*

FIGURE 2.2: Storytelling via cultural archetypes.

The combination of the four cultural archetypes is less about force and more about fit. Sometimes the story of the individual is the best fit (for example, the story of *how* I learn), while the story of the collective (for example, what we decided was the most plausible and effective solution after our inquiry) may be more applicable in other circumstances. The same is true for the written versus the oral tradition.

Performance Assessments

Storytelling invites an opportunity to rethink our overreliance on selected-response assessment methods in schools (especially middle and high schools). It is an opportunity to emphasize the constructed-response method instead, where students produce rather than pick an answer. Not only is this more cognitively rigorous, but constructed-response methods also offer the opportunity to increase our use of performance assessment. According to the American Educational Research Association, the American Psychological Association, and the National Council on Measurement in Education, *performance assessments* are demonstrations of mastery that simulate the context or conditions in which the intended learning or skills are applied in reality (Lane, 2013). Researcher Suzanne Lane (2013) further explains performance assessments as follows:

> Because a defining characteristic of performance assessments is the close similarity between the performance observed and the performance of interest, they are often contextualized by linking school activities to real-world experiences. They can take the form of demonstrations, oral performances, investigations, or written products and may involve collaboration or reflection. (p. 313)

In other words, performance assessment is how we meet this cultural moment in history where storytelling is centered.

Performance assessments are typically assessed according to a rubric, since authentic demonstrations of learning are less about right and wrong and more about degrees of quality (that is, authenticity). Judging the degree of quality requires teachers to draw an inference; the teacher will observe the demonstration and evaluate whether *that* demonstration matches *this* description on the rubric. Educator Dylan Wiliam (2020), following educational psychologist Lee J. Cronbach's (1971) lead, defines *assessment* as "a procedure for drawing inferences . . . we collect evidence from the students, from which we draw conclusions" (p. 22). These conclusions can be about the learner's *next steps* (that is, the formative purpose) or about the learner's current standing (that is, the summative purpose). If assessment is about drawing inferences, and using rubrics facilitates those inferences, then using rubrics with performance assessment (specifically storytelling) would be most appropriate.

Rubrics are pivotal when it comes to cultural responsivity and equity in schools. Research on grading over the past century shows that grades based on fewer, more discernible levels that clearly articulate success criteria are more reliable (that is, consistent among teachers) than the 0 to 100 percent scale (Guskey & Brookhart, 2019). In other words, using rubrics ensures a student's grade is not dependent on who their teacher is.

Rubrics also minimize the role of implicit bias in assessment. Education scholar David Quinn (2021) finds that "racial stereotypes can influence the scores teachers assign to student work. But stereotypes seem to have less influence on teachers' evaluations when specific grading criteria are established in advance." Consider the following findings by Quinn (2021):

> When teachers evaluated student writing using a general grade-level scale, they were 4.7 percentage points more likely to consider the white child's writing at or above grade level compared to the identical writing from a Black child. However, when teachers used a grading rubric with specific criteria, the grades were essentially the same.

All people have bias (Payne, Niemi, & Doris, 2018). The first step to mitigating bias in assessment is to admit its existence. This admission is not an admission of malicious intent—it's about awareness. Admission is the only way educators can ensure the most inclusive assessment culture in a classroom or a school, but this is easier said than done because admitting to something that sounds so detrimental is not easy for anyone. While there may be other confounding factors (for example, sample size or rubric training) that make generalizing the results of this research challenging, common sense would suggest that once criteria are predetermined and clearly articulated, teachers would be less susceptible to implicit bias. By employing constructed-response assessment methods and rubrics, teachers can almost eliminate implicit bias within their classrooms and ensure reliability among colleagues who teach the same grade-level subject.

Competency Connection

Assessment itself is a competency, meaning it is a skill that students can and need to learn if they are to assess themselves as learners (both the *what* and *how*). It may not always be referred to that way, but assessment is an essential competency embedded in the learnings and skills identified as essential for the 21st century. For example, to assess *how they learn*, students will need to *think critically* about both their strengths and areas in need of strengthening. We'll save the deep dive into specific critical competencies—critical thinking, collaboration, creativity, communication, digital citizenship, social competence, and self-regulation—as Cassandra Erkens, Tom Schimmer, and Nicole Dimich (2019) present them for chapter 3 (page 57), but for now a more meta approach to *assessment as a competency* is in order.

Assessment as a Competency

Assessment is present throughout the 21st century competencies. Consider the following examples.

- *Critical thinking* involves elements of assessment.
- When students *evaluate*, they are assessing (that is, judging effectiveness, quality, impact, and so on).
- When students *synthesize*, they are assessing (that is, determining which information is most critical to include).
- When students *analyze*, they are assessing (that is, closely examining elements to gauge relevance, importance, impact, and so on).
- *Collaboration* involves elements of assessment, such as evaluating the quality of ideas generated or the effectiveness of the collaboration itself.
- *Creative thinking* and *innovation* require ongoing assessment of plausibility, practicality, potential implementation challenges, and possible outcomes.

Students need to learn the fundamentals of assessment. Not only will this knowledge drive their ability to self-assess and self-regulate their learning, but it will also help them judge the credibility of the information they consume. Figure 2.3 (page 46) demonstrates how the assessment tenets correlate with students' ability to assess a source's credibility.

Assessment Tenet	Assessing the Credibility of Sources
Assessment purpose	Determine a clear purpose for why you are seeking information and your intended use for that information.
Assessment architecture	Identify what outcome is driving your search for information.
Accurate interpretation	Use established criteria to judge the credibility of sources.
Instructional agility	Adjust the purpose, outcome, or criteria based on what you have accessed, should it be necessary.
Communication of results	Communicate to self and others both the strengths and what needs strengthening within your judgment of the credibility of sources.
Student investment	Self-direct, manage, and monitor the entire process as outlined in the previous items.

FIGURE 2.3: Six assessment tenets and judging the credibility of sources.

This is just one example of how assessment permeates the critical competencies of the 21st century and why students must be able to self-assess. As a competency, assessment reaches into the past, the present, and the future.

Assessment of the Past, Present, and Future

Assessing the past means we can learn from mistakes and confirm past successes. As students look back, they can be better equipped to make decisions or set a direction in the present moment. An assessment of the past, especially the more distant past, can bring the necessary clarity to the results of decisions, directions, or developments. To make better decisions in the future, we must be able to look back and evaluate our experiences.

In the present moment, we need to make decisions in real time. The onslaught of information makes it even more critical that students can assess the credibility of what they are consuming. The relentless presence of fake news, along with the proliferation of AI, makes the competency of assessment (in this case of assessment as critical thinking) all the more important. Assessing the present moment also allows the collective to check in about how *we* are doing as a collaborative team. Are we adhering to established norms and processes? Does everyone feel their voice is being heard? Do the roles we've established still suffice? What evidence do we have to support the assertions one way or the other?

Assessing the future is about using our judgment to predict what solution will solve a problem or predict the potential outcomes of the many pathways to choose from. *Design thinking*—a human-based approach to innovation—includes assessing the present challenges that will transform products, processes, and services to create a more desirable future. Addressing any problem requires us to envision the future and determine what's necessary to realign or recalibrate our course toward a more seamless existence. This is no small feat; however, it will be exponentially more difficult without the necessary competence with assessment.

Our assertion that assessment is a competency reinforces why the tenet of *student investment* is a "first among equals" when it comes to our assessment literacy. When we adhere to the other five assessment tenets by clarifying our purpose, designing rigorous assessment methods, aligning our interpretations of success through rubrics, and demonstrating agility in response to the results, we create the conditions for students to become assessors on their own behalf.

The Story of What I'm Learning

Stories are a viable assessment method that can uniquely reveal a depth and breadth of understanding about what students are learning—namely, the standards in the curriculum. However, it's important that those stories align with sound assessment practices to ensure accuracy.

Target-Method Match

Whether our approach to assessment is traditional or progressive, it is essential that we choose the appropriate assessment method. Chappuis and Stiggins (2020) write the following in *Classroom Assessment for Student Learning*:

> Assessment methods are not interchangeable. To ensure accurate assessment results, the overriding criterion for selection of method is consideration of the type of learning targets to be assessed: Some assessment methods are better matches for certain types of learning targets than others. (p. 105)

Chappuis and Stiggins (2020) refer to this finding as *target-method match*. As inclusive, equitable, and expansive as storytelling is, to be a viable approach to assessment, it still needs to be the right fit for the standard being assessed. The good news is there are only three assessment methods, as outlined in table 2.1 (page 48).

Table 2.1: Three Assessment Methods

Assessment Method	Description	Format Examples
Selected response	Learners select the correct answer from a finite list of possibilities.	Format examples include multiple choice, true or false, and matching.
Constructed response	Learners must construct an answer that shows evidence of thinking and provides a thorough explanation or demonstration of their understanding of the learning goal.	Format examples include essays, projects, and oral presentations.
Performance assessment	Learners demonstrate their knowledge or skill in a simulation of the context in which the knowledge or skill is meant to be applied. This can often (not always) be a demonstration that must be seen or heard to be assessed.	Format examples include essays, projects, and oral presentations, as with constructed response. The task is authentic and replicates (as much as possible) what an adult in that field would typically do.

Consider two important reminders. First, consider the distinction between the *method* and the *format*. While assessment methods are not interchangeable, formats are. Once a teacher has identified the appropriate assessment method, they are free to choose any format (oral, written, visual, or any blend of the three). Students themselves could also choose the format. Second, performance assessment is really a subsidiary of constructed response. While there are examples of selected response in authentic, professional settings (for example, certification testing), most professions are about developing or *constructing*. This is why the formats for both performance assessment and constructed response are the same; it's the task that reveals the authenticity.

Humanized Course Content

Telling a story is a performance assessment (that is, an authentic constructed response) as it *humanizes* the content or skills that students are learning. There are the facts, events, procedures, and processes, but there is also the story that underpins all those things. Storytelling is the thread that ties together the events; it's the reason why certain processes became necessary and normalized. Learning is a human experience, so being able to humanize what they are learning will serve to deepen student understanding.

For example, World War I began in 1914 after the assassination of Archduke Franz Ferdinand of Austria. That event sparked an unprecedented war across Europe that lasted until 1918. But why? What is the *story* that underpins World War I? Students could *tell the story* of how alliances—whether countries or personal friendships—are susceptible to acute events. Students could also tell the story that every downside has an upside. The resulting death and destruction of World War I was unprecedented; however, it also resulted in a boom of innovation and economic recovery. The United States, for example, had been in a recession for nearly four years prior to the war. While the United States remained neutral for most of the war (only entering militarily in 1917), the European countries almost immediately began purchasing goods from the United States, causing an abrupt reversal of the economy. Once the United States entered the war, the boom was more significant as production and innovation had to increase. Unsurprisingly, after the war ended in 1918 came the Roaring Twenties.

So, what is the story of World War I? Is it the dawn of global interconnectedness? Is it the story of collective identities through the growth of nationalism? There are so many stories to tell. As students tell the story of World War I through their personal and cultural lenses, a student whose family has lived in the United States for generations might tell a different story than the student whose ancestors lived in Serbia or Austria in 1914. Events and facts are what they are, but they become humanized as students tell the story of what those events and facts mean and how they impact their worldview.

Students could even zoom out and examine the story through overarching themes. For example, they might ask such questions as, "What's the story of scientific breakthroughs?" "What story does every political revolution have in common?" or "How does music reflect the story of society?" Finding a story structure (such as those explored in chapter 1, page 13) and providing the opportunity for students to humanize events and things in our society will create meaningful connections that can potentially deepen their competence within any subject area.

The Story of How I'm Learning

Nothing will rehumanize assessment more rapidly than when students tell *their* story as learners. Examining themselves and reflecting on *how* they are learning allows them to be more self-regulatory. Students will come to know, for example, the conditions that maximize their learning, the strategies for overcoming initial misunderstandings, and methods for getting unstuck. The story of *what* they're learning is about the curricular standards; the story of *how* they learn is about themselves.

Metacognition

Metacognition is generally the ability both to be aware of one's cognitive processes (metacognitive knowledge) and to regulate them (metacognitive control; Fleur, Bredeweg, & van den Bos, 2021). Research consistently shows that higher achieving students exhibit higher levels of metacognitive knowledge about a given subject and are more skilled at regulating their cognitive processes (Baker, 2010). While there are a variety of definitions for metacognition in the field (Azevedo, 2020; Norman et al., 2019), this variety is more nuanced and does not detract from the big ideas that students develop their awareness of their own thought processes and the patterns behind them. Humanizing students' development of knowledge and skills through their own stories can add an emotional dimension to what might otherwise be a clinical exercise.

One dilemma in the research on metacognition that schools should pay attention to is the distinction between *domain-generality* and *domain-specificity* (Azevedo, 2020). If metacognition is domain-general, there's an expectation of transfer; metacognition is taught concurrently, and teachers expect students to transfer the knowledge and skills to new learning situations. If metacognition is domain-specific, metacognitive knowledge and skills are taught separately within each subject. The answer for schools is balance. The most efficient and effective approach to teaching metacognition is likely through a universal (domain-general) approach to establish some consistency across classrooms; it clearly would be challenging for students to navigate different metacognitive processes in each of their classes, especially at the secondary level, where students often have several different teachers. However, some subject-specific (domain-specific) nuances or adjustments might be necessary to account for differences in how the processes are carried out. For example, a student who finds one subject less than favorable might reflect on how to become more invested in the learning, while in other subjects where they thrive, their reflection might revolve around accelerating their expertise.

Assessment of Self

For the purpose of clarity, we differentiate *self-assessment* as a focus on curricular standards or competencies (*what* I'm learning; the standards) from the *assessment of self* as a metacognitive act (*how* I'm learning; the students' habits of learning). This is not a distinction made in academia; rather, it's a simple way to clarify the locus of attention. The assessment of self may initially be challenging for some students if it isn't habitual or if it's uncomfortable. Teachers should be patient with students as they develop both the will and the skill for the assessment of self. Building the will and the skill could take years. For example, a grade 1 teacher may introduce metacognitive processes and practices, but the students may finish the school year with underwhelming skill and will. The students may not actualize the skill and will until midway through grade 2 or grade 4. We must stick with it. If it's not habitual for teachers, it won't be habitual for students.

As students tell the story of how they learn, they can utilize a number of different strategies (that is, skills) to reveal the substance of their story. Researcher Chris Drew (2023) offers the following thirteen strategies teachers can use.

1. **Self-questioning:** Self-questioning involves pausing throughout a task to consciously check your own actions.

2. **Meditation:** Meditation involves clearing your mind. We could consider it to be a metacognitive strategy because meditators aim to—(a) clear out the chatter that goes on in our heads, (b) reach a calm and focused state that can prime students for learning, and (c) be more aware of our own inner speech.

3. **Reflection:** Reflection involves pausing to think about a task. It is usually a cyclical process where we reflect, think of ways to improve, try again, then go back to reflection.

4. **Awareness of strengths and weaknesses:** Central to metacognition is a person's capacity to see their own strengths and weaknesses. Only through looking at yourself and making a genuine assessment of your weaknesses can you achieve self-improvement.

5. **Awareness of learning styles:** If you are aware of how you learn (that is, the way your brain processes information!), you may be able to use your strengths and work on your weaknesses more efficiently.

6. **Mnemonic aids:** Mnemonic aids are strategies you can use to improve your information retention. They involve using rhymes, patterns, and associations to remember.

7. **Writing down your thinking:** This is about ensuring you are employing the right thinking processes and can show others how you went about thinking about the task.

8. **Thinking aloud:** You have to talk through what your brain is doing, making those thinking processes explicit. Teachers will often ask students to speak out loud about what they're thinking. It not only helps the student be more conscious of their cognitive processes, it also helps the teacher identify areas where the student is going astray.

9. **Graphic organizers:** The ideal graphic organizer will allow us to spill our thinking out onto a sheet or screen and shuffle and sort our thoughts to help us organize our minds better. By using a graphic organizer, we are more effectively thinking about our thinking.

10. **Regulation checklists:** A regulation checklist can either be task-based or generalized. A task-based regulation checklist is usually created before a task begins. A general regulation checklist provides regulation strategies that can be used across any task.

11. **Active reading strategies:** Active reading strategies are strategies that ensure you are concentrating while you read and actually comprehend the information.

12. **Active listening strategies:** Active listening strategies are strategies students use to ensure they are listening attentively.

13. **Planning ahead:** When we plan ahead, we often have to think about how we'll go about a task. We might call it our "plan of attack." Planning ahead involves thinking about what we're going to do in order to complete a task.

Visit https://helpfulprofessor.com/metacognitive-strategies for a complete description of all thirteen strategies.

Three Cautions to Consider

There are three important cautions to note. First, teachers should approach the *awareness of learning styles* strategy through the lens of helping students become aware of their most and least favorable ways to learn, but not as an endorsement of the now debunked learning styles literature (see American Psychological Association, 2019). The idea is not to identify one's learning style and lock into it but to understand one's preferences and then to actively work to stretch those preferences into a multitude of experiences.

Second, in the service of building habits, teachers would be wise to select a few strategies to utilize consistently. Variety could be favorable, but too much variety might lead students to spend too much time asking what to do instead of immersing themselves in the experience. Habits often unfold without thinking; for example, rarely does anyone think about driving while they are driving as there is an automaticity to it. Too many strategies may lead to cognitive overload and lack of habit formation.

Finally, it's important for teachers to stay active through the metacognitive processes. *Introspection illusions* is an idea first put forward by psychologists Richard Nisbett and Timothy D. Wilson (1977) and refers to the cognitive bias that causes human beings to overestimate their ability to understand their own mental states and the motives for their actions. The impact of introspection illusions may have students initially not seeing themselves in the most accurate or favorable light. The balance for teachers will be about staying actively involved throughout these processes to ensure accuracy without centering themselves, which neutralizes the metacognitive impact for students. There is no metacognition if a teacher tells a student what they are thinking. At the same time, accuracy matters since acting on inaccurate thoughts or information may lead to misguided decisions about next steps. The teacher is the mentor of student metacognition, not the main character.

Summary

For storytelling to take its rightful place as a viable assessment method, both teachers and students need to be well-versed in the fundamentals of sound assessment practices. Unlike assessment that simply counts right from wrong, assessment through storytelling requires teachers to make inferences about the degree to which the students have met the learning goals. Well-designed story prompts and clear criteria will go a long way to allowing for descriptive feedback and subsequent action by the student. Additionally, student investment in assessment occurs when assessment and the self-regulation of learning engage in a symbiotic relationship. Teachers can use assessment to teach students to be more self-regulatory about their learning; because they are teaching students to be more self-regulatory about their learning, students' assessment results tend to improve.

Assessment through storytelling creates the opportunity for teachers (and schools) to be more culturally expansive and to create 21st century competency relevance. Anchoring the storytelling efforts around cultural archetypes will ensure that students feel seen and that the approach to assessment through storytelling doesn't *otherize* them within the classroom. Also, assessment itself is a competency as it underpins the other competencies schools focus on. Students who understand the fundamentals of assessment will be better positioned to deepen their skills and dispositions within the competencies of record that schools and districts prioritize.

With those assessment fundamentals, students can both *self-assess* and practice *assessment of self.* Self-assessment provides the opportunity to tell the story of *what* they're learning. Students will examine the degree to which they have met the target or standard and identify their next steps on the pathway to excellence. The assessment of self is the metacognitive opportunity for students to tell the story of *how* they are learning. Students can use metacognitive strategies to uncover their thoughts and feelings, to closely examine what they can do to maximize their chances for success, to understand their own thinking, and to create new habits of learning that bring out their best.

Chapter 2 Discussion Questions for Learning Teams

Journal your response to the following prompts in the space provided. Share your thoughts during team discussion.

1. What quote or passage encapsulates your biggest takeaway from this chapter? What immediate action (small, medium, or large) will you take because of this takeaway? Explain both to your team.

2. What is the current status of your assessment literacy? Is your grasp of the six essential tenets of assessment strong, mixed, or at a novice level? Explain. What about your faculty as a whole?

3. How habitual is your use of assessment to teach students to be more self-regulatory about their learning? What aspects do you feel are strong and what aspects do you feel need strengthening?

4. How habitual is your use of cultural archetypes for assessment design? What aspects do you feel are strong and what aspects do you feel need strengthening?

5. What is your current level of comfort and competence with the distinction between students *answering test questions* and *telling the story* of what they are learning? What's clear and what needs clarification?

6. To what degree (a great deal, somewhat, not at all) are metacognitive practices and processes habitual in your classroom? What is strong and what needs strengthening? What about as a school?

7. How open (a great deal, somewhat, not at all) will your students be to telling the story of *how* they are learning? What aspects of your classroom culture (or school culture) do you feel need to be addressed to increase the students' level of openness to the assessment of self?

Rehumanizing Assessment © 2025 Solution Tree Press ▪ SolutionTree.com
Visit **go.SolutionTree.com/assessment** to download this free reproducible.

Chapter 3
CRITICAL COMPETENCIES THROUGH STORY

In an information-rich society, schools no longer need to prioritize imparting knowledge to students; instead, schools can now focus on using knowledge to develop critical 21st century competencies. The critical competencies are not a discrete set of skills that students simply *do*; rather, they are dispositional defaults determining who students eventually *become*. Storytelling provides rich, authentic evidence of these critical competencies.

This chapter discusses education's shift to ensure that students know what to do with their learning in response to accelerating technological advances. In a time when access to information is more efficient, students must become discerning about how to use that information in service of the collective. This chapter notes that the move toward critical competencies is a global phenomenon and examines how policies around the world are shaping their role in education. Storytelling is a viable way to assess students' grasp of the competencies, empowering them to demonstrate what and how they are learning.

The Big Idea

Access to knowledge and information has never been more efficient and has disrupted our traditional views of the purpose of school. What matters now is that students can *do something* with knowledge and information. In other words, they must develop the necessary critical competencies to be highly adaptable in this age of acceleration.

Adaptability and the Age of Acceleration

The *Great Acceleration*, a term coined by researchers Will Steffen, Paul J. Crutzen, and John R. McNeill (2007), refers to the post–World War II surge in human activity—particularly industrialization, urbanization, and resource use—that led to significant (that is, *accelerated*) environmental and social changes. One need only look to Moore's Law to see evidence of this acceleration. In the mid-1960s, Intel cofounder Gordon Moore (1965) predicted that the speed and power of microchips would double every one to two years, a prediction that continues to be accurate decades later. Consider the invention of the smartphone. It took humanity until the first decade of the 21st century to invent the smartphone, but since that time, smartphones have gone through an exponential number of changes and advancements.

Human adaptability has typically been on a steady incline; most people are more adaptable than the older generation but less adaptable than the younger generation. Again, adaptability to technology alone illustrates this. However, given that the acceleration of technological, social, and environmental impacts is exponential for the first time in our history, human adaptability is being outpaced. This leaves people feeling completely overwhelmed and constantly behind (Friedman, 2016). Advancements that used to take years now take months or even weeks. The accelerating pace of change requires a higher level of adaptability.

For students, this means that adaptability grows as they develop the skill and will of critical 21st century competencies. Rather than trying to predict what the future will look like to determine what students should learn (an impossible ask), educators would be wise to focus on those skills and dispositions that increase *adaptability*. Being a critical thinker, a clear communicator, a collaborator, a creator, and an innovator makes students highly adaptable and intellectually nimble. The effectiveness of a 21st century learning environment cannot be dependent on the collective best guess as to what the world will look like thirty years into the future because we can't afford to be wrong. Instead, we need to equip all students with *adaptive expertise*.

Means and *Ends* Switching Places

Traditionally, teachers were the knowledge keepers; they vetted any misinformation or misunderstandings prior to imparting knowledge to students. Students could trust the information they received was true, or at least true given what society knew at the time. That era is over. Acquiring information is the simple part; the challenge now is doing something substantial and sophisticated with that information.

Technology, and specifically the emergence of AI, has created a need for consumers of information to be more discriminatory than ever. Given the way misinformation has blurred the lines of reality, students must be able to distinguish fact from fiction. That doesn't develop without intentionality. The ability to use critical thinking to identify trustworthy sources of information is more important than ever. There is arguably too much information available and the ability to cut through the noise is one of many skills schools have been compelled to address as society accelerated into the 21st century.

To remain relevant, the education system is adapting. Not everywhere, of course, but more and more education systems are recognizing that the ubiquitous access to knowledge and information allows the focus to shift to *doing something* with that knowledge and information—thus the focus on critical competencies. The overemphasis on memorization in the past hindered some students from thinking at a more sophisticated level. Now, *thinking* sits at the forefront and the information needed to think is at students' fingertips. While learning curricular content used to be the *end*, it is now the *means*. Teachers used to put students into collaborative groups to do a project centered on learning curricular content. Now, teachers are using curricular content to teach collaboration. The means and ends need to switch places. Education can't exist in a 21st century society with 20th century curriculum and pedagogy.

Knowledge, Skills, and Attitudes

Despite the repositioning of knowledge and information, knowledge still matters. Whether students are innovating, creating, collaborating, or critically thinking, they have to think about something. While memorization may not be necessary, it is advantageous to know things or at least know where to efficiently access information to allow them to more seamlessly develop their capacity with the competencies. False dichotomies are not helpful; it's not content versus competencies. Rather, it's competencies through content and it's the specifics of the competencies that highlight the difference between the superficial and the meaningful. *Content* is always needed (that is, students have to think about *something*) but it is the means to an end; teachers use science content, for example, to teach collaboration. There is a big difference between *cooperation* and *collaboration*.

The skills of the competencies are where the depth exists. Teaching students to collaborate means teaching them, among many things, how to establish roles and responsibilities, come to consensus, productively disagree with one another, and resolve conflict. That piece was often missing when teachers traditionally asked students to produce group projects. Critical thinking and innovation often involve the construction of knowledge or an innovative solution to an existing dilemma. The skills of analysis, synthesis, evaluation (that is, assessment), hypothesis, and prediction (to name a few) are all necessary to think critically. Critical thinking often depends on content proficiency, making it difficult to assume its transfer to other contexts (Abrami et al., 2015; Willingham, 2020). Nonetheless, it would be a desirable outcome that students not just *do* the competencies but *become* the competencies.

Students must become critical thinkers, collaborators, creators, and innovators as a default disposition. And they must achieve a level of automaticity that extends beyond the school environment. Again, teachers can't take this for granted; they must intentionally make connections between the competencies and the students' outside world. For instance, teachers could ask students for examples of how they used critical thinking skills on the weekend, at home, or with their friends. What problems did they solve? Did they collaborate with someone to solve a problem or complete a project? Did they use any of the skills they learned at school? Teachers might also provide hypothetical scenarios for students to grapple with that illustrate their ability to transfer skills. Making that connection will bring obvious relevance to what the students may perceive as just another required set of learning outcomes.

Cultural Connection

The global movement toward competencies is gaining momentum. While this movement takes on various names and degrees of implementation, there is a collective sense of urgency to meet the moment internationally. Examples emerging from around the world illustrate that the move toward competency-based education is not uniquely North American. In the following sections, we look at a few examples in close detail.

Kenya

In 2017, the government of Kenya launched a new competency-based curriculum. Generally, people welcomed the move due to long-standing concerns over the former curriculum's preoccupation with examinations, heavy workloads, and a teacher-centric instructive approach (Mills, 2023). This monumental shift grew out of the 1998 report of the Commission of Inquiry Into the Education System in Kenya.

Kenya's national curriculum policy states, "The challenge for educationalists worldwide is to prepare learners for current realities without limiting their ability to succeed in the larger community and the global realities of work and life in the 21st century" (Ministry of Education, Science and Technology, 2015, p. 1). Specifically, one of the objectives outlined in the policy is to establish a competency-based education "that emphasizes the importance of producing learners who can take initiative and creatively innovate products and processes that spur talents and development of values" (p. 14). The emphases on taking initiative (student driven) and being creatively innovative (critical and creative problem solving) underpin the Kenyan government's recognition that they need to modernize their education system.

Even their assessment policies align with a modern paradigm. Consider the following statement from Kenya's national curriculum policy on assessing competencies:

> To enhance comprehensive understanding of the progress made by learners at all levels, [the Ministry of Education] will pursue the following policies:
>
> - Establish mechanisms for conducting both formative and summative evaluation as a means of achieving comprehensive results of learning outcomes;
>
> - Create an enabling environment for performance based learning, and transform assessment to check knowledge, skills and abilities required for the performance of certain tasks; and
>
> - Initiate organizational linkages and networks to promote adoption and implementation of competency based assessment. (Ministry of Education, Science and Technology, 2015, p. 19)

The intent to use both formative and summative evaluation and the emphasis on performance-based learning clearly align with 21st century goals. That said, how the policy is operationalized in schools will make the difference between success and failure.

India

In 2020, the government of India approved the National Education Policy (NEP) that ushered in large-scale, transformational reforms for students from ages three to eighteen, as well as higher education. This policy replaced the thirty-four-year-old policy introduced in 1986 and marked a significant shift in the educational priorities for India:

> [The NEP] seeks to "ensure inclusive and equitable quality education and promote lifelong learning opportunities for all" by 2030. Such a lofty goal will require the entire education system to be reconfigured to support and foster learning, so that all of the critical targets and goals (SDGs) of the 2030 Agenda for Sustainable Development can be achieved. (Ministry of Human Resource Development, Government of India, 2020, p. 3)

The rationale for the policy is compelling and clearly indicates a shift in alignment with other jurisdictions around the world seeking to bring their school systems into the 21st century. The policy cites a rapidly changing knowledge landscape, dramatic advances in technology, and the need for multidisciplinary abilities. The NEP also asserts that climate change, increases in pollution, and depleting natural resources demand a new and differently skilled labor force and the rise of epidemics and pandemics calls for collaborative research in infectious disease management. All of this requires the educational system to quickly and significantly shift focus:

> Indeed, with the quickly changing employment landscape and global ecosystem, it is becoming increasingly critical that children not only learn, but more importantly learn how to learn. Education thus, must move towards less content, and more towards learning about how to think critically and solve problems, how to be creative and multidisciplinary, and how to innovate, adapt, and absorb new material in novel and changing fields. Pedagogy must evolve to make education more experiential, holistic, integrated, inquiry-driven, discovery-oriented, learner-centred, discussion-based, flexible, and, of course, enjoyable. The curriculum must include basic arts, crafts, humanities, games, sports and fitness, languages, literature, culture, and values, in addition to science and mathematics, to develop all aspects and capabilities of learners; and make education more well-rounded, useful, and fulfilling to the learner. Education must build character, enable learners to be ethical, rational, compassionate, and caring, while at the same time prepare them for gainful, fulfilling employment. (Ministry of Human Resource Development, Government of India, 2020, p. 3)

Students telling the story of their learning and how they learn aligns seamlessly with the previous policy statement. Not only would it fulfill the NEP's curricular goals, but it would also certainly allow the students a learner-centered, artistic, fulfilling, and enjoyable education experience. The policy emphasizes the need to reduce curriculum content to enhance essential learning and critical thinking as well as experiential learning that includes "story-telling-based pedagogy" (Ministry of Human Resource Development, Government of India, 2020, p. 12).

Specific to assessment, the NEP proposes the establishment of a national assessment center called PARAKH (Performance Assessment, Review, and Analysis of Knowledge for Holistic Development) to establish norms, standards, and guidelines for student assessment. The PARAKH mandate, among several things, is tasked with the responsibility of "encouraging and helping school boards to shift their assessment patterns towards meeting the skill requirements of the 21st century in consonance with the stated objectives of [the NEP]" (Ministry of Human Resource Development, Government of India, 2020, p. 18). Students will still be required to take exams at certain intervals and will still focus on basic skills and knowledge, but they will also be assessed on their "relevant higher-order thinking skills and their application of knowledge in real-life situations, rather than rote memorization" (p. 18). This approach to assessment would meet the moment of a 21st century education for students in India.

British Columbia

In Canada, the province of British Columbia introduced a revised curriculum in 2015 that replaced prescribed learning outcomes with curricular competencies. The change was significant as many saw the previous curriculum as too prescriptive and restrictive. Highlights of the redesigned curriculum in British Columbia (BC) include:

- **Personalized Learning:** The redesign of BC's curriculum provides flexibility to inspire the personalization of learning and addresses the diverse needs and interests of BC students.

- **Ecology and the Environment:** Revisions to the Science curriculum were made to ensure better representation of ecology and environmental learning.

- **Historical Wrongs:** The curriculum includes the history of the Asian and South Asian communities and their contributions to the development of our province—as well as the injustices they experienced.

- **Aboriginal Perspectives and Knowledge:** Aboriginal culture and perspectives have been integrated throughout all areas of learning. For example, place-based learning and emphasis on indigenous ways of knowing reflect the First Peoples Principles of Learning in the curriculum.
- **Flexible Learning Environments:** BC's redesigned curriculum provides teachers with great flexibility in creating learning environments that are relevant, engaging, and novel. Flexible learning environments give consideration to local contexts and place-based learning. (Government of British Columbia, n.d.a)

While literacy and numeracy remained at the heart of the redesigned curriculum, the real shift was the establishment of core competencies necessary for students to engage in deeper learning. They include *thinking* (critical and creative thinking), *communication* (including collaboration), and *personal and social* (positive personal and cultural identity, personal awareness and responsibility, social awareness and responsibility) competencies. These core competencies are embedded within every subject and are identified as *curricular competencies*; they are the core competencies contextualized within each subject area. Visit https://curriculum.gov.bc.ca for more information on the BC curriculum.

One aspect of the revised BC curriculum relevant to storytelling is the focus on personalized learning and the emphasis on the whole learner. The British Columbia Ministry of Education (Government of British Columbia, n.d.c) defines *personalized learning* as a student-centered education tailored to individual needs that is responsive to the passions, interests, aspirations, and needs of students. Encouraging teachers to tailor their assessment methods to include students telling the story of what they are learning would honor those students for whom storytelling is a passion and interest. Additionally, the emphasis on *personal awareness* as a core competency provides a seamless alignment to telling the story of how students learn. The metacognitive exercise of personal awareness would translate nicely into a student narrative about how they learn.

The other aspect relevant to storytelling is the purposeful integration of Aboriginal perspectives and knowledge. Because storytelling is synonymous with Indigenous ways of knowing, not only does storytelling provide an expansive approach to assessment, but it also has a clear and obvious cultural connection to British Columbia. In partnership with the First Nations Education Steering Committee (FNESC, n.d.), the Ministry of Education consulted with Indigenous elders, scholars, and knowledge keepers, and together developed the First Peoples Principles of

Learning. Consider a few of the principles that make storytelling an important approach to assessment and learning:

> Learning is holistic, reflexive, reflective, experiential, and relational (focused on connectedness, on reciprocal relationships, and a sense of place).
> Learning is embedded in memory, history, and story.
> Learning requires exploration of one's identity. (FNESC, n.d.)

Visit the First Nations Education Steering Committee's website at www.fnesc.ca /first-peoples-principles-of-learning to view the full list of principles.

Nothing is more holistic, experiential, or closely aligned with one's identity than storytelling. Learning being embedded in memory, history, and story overtly endorses storytelling as a way of learning and, therefore, assessing. Storytelling as a viable and authentic means of learning and assessment is apparent throughout the revised BC curriculum.

Implementation Is the Key

While the previous examples highlight how a focus on competencies is relatively widespread, it is important to recognize that there is a difference between a policy document and full implementation at the classroom level. Policies don't always guarantee implementation, and even when implementation occurs, it takes time to go to scale. Implementation will be the key to manifesting the visions articulated throughout this section, but an unwavering commitment to the modernization of the education systems worldwide is the only way it can begin.

Competency Connection

Globally, the four Cs (critical thinking, creativity, collaboration, and communication) are ubiquitous (Battelle for Kids, 2019). After that, the list of additional competencies globally is long, diverse, and debatable. For our purposes, we'll narrow the focus to seven critical competencies (three in addition to the four Cs) that foster the development of student agency.

The seven critical competencies outlined in the book *Growing Tomorrow's Citizens in Today's Classrooms: Assessing Seven Critical Competencies* (Erkens et al., 2019) underpin the exploration of story as a viable and authentic assessment method. Consider this brief description of each of the seven critical competencies:

1. **Self-regulation:** Individuals and collaborative teams must understand what they know and what they don't know and how to navigate and learn when they don't know. *Self-regulation* is the ability to recognize the conditions and situations that motivate or shut down people— whether as individuals, teams, or systems. Self-regulation is the ability to independently monitor progress and deal with defeat, yet still persist—by learning from previous experiences.

2. **Critical thinking:** Individuals and teams must think critically to analyze, evaluate, and synthesize ideas and information to understand issues, concepts, and other phenomena. Critical thinking helps make sense of the world and sheds light on steps to create progress. Individuals, teams, and systems must critically evaluate sources of information and determine credibility. Given the plethora of information at one's fingertips in the modern world, the ability to identify surface-level insight, fluffy ideas, meaningful insights, valid information, or plausible ideas is essential.

3. **Collaboration:** Individuals, teams, and systems must work together to communicate and apply information, and creatively solve problems and develop innovative solutions to the world's most pressing challenges. Individuals, teams, and systems must bring together diverse perspectives, work through conflict productively, generate solutions, and create new ideas or products.

4. **Creative thinking:** Individuals, teams, and systems must put unique, competing, and unrelated ideas together to generate new and more innovative solutions. This is imperative to deal with changing demands, changing climate, changing technology, and changing social conditions. Each of these contexts provides rich opportunities for creativity to thrive.

5. **Communication:** Verbal, written, and digital communication [are] essential to effectively collaborating, problem solving, and creatively engaging with diverse individuals and groups. Learners must use different [media] to clearly articulate and share ideas, as well as debate and provide counter-ideas and counterarguments. Innovation depends on sharing ideas clearly, building on ideas fluidly, critiquing ideas productively, and defending ideas thoughtfully.

6. **Digital citizenship:** Learners must become digital citizens who understand how to ethically, productively, and proactively conduct themselves online. Digital citizens are globally competent and understand the etiquette of communicating with diverse individuals and groups in a variety of online venues. Digital citizens seek to understand diverse points of view and perspectives.

7. **Social competence:** Learners in this new context must be socially aware and learn how to use all the critical competencies to contribute solutions to the larger issues plaguing local and global communities. Socially competent individuals see how the health and education of both the individual and groups contribute to the whole. Socially competent humans use the critical-thinking competencies to make their own circles, as well as the larger community's, more inviting and inclusive places for all. Individuals and groups that serve the larger community feel connected and part of creating the world in which they would like to live. (Erkens et al., 2019, pp. 4–6)

Some competencies (for example, critical thinking) will be relatively easy to develop, as elements of them already exist throughout many curricular standards. For example, students are already being asked to analyze, evaluate, synthesize, and hypothesize. Other competencies, such as collaboration, may need further development since few standards stipulate that they be met collectively.

While the competencies are listed separately, they should not be viewed as separate silos; rather, they should be viewed as integrated skills and dispositions. Critical thinking and problem solving often involve an element of creativity and can be done collaboratively. Life is not siloed and dilemmas don't come neatly packaged. The more teachers can create integrative opportunities, the easier it will be for students to integrate these skills into their everyday lives. This approach will be accelerated if we position content or subjects as the means and competencies as the end! The following sections provide more detail about three of the competencies.

Digital Citizenship

One of the competencies that we will not address directly in the book is digital citizenship. Digital citizenship is important since students often tell their stories digitally, but for the purposes of this book, we will position this competency on the periphery as a method rather than a means. While digital citizenship is a critical competency worthy of exploration on its own, it has a natural and essential interdependency with the other critical competencies (Erkens et al., 2019).

When most people think of *citizenship*, they think of being respectful, polite, responsible, and positive; *digital citizenship* is exactly that in a digital world. Given the fact that the digital world can be anonymous, it is even more crucial that this citizenship becomes habitual within our students as they grow into adulthood. Teachers must intentionally address, nurture, and establish the habits and dispositions students need to cultivate in a largely text-dominated world. According to Mike Ribble (n.d.), a pioneer in this field, there are nine elements of digital citizenship: (1) digital access, (2) digital commerce, (3) digital communication, (4) digital literacy, (5) digital etiquette, (6) digital law, (7) digital rights and responsibilities, (8) digital health and wellness, and (9) digital security.

The challenge is that although digital citizenship is frequently espoused, what it means to be a digital citizen has different connotations depending on who is referencing the term. Defining digital citizenship is further complicated by the fact that some academics subscribe to the theory that it centers on the individual's responsible use of technology while others believe it's an extension of democratic citizenship that may include both civic agency and community involvement (Davis, 2020).

Despite the disagreements in academia, there are several habits and dispositions that epitomize digital citizenship. Digital citizenship often begins with empathy since it is impossible to hear someone's tone or see their facial expressions in a text-dominated space. As a result, it's easy for users to make harsh judgments about someone's intent online. A related concept is *digital wellness*, which is the habit of disconnecting from the digital world for mental and physical health. Of course, digital citizenship also includes understanding the technicalities of the digital world in terms of how the internet works, how to use data appropriately and respectfully, and how to remain safe and secure. It is an important 21st century competency that requires intentional action and continual practice.

Communication

Communication is another competency that we will not specifically address in the remaining chapters of the book because storytelling *is*, of course, communication. However, through story, students can go deeper in their speaking and listening skills.

Strong communicators anticipate the potential interpretations of their messages and then select the most appropriate means to elicit a favorable response from the receiver. The most favorable story structure and means of communication can create a compelling story. Likewise, strong receivers of messages know how to infer, recognize nuances, consider the context and the subtext, scrutinize credibility, and then examine potential pros and cons before simply accepting a message at face value. Though many people excel at communication, there really is nothing simple about communication.

Whether verbal or nonverbal, communication means conveying one's thoughts, ideas, feelings, concerns, and solutions. Effectiveness rests with the healthy and productive manner with which those messages are delivered and received. Conveying the story of what they are learning and how they learn will require students to consider the healthiest and most productive ways to deliver their stories and think about how those stories will be received. One might communicate *their* truth, for example, but that truth could be misunderstood or be harmful to the receiver. Communicating with fierce determination regardless of the fallout could be an unintended consequence that takes away from the intended message. Of course, there are times where the receiver might need to hear a tough truth and that has to be acceptable, but in most cases telling our stories includes considering how our stories might land with others.

Self-Regulation

At the heart of storytelling is *student agency*, meaning that students are the primary decision makers of their learning through voice, choice, motivation, ownership, and self-efficacy. According to the Organisation for Economic Co-operation and Development (OECD, 2018), student agency "does not mean functioning in social isolation, nor does it mean acting solely in self-interest. Similarly, student agency does not mean that students can voice whatever they want or can choose whatever subjects they wish to learn" (p. 4). Agency must be contextualized (both socially and academically) if it is to fulfill the promise of an enhanced, personalized learning experience.

With digital citizenship, learners are engaged in actively discussing and determining what it means to be respectful and responsible in the digital space; they are the arbiters (in an age-appropriate way) of what is and is not appropriate (that is, they have agency) for their peers and others. There will, of course, always be teacher guidance and advising as students develop their own understandings of what constitutes appropriate digital norms. Ultimately, however, the goal would be to transition to a primarily student-driven and student-regulated model, at least within the context of the school, as students tell the story of what and how they learn. Hopefully, these norms extend beyond the school environment as well.

The agency developed within the digital space can and does overlap within the expanded context of social competence (a competency more fully explored in the next chapter). Ideally, students should have agency in developing positive and productive social norms within the school setting. With the guidance of their teachers, students adhere to social norms and begin to thrive as their social competence grows. With time, students gain the competence to adapt to a variety of situations and know what social skills best fit without adult supervision. When telling the story of *what* and *how* they learn, students would have the social competence and awareness to both self-monitor and monitor others in real time to know how a story is landing.

The overarching competency of all of this is *self-regulation*. Being able to *regulate* oneself means having the ability to independently monitor progress, deal with defeat, yet still persist—by learning from previous experiences (Erkens et al., 2019). There are several different perspectives in academia about self-regulation. However, these perspectives share many common features, including the idea that self-regulation involves being behaviorally, cognitively, metacognitively, and motivationally active in one's learning and performance (Schunk & Greene, 2018). All of these actions are essential to storytelling as a viable assessment method.

While there is a tendency to explore self-regulation through the lens of motivation, the much broader application lands within both the cognitive and affective domains. While students are telling the story of what they are learning, it is important for them to monitor how they feel; for example, are they feeling hopeful and efficacious about achieving a learning goal? Students self-regulating while telling the story of how they learn is at the heart of the experience since the metacognitive process is about developing a deep understanding of the conditions and habits that maximize students' potential success. The story of how one learns can be deeply personal, so it is important for students to regulate their emotions and develop coping strategies when regulation eludes them, even if momentarily.

The Story of What I'm Learning

Stories are a viable assessment method that can uniquely reveal a depth and breadth of understanding about what students are learning. However, it is not only content understanding that will be revealed, but also evidence of competency development. The challenge we face as educators is choosing which competency to prioritize.

Competencies Aren't Silos

Two things are important when assessing critical competencies through story. First, we know the competencies do not, operationally, exist in silos. Rather, there is natural overlap between them. The overlap exists, for example, when students are collaboratively problem solving to communicate an innovative or creative solution to the dilemma at hand. Despite teaching the critical competencies (at times) separately, teachers would be wise to seek opportunities to merge them since that's where authenticity lies. Second, while there is a fusion between the competencies, it is also wise to establish a point of emphasis or priority for assessment since it can be challenging to assess everything at once.

Students could create a science-themed podcast where they would tell the story of scientific phenomena, experiments, or even the biographies of influential scientists. Science fiction storytelling would allow students to use their scientific knowledge and skills through an imaginative process to create a narrative that illustrates their understanding of scientific processes and principles. Each of these examples could also be done through collaborative student teams. Teachers would be able to assess the students' willingness to think with creative intent (and collaborate) through the substance of scientific principles.

In physical education, students could create and then role-play scenarios that involve skills, movement, and overall fitness. The scenarios could incorporate critical and creative thinking that involves physical movement and strength. For example, "You're locked out of your house but there is an open window on the second floor. Hypothetically, what strength and agility would you need to climb up to the second floor and enter your home?"

In history, students could create storyboards or comics that depict certain historical events or write a journal or diary from the perspective of someone who lived through a particular time or event. What if social media existed during the American Revolution? Podcasts or radio dramas could also be an effective way to infuse research, writing, collaboration, creativity, communication, critical thinking, and more.

Find a Natural Fit

Rather than forcing it, finding the best and natural fit for students' particular learning is key. It's unlikely that teachers can emphasize every competency for assessment simultaneously, so planning with the totality of the experience in mind is both wise and manageable. All competencies could exist to some degree within a robust task, but the question is what to emphasize when it comes to assessment. The critical competencies are already encapsulated to varying degrees within current curricular standards. Critical thinking and communication are embedded throughout, while creative thinking and collaboration may require some intentional design. Digital citizenship, social competence, and self-regulation can be infused throughout the processes as students use storytelling throughout the range of learning experiences teachers create. Students will refine their skill with the competencies with practice.

The Story of How I'm Learning

As students tell the story of how they are learning the competencies, it will be important to proactively establish (or co-create) criteria students can use to monitor themselves.

Structure and Predictability

Creating tools, structures, and predictable routines for metacognitive monitoring will go a long way to helping students establish the habit. Single-point rubrics, which outline specific criteria while leaving room for open-ended feedback or reflection, can be advantageous to find the balance in not being too tight or loose with criteria. Figures 3.1 and 3.2 are examples of single-point rubrics students can use to reflect on their willingness to think with creative intent.

Things I Am Good At		Things I Could Do Better
	Preparation: I had a very interesting question and I wanted to find the answer.	
	Incubation: I found many different ways to answer my question.	
	Illumination: I had a spark that led to a new way of thinking about my question.	
	Evaluation: I asked for feedback and others thought my ideas would work.	
	Implementation: I was able to solve the problem or create something new with my idea.	

Source: Adapted from Erkens et al., 2019.

FIGURE 3.1: Single-point rubric for creative thinking (elementary school).

Visit go.SolutionTree.com/assessment for a free reproducible version of this figure.

Strengths		Opportunities to Improve
	Preparation: I was truly curious about something that required further investigation.	
	Incubation: I played with a lot of ideas, even from different areas of study. I was able to blend ideas, imagine new possibilities, and construct possibilities.	
	Illumination: As I was playing with my ideas, I had new insights or aha moments that caused a spark of excitement. I was confident my ideas were original and would be exciting to others too.	
	Verification: I was able to test my ideas to make sure they were plausible or pleasing to others. I gathered feedback because I wanted to know what wouldn't work as much as what would work. I listened to feedback when I thought it was relevant and made focused revisions as needed so that I could produce an excellent product, performance, or solution.	
	Implementation: I was able to complete my task and bring my project to life. I successfully moved it from an idea to a reality.	

Source: Adapted from Erkens et al., 2019.

FIGURE 3.2: Single-point rubric for creative thinking (secondary school).

Visit go.SolutionTree.com/assessment for a free reproducible version of this figure.

The criteria in figures 3.1 and 3.2 are examples of tools students could use to gather their thoughts before they tell the story of how well they think with creative intent. What are their strengths? What needs strengthening? What obstacles did they face and how can they overcome them proactively next time? What puts them in a creative flow? These are all reflection points that teachers can facilitate with a simple tool that organizes the student's thinking as they craft their own personal narrative.

Making this metacognitive process a part of the reporting system would be a desirable outcome as well, though not through the traditional means most systems have used. The reporting would not be for the purpose of yet another grade but for some accountability toward personal growth, with that accountability being internal (within the student) rather than externally coerced.

In British Columbia, for example, the Ministry of Education has articulated that students are responsible for assessing their own growth in the core competencies, but there are ways for teachers to create meaningful opportunities to assist students in doing so:

- Teachers can use the sub-competency profiles and illustrations to support students in their growth as educated citizens.

- Providing students with meaningful tasks and activities, where they can explicitly reflect on where and how they are using the core competencies, will further their development in Communication, Thinking, and Personal and Social. The illustrations for each sub-competency provide examples of rich tasks, activities, and feedback.

- The Core Competencies are embedded within the curriculum and are naturally supported when students engage with the Big Ideas and Curricular Competencies in each area of learning. Examples of explicit connections with Big Ideas can be found in the "Connection" section for each sub-competency.

- Teachers support students in assessing their own growth in the Core Competencies. (Government of British Columbia, n.d.b)

The support teachers will provide to students is likely to come when they highlight the connections between the specific curricular competencies within each subject area. The story of how they learn could be filled with successes and challenges, and it is within those connections that the substance of the stories will be found. Consider the following fictional example of what a high school student *could* express when telling the story of how they learn critical competencies:

> *I really enjoy the social part of collaboration and also working together with my classmates, but I do find it challenging to stay focused when everyone gets excited and starts talking at once. I find I can't focus on one thing and then I forget what everyone says, and I get rattled. I remember this from birthday parties when I was a little kid as well; I get overwhelmed. One time in my English class, our group (collaboration) was analyzing (critical thinking) a short story to determine its theme and everyone was leaning in and almost yelling what they thought with no rhyme or*

reason. Finally, I just raised my hand and asked the group if we could each take a turn because there are a lot of good ideas and we are not hearing each other. I was really proud of myself because I'm usually not that bold, but they agreed. I also suggested we write down everyone's ideas so that we don't forget, especially when it came to the evidence that would support the claims they made about theme.

The student might communicate this story through various media, but the main message is the same: this is how I most effectively collaborate with my group members. Students might initially need some sentence starters or prompting to build the habit and identify the substance of their learning, but the goal is metacognitive independence. Digital or physical portfolios could provide a more substantive way for students to self-report their growth within each of the competencies.

Teachers as Role Models

Teacher role modeling is another way to support students in building desired habits. Teachers could share the story of how they learn with their students to illustrate their own strengths and challenges as they grow professionally or personally. This can give students a firsthand view as to how their teacher thinks critically and problem solves. Learning experiences aren't linear, which gives the teacher the opportunity to share how they overcame obstacles. For example, a teacher who is learning to play golf could reveal, "I was trying to stop slicing every drive. I kept opening my club face, so I started hitting half-swing shots at a slower tempo to try to correct my swing." This models critical thinking and a solution-focused mindset. It's not, "I'm bad at golf," but rather, "How do I fix this?"

A teacher could also share their internal successes, frustrations, and challenges as they learn something new, such as a new instructional strategy, or how to play the piano or build a backyard patio. Sharing their internal dialogue for working through an issue can be most helpful for students inexperienced at self-reflection and metacognition. Learning something new is not just clinical. There are always emotional ups and downs when learning something new, and revealing those (to a point) can demonstrate for students how to manage their own self-talk. For example, a teacher could say, "I felt myself getting frustrated trying to ensure that I got the measurements right for our backyard. When I get frustrated, I don't think straight. So, I took a deep breath, refocused on the process I needed to follow, slowed down, and got it right." It shows that the teacher is human and that it's normal to experience and manage emotions when learning.

The overarching benefit is the modeling of lifelong learning. Students benefit from seeing that learning is not restricted to K–12 experiences and that it can be a lifelong endeavor (if we choose). There are no grades or scores attached to so many things adults choose to learn, which sets a tone of curiosity and knowledge or skill seeking. It sends the message to stay inquisitive long after their formal education has ended. We can't overlook the impact that modeling could have on our students. Teachers describing how they learn could make them more relatable and potentially reframe for students what it means to be a learner.

Summary

Adaptability through developing critical competency skills and dispositions is the way forward in education. Access to information has never been more efficient. However, students need the skills to recognize what information is credible, what innovations they need, and what collaboration looks like, as so many societal issues and dilemmas exist beyond ourselves, our communities, and even our countries. The critical competencies reposition curricular content as the means to an end since students will always have to think, collaborate, and innovate about something. The end becomes the skills and dispositions that are, under the best circumstances, fluid throughout their lives both in and out of school.

The move toward critical competencies is a global phenomenon. Cultures and countries around the world recognize the need for students to develop these skills and dispositions for success in the 21st century. While there may be some nuanced contextual and cultural differences in implementing the plans, the big ideas are universal and expanding their reach throughout the world. Most critical to this movement is the consensus that these competencies must be assessed to substantiate the claims both students and teachers make regarding the authentic development of the competencies. Again, there may be various degrees of implementation at this point, but the global recognition that this shift is necessary is clear.

Storytelling fits seamlessly with the need to assess critical competencies. There are facts, there are skills, and then there is the *story* of what students are learning. Telling the story that underpins their learning humanizes it so there is no knowledge vacuum or silo. Telling the story of how they learn shines the light of assessing the competencies on the students themselves. When they are metacognitive, they think critically about themselves, communicating their self-observations, thinking of creative ways to overcome obstacles, and potentially seeking ideas and support for continual growth. The story of *what* and *how* they learn is how students will reveal their growth with the skills and dispositions of the critical competencies.

Chapter 3 Discussion Questions for Learning Teams

Journal your response to the following prompts in the space provided. Share your thoughts during team discussion.

1. What quote or passage encapsulates your biggest takeaway from this chapter? What immediate action (small, medium, or large) will you take because of this takeaway? Explain both to your team.

2. In what ways do you use storytelling to allow students to demonstrate critical and creative thinking? What new ideas come to mind after reading this chapter?

3. What are some specific (small, medium, or large) examples of how you already use storytelling to develop collaboration and communication skills within your students? What new ideas come to mind after reading this chapter?

Page 1 of 2

Rehumanizing Assessment © 2025 Solution Tree Press • SolutionTree.com
Visit **go.SolutionTree.com/assessment** to download this free reproducible.

| REPRODUCIBLE | 79 |

4. Which of the critical competencies described in this chapter do you feel is a natural fit for your subject area or grade level? Why?

5. How do you, or could you, integrate digital storytelling or other technology tools to enhance both traditional and 21st century storytelling techniques in a culturally responsive manner?

6. How have you incorporated self-assessment into storytelling activities or assignments?

7. What examples do you have of tools or methods you use, or could use, to facilitate students' self-reflection on their competencies?

Page 2 of 2

Rehumanizing Assessment © 2025 Solution Tree Press • SolutionTree.com
Visit **go.SolutionTree.com/assessment** to download this free reproducible.

PART 2

LEARNING THROUGH STORY

In this part of the book, we build on the research foundation we set in part 1 (page 11) to explore practical strategies for implementation. Each chapter is organized around a central concept drawn from a cultural perspective on storytelling.

For instance, conflict is the central concept of chapter 4 (page 83), drawn from the classical understanding of story as having a beginning, middle, and end organized around a central confrontation or conflict. With this concept in mind, we explore the role of productive struggle in learning, especially as it relates to interpersonal struggles, and describe ways for students to tell these stories as evidence of learning.

Chapter 5 (page 109) focuses on a four-part Japanese story structure called Kishōtenketsu that is organized around reconciliation, or the restoration of harmony. Drawing from the story structure, we explore different opportunities for students to reconcile the big ideas across units, or differing strengths in collaborative endeavors.

The remaining chapters are grounded in the concepts of perspective, reflection, imagination, and craft. There is no intended order to read these chapters in, so feel free to choose a concept you would like to explore in your space to begin. As you read, use the graphic organizer in the epilogue (figure E.1, page 242) to take note of the different strategies you will commit to trying.

Chapter 4
CONFLICT THROUGH STORY

Western story structures all have one thing in common: a central conflict. Whether it is internal (within the character themselves) or external (against others, nature, or society), it is this tension that forces the character to make a choice and move the story to resolution. Telling the story of how conflicts are untangled is essential for students as they learn how to approach struggle productively and unlock deeper learning about course content, themselves, and each other.

This chapter examines conflict as a force that drives story forward, providing the opportunity for productive struggle. By facing the internal and external conflicts in their lives, students can learn to recognize their tragic flaw, practice vulnerability, and embrace imperfection in the learning process. Students must master self-regulation and social competence to successfully navigate a pluralistic society and the inevitable conflicts that arise. This chapter concludes by offering three tools teachers can use to support students to tell the story of how they're learning: (1) conflict exit tickets, (2) conflict resolution story circle, and (3) the learning pit story.

The Big Idea

Conflict is the engine that moves a story forward. It is what creates a problem that a character must resolve, leading them to make choices that will impact the resolution. It is the catalyst for learning, not a dead end. In the following sections, we examine conflict as productive struggle, as well as external and internal conflict.

Conflict as Productive Struggle

Culturally we often talk about conflict as if it's a problem, something to avoid. Rather than see conflict as negative, it is helpful if we think of conflict as neutral, an unavoidable byproduct of being alive, and recognize that it is our aggressive, dominant, or competitive *responses* to it that are the problem (Deutsch, 1973). If we can work through our avoidance of conflict, we might even see it as beneficial. In the workplace, research supports the benefits of *task conflict*, or a struggle over ideas and opinions, which leads to heightened creativity and decision making in teams (Jehn, 1995). If we imagine classrooms as a microcosm of the future workplace, we can see how conflict is a necessary element of the critical competencies we wish students to develop.

The presence of conflict in story has a long history in Western discourse. Around 335 BC, Aristotle (2008) famously wrote in *Poetics* that a great story must have a beginning, middle, and end in sequential order and that the middle must be a confrontation of some kind. Using language like *confrontation* speaks to the negative perception of conflict as it alludes to a battle where one side will emerge victorious while the other perishes. This perception of conflict in Western cultures is visible throughout our history of colonialism, in which acquiring land was the prize for winning the conflict with Indigenous people already living there.

However, as we've updated our cultural narrative, trading conquest for coexistence in diverse nations, so too must we update our narrative of conflict. In 2014, the National Council of Teachers of Mathematics (NCTM) brought a relatively new phrase into the educational lexicon: *productive struggle* (Caldwell, Kobett, & Karp, 2014). As the name implies, this is the type of struggle that results in progress, deeper learning, and creativity (Aljarrah & Towers, 2022; Hiebert & Grouws, 2007). *Unproductive struggle* leads to frustration and disengagement. The key differentiator between the two types of struggles is the role of an expert practitioner—the teacher—to offer coaching and feedback that builds on students' thinking rather than ending the struggle with an answer or letting it stall out with a vague response (Warshauer, 2015). As the NCTM describes, productive struggle marks the difference between learning mathematics through replication and learning mathematics with understanding while also developing the behavioral attribute of perseverance. What if we told a story of school as a space where students receive opportunities to embrace conflict and be challenged to make important decisions in response? What if we affirmed that each student is the main character in their own life story? After all, as educational leadership expert Margaret Wheatley (2009) describes, it is our "willingness to be disturbed" (p. 34) that is fundamental to our learning, creativity, and ability to collaborate.

External Conflict

External conflict is defined by a challenge a character faces when they clash with a force outside their control. We hide our eyes as characters shrink in terror due to unexplained, supernatural forces like ghosts, monsters, or magic. In the movie *Dante's Peak* (Donaldson, 1997), for example, we stay glued to our seat as characters race to evacuate their small town after the eruption of a volcano. In *The Hunger Games* (Collins, 2008), we feel pride as characters decide to eat the poisonous berries together, thus revolting against a societal norm that has led to widespread suffering in their communities. While these fictional conflicts don't occur in the classroom, there is one external conflict that happens in schools daily: the timeless clash between people.

Conflict between students is such a common occurrence in the social hierarchy of the school environment that countless studies and programs have aimed to teach students conflict resolution skills, with demonstrably improved learning outcomes (Garibaldi, Blanchard, & Brooks, 1996; Gillies, 2016; Johnson & Johnson, 1995, 2001; Lantieri, DeJong, & Dutrey, 1996).

One such program emerged out of the renewed focus on peacemaking after World War II and aimed to teach conflict resolution through a series of critical steps. The first step was to establish a culture of cooperation over competition across the school. The second step was to provide explicit instruction that shifts the perception of conflict from something that involves anger and hostility to instead see it as a desirable catalyst for learning. The third step was to employ a dispute-resolution protocol that emphasized a win-win mindset. The final step was to involve a neutral third party to support mediation, such as a randomly assigned peer mediator in a classroom (Johnson & Johnson, 1996). While well-intentioned, schools often implement such conflict resolution approaches in a top-down manner, which fails to capture the nuances of students' lived experiences (White, 2003).

An alternative to the top-down approaches of teaching conflict resolution is to listen to and seek insight from students' stories as they negotiate conflict in school. After all, students quickly see through scripted programs featuring outdated scenarios. Taking on the role of the expert is a powerful motivator, especially when students can share their stories as valuable teaching for their peers. In his master's thesis at the University of British Columbia, Vincent White (2003) explored themes that emerged after listening to stories of conflict resolution from middle school students. He listened to students who had been identified by their teachers as having exemplary social competence to see if he could distill wisdom that better reflects the realities of youth. One of his key findings is the power dynamics at play in this interaction. While the students were empowered to be the authority on the topic, the adult still played an analytical role to the experiential knowledge of the student "through the use of open-ended questions asked in a tone of genuine perplexity" (p. 99). White (2003) suggests using some of the core themes that emerged to start an authentic conversation with students about potential sources of conflict and how they would respond to them. Those themes are presented later in this chapter as a starting point for a story circle (page 28).

Interpersonal conflict is pervasive in schools and only seems to be getting more pronounced as our culture faces increasing polarization. Now, more than ever before, teachers are being called on to help resolve conflicts that involve race, sexual identity, ethnicity, and political identities while also being policed for talking about these very topics. We would be remiss if we did not also talk about the conflict we are facing with the introduction of AI software like ChatGPT, allowing students to produce seemingly human-generated writing in seconds. Many schools respond with hostility to this technology, placing bans or increasing the surveillance of student work. Rather than responding to this external conflict with hostility, we can lean into the complexity of the challenge and recruit students as allies to seek a resolution. By asking open-ended questions with genuine curiosity and empowering students as storytellers, teachers can model a productive response to external conflict.

Internal Conflict

While a character might face many external conflicts throughout the course of a story, a deeper internal conflict often lingers until they are finally forced to confront the biggest challenge of all: changing themselves. What makes an internal conflict so much harder to confront are the deeper values of the character that are being called into question. When it comes to facing ourselves, the stakes are always higher. However, it is through the process of confronting and overcoming internal conflict that we gain self-awareness and increase the quality of our life. However, this type of growth doesn't come easily. Anyone who has ever felt conflicted knows it's an exceptionally distressing feeling that can consume our minds and leave us feeling stuck. It's a deep pull toward something better while feeling trapped by our own limiting beliefs.

When listening for an internal conflict in the words of others, there is one telltale word: *but*. If we think about the many internal conflicts that students face in K–12 schooling, we can see this in action:

> *"I need to get an A on my test for my parents to let me play on the basketball team, but I don't have time to study outside of my grueling practice schedule."*

> *"I'm terrified of speaking in front of my peers, but English is my favorite class and the teacher says we all need to perform a slam poem."*

> *"I want to be a professional skier and my career is already taking off, but I have to attend all of these classes that aren't relevant to my future at all."*

Do the previous scenarios pique your curiosity? How will these conflicts play out? What decisions will the characters make? Will the basketball player resort to cheating to do well on the test, or advocate for extra time to study? Will the lover of English face her fears and discover her voice, or succumb to the whispers in her mind and be "sick" the day of the poetry slam? Will the skier eventually drop out of school, or learn to find the relevant skills amid the irrelevant content? Of course, we always hope for a happy ending, but what is the likelihood of that resolution if our students are never provided the space to make these internal conflicts known to compassionate mentors along their educational journey?

The role of the mentor is integral to stories humans have told throughout history. This character often appears once the main character accepts a call to adventure and crosses the threshold from their ordinary world into a new one (Campbell, 2008, original work published 1949). The mentor is often older, wiser, and quickly becomes a trusted adviser to the main character. Think Obi-Wan Kenobi to Luke Skywalker, or Dumbledore to Harry Potter. If students trust us enough to accept struggle as they step into a new learning journey, then we can remember that probing questions and affordance are useful tools for us as mentors. *Probing questions* are when we build on a student's thinking and encourage self-reflection, while *affordance* is giving them space to continue the work on their own (Warshauer, 2015). A great mentor sees the potential in us long before we see it in ourselves.

Cultural Connection

There is a dichotomy that we must confront. On the one hand, society tells us that vulnerability is desirable and welcomed, and being your authentic, imperfect self is most humanizing. On the other hand, schools revile mistakes, missteps, and flaws in the impossible search for perfection as students strive for the Holy Grail of 100 percent. No one is perfect, yet within our schools, fixing all mistakes and missteps to become "perfect" is an implied goal. By focusing on seeing our tragic flaw, embracing vulnerability, and inviting imperfection into school culture, we can come to a more balanced view.

See Your Tragic Flaw

We've discussed the need for better conflict resolution externally and internally, but what about the stories where the character succumbs to conflict? One of the most well-known models of analyzing plot structure was designed by 19th century German playwright Gustav Freytag (1863). Commonly known as Freytag's Pyramid, this model begins with exposition and an inciting incident, then proceeds through rising action. The pyramid reaches its peak with the climax, then finishes with falling action and resolution (Glatch, 2024). However, Freytag never intended his model to be used to analyze plots with happy endings; it was intended to tell the story of tragedy.

Without this crucial piece of information about the model's original design, English teachers around the world who use this "plot roller coaster" to help students understand story miss out on a powerful discussion about internal conflict. When it comes to tragedy, an essential ingredient to the catastrophic outcome for a main character is their tragic flaw. This idea dates to Aristotle's *Poetics*, in which he used the term *hamartia* to refer to the qualities, beliefs, and values that lead to a character's downfall. Aristotle never intended this "flaw" to signify a character's moral failing, but rather to describe how certain qualities lead to poor decision making that can negatively impact an outcome. The most negative of these qualities is an inability to tolerate vulnerability.

Embrace Vulnerability

We are experiencing a seismic cultural shift in our willingness to resolve conflicts both externally and internally, and Brené Brown has a lot to do with it. As of 2024, Brown's (TED, 2011) viral TED Talk "The Power of Vulnerability" has seventeen million views, which marks a first for a researcher (though she would prefer we call her a *storyteller*). Her work has caused an explosion of interest in what researchers call "the affective domain," or that which deals with emotions. In the video, Brown tells the story of embarking on her PhD to empirically understand human connection. To do this, she interviewed thousands of people and discerned themes from the stories they shared. One trend she noticed immediately was that when they were asked to talk about love, they described heartbreak. When asked to describe belonging, they told of feeling excluded. But this wasn't true with everyone she interviewed. Brown noticed that there is something unique about those rare few who tell stories of courage, compassion, and connection. That distinction is a *willingness to talk about their struggles*.

Brown discovered that those who are the most connected, compassionate, and courageous are those who can best tolerate shame, or the feeling of not being good enough. They understood that shame was a byproduct of sharing their whole selves, imperfect and flawed, and that this wholeness was what allowed them to connect with others. This truth can be seen in the student who says, "I'm not sure how to solve this problem. I do know how to find the equation within it, but I don't know how to solve it. Can you give me a hint?" Brown came to call this group *wholehearted*.

Invite Imperfection in School Culture

It is predictable that Freytag's Pyramid was rebranded in our schools to tell the story of success and happy endings when we consider our cultural aversion to failure in the education system. By adopting the habit of grading everything students do and recording those scores in a gradebook, teachers are inadvertently sending the message that mistakes could have devastating effects on your overall grade. For instance, if a student were to score a 0 on an assignment in a traditional, percentage-based grading system, it could take upward of nine perfect assignments to recover their former score due to the mathematical anomaly that an F is worth 60 percent of a grade (depending on the cutoff for failure). The message is clear. Don't make a mistake, or else.

However, if we put aside the many tragic outcomes from popular fiction that involve death and devastation, the tragic outcomes that students experience in school might instead be an opportunity for deep learning about themselves to heal their tragic flaw and achieve a different outcome in the future. Some "tragedies" that students often face in school include missing assignments, starting a fight, cheating, or demonstrating defiance. Each of these outcomes starts with a flawed belief or mindset that leads the student to make the decisions they did. Traditionally, schools have been places that label and punish students for these outcomes rather than holding space for them to untangle their internal conflicts and be better equipped to resolve their external clashes. The point here is not to discredit the appropriation of Freytag's Pyramid to stories of success, but rather, to argue for the equal representation of Freytag's *tragic* Pyramid to help students become more successful, self-regulating learners.

Competency Connection

A student's unwillingness to learn could be the result of an internal conflict. The will and skill to learn can be neutralized by external factors that create a dilemma. Being able to self-regulate and think metacognitively, as part of their overall social competence, can reveal this conflict, allowing students to self-manage as they learn. In the following sections, we look more closely at self-regulation, social competence, and interpersonal and intrapersonal skills.

Self-Regulation

By definition, *self-regulation* is "a cross-cutting competency rich with a host of robust skills and processes working in tandem in timely and purposeful ways" (Erkens et al., 2019, p. 42). Therefore, *self-regulated learning* is "a process that assists students in managing their thoughts, behaviors, and emotions in order to successfully navigate their learning experiences" (Zumbrunn, Tadlock, & Roberts, 2011, p. 4). The crucial importance of this competency emerges when we reflect on the rate of change in our world today. Every industry is being bombarded by a need for employees to rapidly upskill and reskill in the face of conflict due to technology, climate, and unprecedented events (OECD, 2019a; UNESCO, 2017). In short, this competency is essential for *everyone* in our world today. To develop it, our first step is to understand how it represents the skill and will of learning.

To better understand the *skill* of learning, we can further unpack that into two subcategories: cognition and metacognition. *Cognition* involves mental skills that aid comprehension. This is where teachers invest most of their time in the classroom, but it is only a small piece of the self-regulated learning pie. Tasks and activities that aid cognition support students in knowing information, then using that information to make connections and solve problems. It is in cognition that the other well-known competency, *critical thinking*, resides. *Metacognition* involves thinking *about* the thinking that cognition requires. While this skill doesn't get the same instructional attention as cognition in the classroom, it is starting to gain more traction as our collective understanding increases.

Now that we have unpacked the *skill* of learning into acts of thinking, let's turn to the *will* of learning to understand the role of our emotions in the process. Across the literature on self-regulation, there are three affective (emotional) domains that significantly impact a learner's motivation to engage in thinking: (1) hope, (2) efficacy, and (3) growth mindset (Erkens et al., 2019). Let's look at each of these in more detail.

1. *Hope* is a sense of grounded optimism that a learner carries with them into a learning experience based on their previous experiences and the culture they are currently immersed in. For instance, if the culture of a classroom is filled with stories of a teacher who is a "hard grader" and only gives out a couple of As per course, a learner's sense of hope may be diminished.

2. If hope is a tendency toward optimism, then *efficacy* is a learner's unwavering belief that they can accomplish their goals, no matter what the context. Teachers can help to develop this belief by highlighting strengths in their feedback, helping learners to see what strategies they already have in their tool kit.

3. *Growth mindset*, a term coined by psychologist Carol Dweck (2006), is "the view you adopt for yourself" that "profoundly impacts the way you lead your life" (p. 6). A growth mindset is the stories a learner tells themselves that attribute their success to their efforts, not to their innate talent or superiority. It's like a beginner's mindset where one tells the story of how they are always learning, versus being an expert who knows all.

To return to this chapter's overarching concept of conflict, when students are demonstrating a lack of *skill* in their learning, they may be feeling conflicted in their *will* to learn. For instance, social identity is often a barrier to a student's willingness to take charge of their learning. They might think, "I don't want to fail this class, but I'm scared my friends will think I'm a nerd if they see me trying too hard." To assess this critical competency, we must invite students to reveal their will to learn through story and make choices accordingly. A practical tool to do this is course letters, which we discuss in the Story of What I'm Learning section of this chapter (page 95).

Social Competence

Even though many still refer to it as one of the *soft skills*, social competence is anything but soft. This competency includes "any behavioral attribute, characteristic, emotional disposition, or action that allows learners to socially adapt so as to align more seamlessly with the most immediate conditions" (Erkens et al., 2019, p. 238). It is this emotionally driven set of skills that is hardest to teach and even harder to learn. And yet, "noncognitive factors such as personality traits, motivation, interpersonal skills, and intrapersonal skills have been found to correlate significantly with educational attainment, workplace productivity, and life earnings" (Zhao, 2016, p. 4).

Within the overarching category of social competence, it's helpful to distinguish two subcategories: *interpersonal* and *intrapersonal*.

Interpersonal and Intrapersonal Skills

Interpersonal social competence is the skills related to interaction and communication between people. Of course, we want to develop students' ability to be empathetic, respectful, and kind toward others, but conflict is inevitable. It is the real test of interpersonal skills. Everyone can get along when there is no disagreement, but when interests clash, this competency is put to the test. Our ability to build our skill set to respectfully engage and work through conflict is at the heart of a peaceful, democratic society. As students progress through the grades in school, our focus shifts to reflect developmental appropriateness. In the elementary years, our focus is on interactions with a single person, whereas by middle school this lens expands to understand how a respectful community functions. By high school, students' lenses expand again to explore interpersonal competence on a global scale. We describe an interdisciplinary project later in this chapter to demonstrate how students can develop this global competence while also achieving standards in all core subject areas (page 98). Specifically, they will explore how war is conflict realized on a global scale, and what we can learn from it.

Intrapersonal social competence is the skills that describe how an individual acts *within* and *toward* themselves. It is how they navigate the discomfort of internal conflict. It involves the management of thoughts and emotions to effectively take action and interact with others. Our ability to manage our inner storyteller is integral to telling stories of successful conflict resolution with others.

At the heart of intrapersonal social competence is *emotional agility*, as coined by researcher Susan David (2016), whereby we gain the skills to navigate and process negative emotions. A lack of emotional agility is "toxic positivity" that often results in numbing behavior like scrolling social media, watching TV, abusing drugs and alcohol, or shopping as means to avoid negative feelings. David (2016) refers to this response as "bottling," which often results in unintentional leaks of amplified, aggressive negative emotion toward others. Alternatively, another antisocial intrapersonal response is brooding, where someone lets their negative emotions consume them to the point that they become stuck and cannot move forward. The goal of emotional agility is to notice and name (with specificity) the negative emotion we are feeling, remind ourselves it's just an emotion and will not last forever, and calm our central nervous system until it passes. To demonstrate intrapersonal social competence, we must rewrite the narrative that emotions are bad and to be avoided, or worse, a shortcoming belonging only to women.

The Story of What I'm Learning

Whether by examining historical events, scientific breakthroughs, or literature within the context of when and where it was produced, conflict is often at the heart of what students are learning. The following sections illustrate how teachers can use struggle statements, course letters, and the story of war to facilitate student learning.

Struggle Statements

A struggle statement is a short, constructed response in which students step inside the perspective of an expert in any specific discipline. To help students think like authors, mathematicians, historians, artists, or scientists, we must uphold one simple truth: The more we know, the more we reveal what we don't know. How can we help students to step inside the cognitive dissonance that resides in someone who has come to recognize the dilemmas of their field?

In the book *Making Thinking Visible*, Ron Ritchhart, Mark Church, and Karin Morrison (2011) offer a routine to allow students to step inside the perspective of another person or group. This routine is a helpful scaffold for students as they work toward creating a struggle statement from the perspective of a practitioner in the field of study. First, they must choose a perspective to step inside. Consider the following examples.

- Historians
- Politicians
- Artists
- Authors
- Musicians
- Athletes
- Mathematicians

The structure requires students to answer the following four questions.

1. What can this person or thing see, observe, or notice?
2. What might the person or thing know, understand, hold true, or believe?
3. What might the person or thing care deeply about?
4. What might the person or thing wonder about or question?

Once students have answered the questions, they can consolidate their understanding into a single struggle statement using the stem, "I desire/fear/must/expect/need _____, but I desire/fear/must/expect/need _____." For instance, an author may think, "I have an expectation from my publisher to sell a lot of books, but I need to write what is in my heart." It's the constant battle between writing for a target audience and writing as personal therapy. The logical path through this dilemma is to embrace the humility that what is interesting to us as the author is not always interesting to readers. Being an author ultimately means being able to make an income from your writing, so we must prioritize the audience.

However, there is perhaps no greater field ripe for internal conflict than science. American theoretical physicist J. Robert Oppenheimer is considered by many to be the father of the atomic bomb due to his role as leader of the Los Alamos Laboratory during the Manhattan Project in WWII. In August of 1945, two of the nuclear bombs he created were dropped on Hiroshima and Nagasaki, Japan, heralding the end of WWII and instantly killing nearly 110,000 civilians (Biography, n.d.). Oppenheimer offers a great example of someone experiencing internal conflict. A student learning about him might write a struggle statement such as, "I have a duty to the United States government to invent an atomic bomb, but I fear what they are going to do with it."

To assess struggle statements, a teacher might invite an author, mathematician, historian, or other professional to join a class virtually and have them read the struggle statements one by one and assess the degree (strongly disagree, disagree, agree, strongly agree) to which they agree with the statement. For instance, an English teacher may share their students' struggle statements with the author. As they read, "I have an expectation from my publisher to sell a lot of books, but I need to write what is in my heart," they respond, "Oh, wow. It feels like someone is truly in my head right now!" before explaining why they strongly agree. They tell a story about a book they have fought to write, despite their initial publisher attempting to water down the idea until it's lost altogether, leading them to explore other publishers. The student who wrote that statement glows with an inner pride as they feel a sense of empathy with a professional author, a moment of powerful feedback. Consider it a meaningful assessment experience providing feedback and further learning.

Course Letters

Our students' previous experiences within a subject area are the biggest indicator of their willingness to engage in the present. With an understanding of self-regulation in mind, developing students' will to learn is integral to strengthening their skill as learners. However, it's hard to figure out how to respond to a student's level of motivation when the only evidence we gather comes in the data from a standardized survey. Rather, we can use story to elicit richer qualitative evidence.

Of all the disciplines students experience in school, the one that carries the most baggage based on past experiences is mathematics. In their book *Dear Math: Why Kids Hate Math and What Teachers Can Do About It*, veteran teacher Sarah Strong and her high school mathematics student Gigi Butterfield (2022) offer a compilation of letters that students wrote to mathematics to offer insight into the anxiety surrounding this subject. These letters reveal the wide diversity of perspectives students carry about the subject, ranging from dreadful to beautiful, and paradoxical to powerful. These emotional stories are important pieces of evidence that reveal a student's level of willingness to engage in learning. For instance, it's more likely that a student will set lofty goals and work hard to achieve them when their experiences have led them to believe the subject is beautiful rather than dreadful.

Of course, there is more to teasing out a good story than simply asking students what they think about a subject. To support students to tell a meaningful story, we must remember to apply the tenets of sound assessment. This means we must provide instruction, exemplars, scaffolds, and feedback as well as demonstrate instructional agility to move each student forward as a self-regulating learner with the will to learn.

A simple structure to help students reflect on and communicate their experiences over the year is a graph. Yes, students can use mathematics for storytelling. All stories have a negative and positive emotional impact that can be measured over time. For instance, figure 4.1 uses a graph to communicate the well-known rags-to-riches story trope.

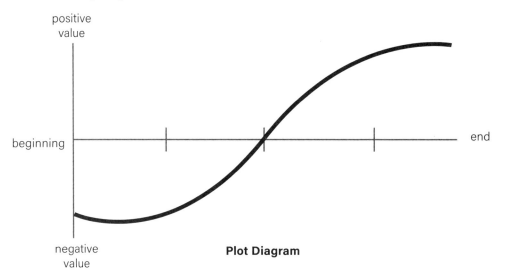

Source: Bunting, n.d.

FIGURE 4.1: Analyzing the rags-to-riches trope's progress from negative to positive.

This graphic representation of the emotional side of story over time presents a powerful template for students to tell the story of mathematics, English, social studies, and so on. Using figure 4.1 as an example, we can invite students to create two graphs. The first charts their general emotional journey in a course over time; the second chooses a specific emotion (fear, anger, joy, boredom, and so on) as a variable that they want to graph more specifically.

After students complete their second graph, invite them to turn and talk with a partner and tell the story of their experiences so far in this course. Be sure to tell students to leave out specific names when discussing the teachers and peers who have been a part of their journey. Consider the following prompts to get the dialogue going.

- What was an especially positive experience for you? What made it so?
- What was an especially negative experience for you? What made it so?
- Was there a turning point in your story?
- What emotions other than the one you chose on your second graph did you feel throughout your story?

At this point, after activating students' background knowledge, introduce the task of writing a course letter where students describe their perspective on a subject based on past experiences. Consider the following instructional sequence that emphasizes clarity, feedback, and an inclusive culture of learning.

1. In advance of instruction, write your own letter to the course you are teaching. Describe the highs and lows of your journey and specifically name the emotions you experienced in response to specific events from your journey.

2. Read your letter aloud to your students and have them notice different elements of it. If possible, print a copy of the letter for each student and give them a chance to read it for themselves a second time and annotate anything they notice. Ask students to share their observations and capture them on the board to create the success criteria for the task.

3. Give students time to engage in independent writing of their own letters. If students finish early, ask them to join you for a conference, and coach them to find ways to strengthen their writing (and thinking) according to the success criteria.

4. When all students finish writing their letters, invite them to join you in a story circle to share them aloud. Always offer the right to pass in a story circle.

5. Ask students to hand in their letters, and tell them you will read each of them and share back what you learned.

Once you have read all the course letters, providing meaningful feedback to the wide diversity of experiences can be challenging but is the essential next step. First, read each letter with empathy, believing the stories that students are telling you about the course. As a teacher of your subject area, you were likely successful in the subject as a student, but your experience of joy does not negate a student's experience of pain. Then, remember that gathering information through this task for a formative assessment means nothing if you choose *not* to adjust your instructional practice using the evidence students provide. Every teacher feels a sense of pride in the instructional tool kit they have built over their career. However, we must be willing to step outside our comfort zone if we hope to change the story that students are telling about our subject area and increase their willingness to engage.

Consider the following formative feedback loop, drawn from the work of D. Royce Sadler (1989), to apply evidence from course letters to instructional agility.

1. Archive the letters in a digital portfolio.

2. Share back key learnings about what has been positive and negative for students.

3. Describe how you want to explore new instructional strategies to increase a positive experience and ask for feedback from students as you implement them.

4. Observe students intentionally, especially those who have had negative experiences, to look for an increased willingness to engage. Conference with them to gain deeper insights and feedback into whether your instruction is changing their perspective.

5. After a period of time, ask students to write a new letter about their experience in your course so far. Scaffold their story by adjusting the grades throughout years in school (*y*-axis) on the previous graphs to be either weeks, months, or units of study.

6. Repeat the feedback loop described above to continue moving all students toward engagement in your course.

Interdisciplinary Project

While the previous section focused on how to understand the emotional impact of an individual course, in this section we shift our attention to a story that is *interdisciplinary*. Another way to rewrite the narratives about different subject areas is to remove the course silos altogether. If we invite students to tell a story grounded in the content of history or science, they will need skills from language arts, mathematics, and the related arts to do so.

To return to the conflict theme of this chapter, one of the most important stories for every human to understand is the story of war. In many ways, war is the result of a lack of internal and external conflict resolution. It serves as a stark reminder that if we can't figure out how to resolve our struggles peacefully on a microlevel, it can lead to macro devastation. However, teaching about war in a social studies classroom is often reduced to a teacher telling a thrilling story of battle to hold students' attention and assessing students' ability to recall names, dates, and events. Instead, how might *numbers* help to tell the story of the hard realities of war? How might ratios and proportions help to paint a picture of a country's devastation?

Tenth-grade students at Harborside Academy in Kenosha, Wisconsin, set out to answer these questions as they engaged in an interdisciplinary project called "Conflict by the Numbers" (EL Education, n.d.). Their challenge was to figure out which of the wars the United States was involved in was most devastating, and why. Of course, since many wars happened at different periods in history, a straight comparison of casualties was not enough, so these high school students had to recruit sophisticated skills of statistical reasoning. To understand the human impact on soldiers, they conducted interviews with veterans and made inferences from the compensation they received. Finally, students had to communicate their findings in a high-quality booklet that placed the data within the larger story of war.

This project elicited evidence of mathematics, language arts, and social studies core standards, and is an example of cross-curricular applicability that is natural, not forced.

The Story of How I'm Learning

Conflict is an inherent part of learning, and as students become more skilled at naming, noticing, and more importantly, managing this conflict, they will more artfully tell the story of how they are learning. Conflict exit tickets, conflict resolution story circle, and the learning pit story are three ways teachers can support students to do this.

Conflict Exit Tickets

As we stated earlier in this chapter, we must rewrite the cultural narrative of school as a place where students embrace conflict and struggle with vulnerability. We need to normalize conflict as an integral part of learning. A formative assessment strategy many teachers are familiar with is exit tickets—a short reflection question or activity students complete independently before leaving the classroom at the end of a lesson. What if we repurposed this activity as a space to honor the struggle? How might we enhance our ability as educators if we better understood where students' learning is blocked, rather than only the content they recall from class?

To set up this style of exit ticket, as shown in figure 4.2, remind students there are different types of conflict that emerge for learners, such as the following.

- **Learner versus learner:** Students conflict with other learners when they struggle to stay on task due to a talkative peer or feel unsafe due to bullying behavior.

- **Learner versus environment:** Students conflict with the environment when their technology fails, or class expectations (such as silence during work periods) do not align with their learning needs.

- **Learner versus content:** Students conflict with content when they feel confused and don't know the next step.

- **Learner versus self:** Perhaps the hardest conflict resides in students themselves as they attempt to move past feeling bored, anxious, frustrated, or hyper.

Exit Ticket	
Name: _____	
Type of conflict: Learner versus learner Learner versus environment Learner versus content Learner versus self	Say more about the conflict you faced today:
How did you try to resolve it? How will you try to resolve this same conflict in the future?	

FIGURE 4.2: An exit ticket for reflecting on conflict resolution.

*Visit **go.SolutionTree.com/assessment** for a free reproducible version of this figure.*

Once students understand the different types of conflicts a learner faces, they can name their own struggle, and most importantly, how they can take steps to resolve it.

When students practice noticing and naming conflict daily, they build a mindset of seeing it as a valuable part of the learning process. However, students who see admitting struggle as a sign of weakness will require a period of unlearning. Recognize that many years of conditioning within the traditional school system culture is pervasive, and predict that some students will respond repeatedly with, "I don't have any struggles at all!" This is why it's essential to set up this daily practice with a conversation about how conflict is normal and even necessary for learning. Of course, some students may genuinely be successful in their ability to navigate conflict, but this exit ticket holds space for their story too.

Conflict Resolution Story Circle

A story circle is a protocol that promotes equality of voice as students practice speaking one at a time and resisting the urge to respond. As conflict is an inevitable part of the K–12 school experience, it can be a perfect topic for a story circle. Until students build enough trust to bring forward their own conflicts, it can be helpful to have examples of conflict to start the conversation. Consider the following examples of conflicts as described by middle school students themselves (White, 2003).

- Insulting each other with put-downs. This can even lead to the possibility of a physical fight, especially among boys who try to act tough around their peers.
- Not showing respect for one another's belongings.
- When kids in older grades try to exert power over kids in younger grades.
- When a student takes advantage of a teacher who is unable to handle the situation properly.
- When kids join in when the class is taking advantage of a teacher. Very few are willing to stand up and tell everyone to stop.

After arranging the class into a circle and re-establishing norms, use the following prompts and questions to promote storytelling and increase vulnerability among students.

1. Read one of the causes of conflict from the list, then ask students to choose one word that describes how they feel when they encounter this conflict. Give them fifteen seconds of silent think time, then ask them to share their word one by one around the circle.

2. For the next round, ask students to share a story of a time they experienced this type of conflict, either as a bystander or being directly involved. Remind them to refrain from using any names.

3. For the final round, invite students to share either stories or ideas of how to successfully resolve these conflicts in a way that promotes a positive relationship for the people involved.

Consider the questions above as a rough framework. Of course, look for opportunities to ask follow-up questions and probe for more clarity and insight as students begin to share their responses. While the list of conflicts provides a starting point, the goal is to get to a place where students contribute their own conflicts to unpack in the circle. The conflict exit tickets students complete at the end of class are another way to gather evidence and themes for a possible story circle topic.

The Learning Pit Story

Though it might sound counterintuitive to the idea of *self*-regulation, there is widespread agreement among researchers that *help seeking* is an important process within this competency (Butler, 1998, 2006; Karabenick, 1998, 2003, 2004; Karabenick & Newman, 2006; Skinner & Zimmer-Gembeck, 2007). After all, seeking others' insights and feedback on the quest to achieve our goals isn't weak; it's resourceful.

Unfortunately, there is a pervasive story in our schools that working independently is ideal, despite the robust research into the benefits of cooperative learning (Slavin, Hurley, & Chamberlain, 2003). Research also reveals that even though students deemed more successful by their GPA are more likely to solicit help, they often do so to demonstrate that they've already mastered the material (Karabenick & Berger, 2013). We must take action to change the cultural narrative that it's weak to seek help to resolve our conflicts.

Prolific author Kurt Vonnegut spent much of his career studying the structure of stories and eventually determined that all our narratives fall into six main "shapes" when plotted on a graph (David Comberg, 2004), like we described in the course letters section (page 95). One such shape he calls "Man in a Hole." Despite the name, these stories can feature protagonists of any gender. A brief synopsis of this structure is that a protagonist starts off doing well, but then something catastrophic happens and they fall into a metaphoric hole that they then need to climb back out of for the duration of the story. In the end, thanks to their courageous efforts, they end up better off than before the story began. The moral of the story is that when we work to overcome our struggles, we grow as a person and advance in life. See figure 4.3 for an illustration.

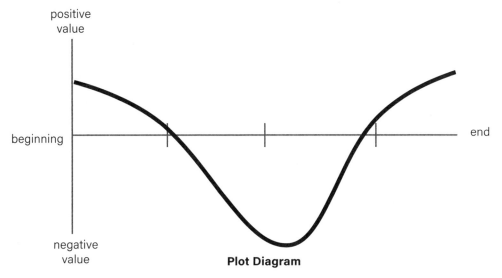

Source: Bunting, n.d.

FIGURE 4.3: Plotting the emotional value of the Man in a Hole story structure.

A classic example of this story structure is the famous film version of *The Wizard of Oz* (Fleming & Vidor, 1939). The main character, Dorothy, is living a decent life in Kansas with her loving family and beloved dog, Toto. However, she's bored. She dreams of a faraway land "over the rainbow" that represents a beautiful utopia. When a neighbor takes Toto away, Dorothy runs away to save him but gets caught in a tornado. The storm carries her away to a foreign land where she must face her predicament and find a wizard who can send her home. With the help of new friends, Dorothy realizes the power to return home was within her all along, resolving her internal conflict of dissatisfaction and yearning for more, and shifting her focus toward gratitude. She simply must click her heels together three times. When she awakes in her bed in Kansas, surrounded by her loved ones, she looks at each of them with fresh eyes as she proclaims her new understanding that there is "no place like home." Like Dorothy—who sought change, realized her challenge, and accepted help to achieve her goals—our learners undergo a journey when they take up learning and fall into the "learning pit."

James Nottingham (2024) writes about the learning pit in his book *Teach Brilliantly*. This concept gives students a visual metaphor to help them understand the process of learning and the role of challenge within it. As you can see in figure 4.4, it is the same shape as the Man in a Hole story structure but shifts the focus where it belongs: on seeking help to overcome struggle and achieving personal growth.

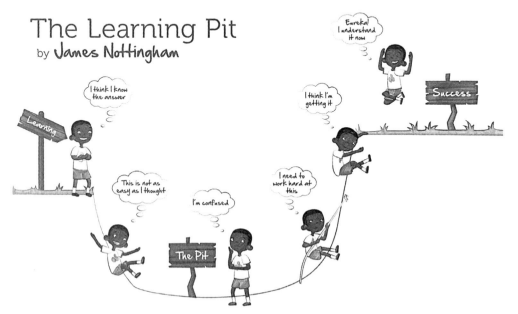

Source: © 2010 by James Nottingham. Used with permission.

FIGURE 4.4: The learning pit.

By providing students a graphic organizer of the learning pit structure, as in figure 4.5, we can gather evidence of students' ability to resolve conflicts and engage in the process of help seeking.

To assess these stories, we can draw from research into help-seeking patterns that differentiate between *avoidant*, *dependent*, and *adaptive* patterns (Ryan, Patrick, & Shim, 2005).

Students who struggle to share a story of pulling themselves out of the pit fall into the avoidant category. It's important to note here that if all students seem to struggle to recall stories of authentic help seeking in your class, you may want to re-evaluate the cognitive complexity of the learning activities that you design. If a classroom is dominated by rote tasks that require more stamina than thinking, students may not feel challenged enough to seek outside support and would rather use their time to get through the pile of work in front of them. If we can eliminate cognitive complexity as an outside factor, the students who fall into the avoidant

Conflict Through Story

What were you working on? What did you hope to learn?	I was working on the script for my digital story. I wanted to learn more about how to create an emotional experience for my audience.
Once you began working toward your goal, what problem emerged that caused you to become stuck?	As I started writing my story, I started to doubt that it was the right story to tell. Compared to other stories it seemed boring.
What did you try on your own to overcome the problem?	I tried to add more of our vocabulary words to make it sound more interesting, but it started sounding even more boring and like I was writing a list.
How did you ask for help from someone else? Did they help solve the problem?	I decided to ask my friend to read it, and they agreed that it felt flat. They asked if I had other ideas. I decided that I needed to restart with a different idea that I remembered my partners liking during the brainstorming activity.
How did you achieve what you set out to learn? What else did you learn?	I ended up writing a different story about my biggest mistake and was able to create a hilarious script that made people laugh. I also learned the value of getting real-life feedback from the audience you are writing for.

FIGURE 4.5: Graphic organizer for resolving conflict and seeking help.

*Visit **go.SolutionTree.com/assessment** for a free reproducible version of this figure.*

category need feedback on the benefits of seeking help and external prompting and encouragement to do so.

The dependent category involves students who have many stories of help seeking to share but will struggle to determine an accurate learning goal. They will instead tell the story of someone else telling them what to do to complete a task. The appropriate response here is to help them to differentiate between achievement and performance goals. *Achievement* goals are focused on understanding and learning, whereas *performance* goals focus on task completion and grades. Emphasizing learning targets and their relationship to larger learning goals is helpful coaching for these students.

Clarity about the intended learning goals brings to life an *adaptive* help seeker, who educational psychology scholars Stuart A. Karabenick and Myron H. Dembo (2011) describe as follows:

> One who begins by accurately assessing that help is necessary formulates an appropriate request for help, understands the best resources available, designs strategies for successful requests, and productively processes the help received to mastery of the material or the ability to solve problems. (p. 35)

These types of help seekers need their habits noticed, named, and celebrated as positive reinforcement. It is by amplifying and sharing the stories of these adaptive help seekers that we can create the conditions for others to learn this valuable self-regulation skill and develop interpersonal social competence.

Summary

Though conflict carries a negative perception, it is an integral part of both stories and learning. As the main character of their school experience, students must learn to productively untangle both external and internal conflicts to unlock learning about the world, each other, and themselves. Even stories of tragedy, where they succumb to conflict, are important opportunities to discover a tragic flaw. Our ability to navigate conflict is directly related to our capacity to navigate uncomfortable emotions. Successfully navigating conflict is at the heart of two critical competencies students need in a pluralistic and volatile culture: self-regulation and social competence. Developing these competencies in the microcosm of the school is critical to build a more cooperative future. On a more personal level, students must be able to navigate external and internal conflicts to maintain positive relationships and mental health.

| REPRODUCIBLE | 107 |

Chapter 4 Discussion Questions for Learning Teams

Journal your response to the following prompts in the space provided. Share your thoughts during team discussion.

1. What quote or passage encapsulates your biggest takeaway from this chapter? What immediate action (small, medium, or large) will you take because of this takeaway? Explain both to your team.

2. How are students in your context currently engaged in productive struggle? Where do you see opportunities for improvement?

3. What are the main causes of interpersonal conflict between students in your context? What internal conflicts do students often share with you?

Page 1 of 2

Rehumanizing Assessment © 2025 Solution Tree Press • SolutionTree.com
Visit **go.SolutionTree.com/assessment** to download this free reproducible.

4. Do you feel there is currently a balance between *cognition* and *metacognition* in your context? If yes, describe it. If no, what would be necessary to make it so?

5. What do you believe is currently the biggest stretch for students in your context, interpersonal or intrapersonal skills?

6. When could you commit to analyzing the information from student course letters with team members to collaboratively design an instructional response? What about conflict exit tickets?

7. Share strategies with your team that you have used with students to teach productive help-seeking behaviors.

Chapter 5
HARMONY THROUGH STORY

Harmony is an ideal state, but as the 21st century is becoming increasingly, unprecedentedly volatile and polarized, it can seem like an unrealistic pipe dream. However, harmony *can* be found in this current reality; it just requires we find peace in a state of constant expansion.

This chapter explores how we can find harmony despite chaotic events unfolding around us, to adapt and create a new normal. We present an Asian story structure called Kishōtenketsu that tells the story of recalibration and reconciliation and show how it can help students cultivate mental and cultural harmony. The chapter concludes by offering three tools students can use to tell the story of how they're learning: (1) the stormy first draft, (2) the sailboat metaphor, and (3) the user manual.

The Big Idea

There are countless opportunities for students within every subject to tell the story of expansion and harmony rather than conflict. Harmony is achieved when students synthesize ideas, concepts, and information. It results when students approach disagreements with collaboration rather than as a conflict to be won, as an opportunity to expand their own perspective by incorporating those of others. *Expansion*, as we use the term in this chapter, refers to a broadening of one's worldview and adaptive expertise. The following sections explore harmony through adaptation, mental disharmony as expansion, and cultural harmony through inclusion.

Harmony Through Adaptation

Our understanding of harmony is often derived from music, where multiple chords played simultaneously create a pleasing sound. We can apply this understanding to our relationships. The *Cambridge English Dictionary* defines *harmony* (n.d.) as "a situation in which people are peaceful and agree with each other, or when things seem right or suitable together." Finding peace means listening to everyone, examining diverse ideas for commonality, and finding mutual agreement about what matters.

Let's turn to epistemology, or the study of theories of knowledge, for three metaphors to illustrate this point: the pyramid, the boat, and the raft. The central question of epistemology is, "How do we know when something is true?" Seventeenth-century philosopher René Descartes's answer, known as *foundationalism* (n.d.), posits that some things are purely true and other truths are derived from that core truth. Think of this as a pyramid with the core truth at the bottom.

There are, however, obvious flaws in Descartes's answer. Challenge any core or subtruth and the pyramid becomes precarious, threatening to tumble; we lose our sense of harmony. Therefore, a new theory called *coherentism* emerged as a more viable alternative. Rather than see truth through a hierarchical lens, coherentism imagines it through a more holistic one, whereby all our truths form a web of beliefs that must continuously stay afloat if we are to be mentally stable (Neurath, 1983; Quine & Ullian, 1970; Sosa, 1980). Philosopher Otto Neurath (1973) offers the powerful metaphor of a boat to explain this theory:

> We are like sailors who on the open sea must reconstruct their ship but are never able to start afresh from the bottom. Where a beam is taken away a new one must at once be put there, and for this the rest of the ship is used as support. In this way, by using the old beams and driftwood the ship can be shaped entirely anew, but only by gradual reconstruction. (p. 199)

Ernest Sosa (1980) builds on Neurath's simile to explain this theory through the metaphor of the raft, meaning it is all our intersecting beliefs that help us to stay afloat, even as we dispose of "logs" that are no longer true. While floating on our raft, we feel a sense of harmony, even as our beliefs are being constantly updated. This theory is one that is helpful in our complex reality today as we strive to stay afloat and maintain a sense of self amid a firehose of information and perspectives.

Mental Disharmony as Expansion

If mental harmony can be thought of as a state of peace, many experiences can lead to a sense of *disharmony*. As the old saying goes, the only constant in life is change, and change will always be a challenge to our inner peace. However, if we can reframe experiences in our lives as an opportunity for expansion, then we are more likely to recalibrate to our inner peace faster. To return to the metaphor from the last section, if we can see change as an opportunity to replace a log on our raft rather than removing the foundation of our pyramid, we can weather the human experience with increased resilience.

To understand this, let's analyze a specific historical change spurred by technological innovation: the invention of the telephone. When the telephone was introduced into North America in the late 19th and early 20th centuries, it sparked social anxiety. Stories took hold in the public consciousness that the telephone would be the end of interpersonal communication, privacy would be no more, and community eroded (Fischer, 1992). Of course, a century later we are living proof that none of these fears came to pass. Instead, we all recognize the importance of the telephone in our lives to stay connected to loved ones who live far away, thereby strengthening our connections to each other and our communities.

The telephone is not the last technological innovation of our time. In the 21st century, we are on the precipice of the diffusion of generative AI into all aspects of our lives. And yet, we must perceive these moments of change as not the collapse of our philosophical pyramid, but the expansion of our raft to include a new log by which we stay afloat. What if we were to teach our students how to see change not as a reason to despair, but as an opportunity to become stronger and more resilient?

In addition to technological disruptions, we are also living through many unprecedented events related to society and our climate. However, in the next section, we want to explore how we maintain our mental resilience in the face of something we believe isn't talked about enough in our school spaces: diversity.

Cultural Harmony Through Inclusion

If the experience of unprecedented events is an avenue for mental disharmony, so too is the experience of diversity in our modern world. Of course, the benefits of diversity are many, but when faced with someone different from us, we may experience feelings of anxiety. Avoiding these feelings of anxiety leads to the like-attracts-like cognitive bias, whereby we seek to surround ourselves with people most like us. The complex problems in our world today demand that we begin to work together in increasingly collaborative teams with diverse backgrounds. This cognitive bias forms a unique challenge for educators who need to prepare students for this reality.

As educators, we are well-versed in the idea that we learn by doing. One of the best ways to learn to value diversity, then, is to be immersed in it—to face the disharmony with an expansive mindset rather than avoidance. This is where inclusion becomes a necessity on the pathway to cultural harmony. While it may be useful for teachers to regroup students based on targeted need from time to time, students benefit from learning alongside peers in diverse, heterogeneous teams. A research-validated practice to achieve this is to randomly group students at the start of each lesson, ensuring students can see the process so they know it's truly random (Liljedahl, 2021). Using a random name picker—there are several free versions online—would be a good choice here. This practice has demonstrated increased engagement, particularly in mathematics classrooms. Students feel the narrative of school shift when they aren't being categorized as "low" or "high" by the teachers, but instead are all esteemed as capable in myriad ways when they work together (Liljedahl, 2021). Later in this chapter, we will discuss collaboration as a competency, but this small action of visible, random groupings on a daily basis is an important stepping-stone for students to rewrite their personal narratives and believe they can work with anyone.

The takeaway is that cultural harmony is not achieved simply by learning about the value of different cultural groups. In fact, research demonstrates that an emphasis on *learning about* diversity can lead to heightened anxiety for those with lower implicit bias when they are faced with cultural differences (van Knippenberg, Haslam, & Platow, 2007). Instead, we need a more holistic approach that emphasizes action. We engage the emotions when we learn by doing, by enacting classroom practices that demonstrate inclusion so that through repeated exposure, students learn to recalibrate to a new normal.

Cultural Connection

Though our Western concept of story is often rooted in a conflict that produces a winner, other story structures around the globe focus on harmony and togetherness rather than opposing forces. The following sections explore this idea more deeply by examining Kishōtenketsu; surface, shallow, and deep culture; and cultural archetypes.

Kishōtenketsu

Kishōtenketsu is a traditional story structure used in Japanese, Chinese, and Korean literature that contains four acts: (1) introduction (*ki*), (2) development (*shō*), (3) twist (*ten*), and (4) reconciliation (*ketsu*). Rather than a direct conflict, this structure offers a cycle of recalibration as events unfold and characters reconcile with the new reality. The most important element is the ten, or twist. This is where something unexpected happens that leads to the ketsu where we see the characters in the aftermath. The key to this structure is the possibility of not having any climactic action at all; the twist can simply offer an opportunity to reset to a new reality.

To understand this story structure, let's see it in action in the film *Parasite*, the 2020 Academy Award winner for Best Picture by director Bong Joon-ho (2019). *Parasite* was the first foreign language film to win the highest honor at the Oscars and paints a fascinating picture of the class struggle in South Korea. Let's unpack the plot of the film to see Kishōtenketsu in action. Consider this your spoiler alert.

- **Act 1: Ki**—We meet the central family of the story, the Kims, who are poor and struggling to make ends meet in their dingy basement apartment.
- **Act 2: Shō**—Through a clever series of cons, the Kim family infiltrates the luxurious home of a wealthy family under the guise of different jobs.
- **Act 3: Ten**—The Kim family discovers there is an even poorer family living below them in the basement of the wealthy family's home.
- **Act 4: Ketsu**—Members of the rich, poor, and poorer families attack the people they blame for their plight at a birthday party in the backyard, leading to injuries and death on all sides. The rich family moves out of the house and a member of the Kim family takes the place of the poorest family in the basement.

As you can see from the example, this story structure doesn't often wrap up in a victorious ending like most Western story structures. Also, be careful not to read into the ending as one class achieving victory over another. The deaths—spoiler alert—that close out the film are a series of misunderstandings due to the different life experiences of each group. Rather than an emphasis on conquest and victory, Kishōtenketsu tells the story of recalibration toward a society grounded in a dehumanizing class system. What perhaps made *Parasite* such a crossover sensation is the Shakespearean ending. However, like most movies of this structure, the focus was on character development, imagery, and a slower pace.

Stories communicate the values of different cultures, and just like food, this can impact our tastes. For many Western moviegoers, this type of structure is boring, representing a story where nothing really happens until the final moments. And yet, this structure upholds a Japanese value of minimalism. Author and professor Henry Lien (2021) argues that we must expand our tastes by moving beyond simply seeing diverse faces in movies to representing diverse themes and structures as well. He offers an invitation for "storytellers to give themselves permission to learn more about story forms and themes informed by other traditions, in addition to including diverse characters," and for "readers to open their minds about what a satisfying story can look like." If we value diversity, we can take action to allow students to tell stories using unfamiliar structures that communicate important values to expand our minds in a Western culture grounded in individualism and competition.

Surface, Shallow, and Deep Culture

To explore a cultural archetype outside of individualism, let's first return to the concept of culture. Remember from chapter 1 (page 13) that culture is a collection of shared stories. Another way to look at it is that culture is the software for the hardware of the brain.

Hammond (2015) further describes culture as having three levels with differing emotional charges: surface, shallow, and deep. *Surface culture* is that which we can see (dress, holidays, food) and has a low emotional charge, meaning challenges to these aspects of culture will not feel especially threatening to the amygdala, the area of the brain responsible for processing emotions. *Shallow culture* includes social norms and etiquette and begins to produce an emotional reaction when different cultures interact, if these norms aren't maintained. The brain perceives the lack of adherence to such norms as a potential threat, increasing the experience of anxiety someone might feel. Finally, challenges to *deep culture*, including beliefs and values, are where we experience culture shock, as they are the mental models through which we analyze all information about the world.

The takeaway here is that our attempts to be "culturally responsive" in a school must move beyond the shallow celebration of surface culture elements like holidays and dress to hold space for deeper cultural elements such as social norms, beliefs, and values. Embracing storytelling as a viable means for assessment will achieve this purpose, but it requires we find harmony in the *dis*harmony of true cultural diversity.

Cultural Archetypes Revisited

In chapter 2 (page 35), we outlined cultural archetypes suggested by Hammond (2015) as a framework for more culturally expansive assessment practices. These archetypes exist on a continuum between individualism and collectivism. North American and most European countries have a high emphasis on individualism in their cultures, which leans toward a celebration of agency and competition, while Latin American, Asian, African, Middle Eastern, and Slavic countries tend toward an archetype of collectivism, meaning they value community, relationships, and interdependence. While the archetype of collectivism emphasizes harmony, we are not giving it preference over the culture of individualism. It's not a zero-sum game. Rather, the inclusion of both collectivism and individualism can lead to cultural harmony across differences.

In the classroom, this means accepting both written and oral evidence as equally valid and assessing both the individual and collective learning outcomes in a unit. While we have ample experience assessing individual learning outcomes, assessing collective ones may seem more challenging. In the next section, we will unpack an approach to assessing the critical competency of collaboration to achieve this goal.

Competency Connection

The collective togetherness achieved through harmony connects seamlessly to the critical competency of *collaboration*. Resolving conflict and returning to harmony is the essence of collaboration, where the team puts its needs above those of the individual.

Collaboration Defined

To honor collectivism, we must provide opportunities for authentic collaboration. Too often, collaboration in a school setting is simply an expectation that students complete a task together, dividing and conquering individual contributions. This is cooperation. However, true collaboration is about mutual interdependence to achieve a common goal. It requires a value shift from individualism to collectivism to recognize that the outcome of a team is far greater than the sum of each individual member. The goal of a collaborative endeavor needs to be lofty enough that interdependence is a necessity. Of course, cooperation is an essential target to help students learn social skills like turn taking and active listening, but these skills are only steps on the ladder to the more sophisticated outcome of collaboration.

Collaboration is hard because it is deeply personal. The first step to becoming a collaborator is to recognize that it is not only a group effort but also an individual one, meaning we need to know ourselves and be willing to communicate who we are to have any hope of working successfully in a group. This is the need for both individualism and collectivism in action. In her 2012 TEDx Talk, communications expert Emily Eldridge makes the personal case for this idea as she reflects on her own inability to collaborate as a driven straight-A student, and how she had to unlearn that bad habit to find success in the "real world." She suggests two important tactics outside of valuing the collective and knowing the goal.

1. **Understand and articulate your unique perspective:** Know what you bring to the table and be willing to articulate it to the group.

2. **Explain your quirks:** Know what about you others might find challenging and clearly communicate it so they can accommodate it.

It can be helpful to organize collaboration into the following categories (Erkens et al., 2019).

- **Collaboration 1.0:** This is what most of us experienced as students in school, where collaboration is used as a vehicle to learn content. For instance, to learn more about ancient Greece, students are put into groups to make a brochure and the resulting product is the focus of assessment. This is the context in which students would likely hear coaching to "make the group effort," as the true goals are cooperating and developing the social skills to play well with others.

- **Collaboration 2.0:** The goal at this level is for students working together to *become better collaborators*. To develop as collaborators, we must help students understand that diversity is a strength and that the conflict inherent in differing opinions is the goal. The healthy conflict we want all students to engage in is *task conflict*, which is aimed at ideas and opinions and has been demonstrated to heighten creativity in teams and enhance the effectiveness of decision making (Jehn & Mannix, 2001).

- **Collaboration 3.0:** As students learn to embrace disharmony as a necessary part of achieving harmonious outcomes, they are ready to engage in collaboration 3.0, where the goal is to work together to solve problems.

We take a closer look at collaboration 3.0 in the following section.

Collaborative Problem Solving

Collaboration 3.0 "requires people to work on common problems or issues together to find innovative solutions or patterns that one person would not be able to solve or discover" (Erkens et al., 2019, p. 110). This is collaboration at its most sophisticated, with students working with people outside of the four walls of their physical classroom. One powerful example of this sophisticated type of collaboration is through a ten-month intensive program for high school students called the Knowledge Society (TKS). In this extracurricular program, students build their background knowledge of emerging technologies like biotech and fintech depending on an area of passion, develop entrepreneurial and innovative mindsets through coaching with a director of their cohort, and eventually consolidate their learning in a capstone project where they are placed on a team and paired with a large organization to become tech consultants. They work with the executives of the company to define a problem they are facing and draw on their diverse team tech knowledge to design a solution. When this program launched in Calgary, Alberta, Canada, Natalie got to witness firsthand the awe of an executive leader as she described how young people could solve problems that had stumped the executive team, hindered by the power dynamics and egos in the room. Hearing the obvious answer to the problem from students still in high school served as a humbling reminder of their own inability to collaborate and helped them get unstuck and move forward on a major project.

Let this story be a reminder that when students receive an authentic problem and audience, as well as the opportunity to develop their passions, they can achieve sophisticated levels of learning that even adults cannot unlock due to their baggage and bureaucracy. What if our youth hold the answers to some of the greatest global challenges of our time? Has an untapped resource for innovation been under our noses all along?

Grading Collaboration

The elephant in the room when it comes to assessing collaboration is grading. If the desired outcome is to work interdependently toward a shared goal, should all members of the team receive the same grade? Or, since we must make an independent effort to contribute to a team, should each student receive a separate grade? With a mindset of harmony, teachers may gather evidence of *both* the individual and team performances to support formative feedback, while the resulting grade will be individual to dissuade one member from doing all the work. We suggest that teachers co-create success criteria for collaboration with students using the following list of core aptitudes. Depending on the design of the collaborative task, teachers may choose to focus on only a few target aptitudes for grading.

- **Displaying curiosity:** Inquire and ask questions to clarify, connect, and generate ideas.

- **Listening:** Actively hear, paraphrase, and summarize others' ideas to deeply understand alternative or competing perspectives.

- **Contributing:** Offer new, radical, and sometimes unpopular views.

- **Committing to work through conflict:** Productively engage in and move through conflict—do not avoid it but also do not unnecessarily incite it for the sake of argument.

- **Consensus building:** Find ways to compromise, balancing practicality and orthodoxy, to provide innovative solutions.

- **Observing:** Observe nonverbal cues and actions to productively and honestly navigate dialogue, conflict, and conflicting ideas.

- **Focusing on strengths:** Capitalize on the strengths of individual team members; presume positive intentions.

- **Focusing on goals:** Position the overall goal over an individual need to be right.

- **Knowing what to do when you don't know:** Embrace uncertainty with questions and a commitment to pursue information and next steps.

- **Synthesizing:** Explore and persevere to synthesize large amounts of information or competing perspectives; blend ideas to co-create and innovate.

- **Sourcing:** Discern the reliability of information by interrogating sources, including the authors' perspectives, organizations, funding sources, and other potential areas of bias. Assess its reliability, realistic potential, and competing and contradictory reports that counter a source's main argument.

To support students in co-creation, choose a few target aptitudes for a task, and co-create what this aptitude looks like, sounds like, and feels like with students. The co-construction process is vital to ensure validity of the resulting summative assessment, which is a combination of teacher observation, student self-assessment, and peer assessment (Erkens et al., 2019). It's key to provide clarity during the co-construction process given that research indicates that much of the feedback students receive from their peers is incorrect (Brown & Harris, 2013). Early investment in clarity helps to get ahead of potential inaccuracies.

When determining a final grade for a collaborative endeavor, teachers may use a criterion-based rubric across four levels, as shown in figure 5.1 (page 120).

Also, a constructed response to capture student reflections on the process is important. While generic questions like "What was your biggest strength as a collaborator?" and "What was your biggest challenge?" can be helpful here, in the next section we explore ways that story may be a more valid and precise means of capturing the twists and turns of working in a team.

The Story of What I'm Learning

Harmony through the story of what students are learning often requires a recalibration of both the collaborative process and the curriculum. Effective collaborative teams see any initial disharmony as an opportunity to grow. The recalibration of curriculum as a return-to-harmony experience will rehumanize course content that can appear, at times, abstract.

Collaborative Recalibration

What story might a student tell to indicate that authentic collaboration has occurred? How will we know that a team tapped into collective wisdom rather than surface-level cooperation? As collaboration is a standard found in every content area and in every grade, these are important questions for teachers to consider. Researcher Bruce Tuckman famously described the story of collaborating as forming, storming, norming, performing, and adjourning, explaining that the clash of strengths and personalities is inevitable (the storming phase), but that by embracing this disharmony, a team is able to truly collaborate (Tuckman & Jensen, 1977).

Tuckman's story of successful collaboration is akin to the Kishōtenketsu story structure. This structure is a powerful way for students to reflect on their individual journey in a collaborative team, with the understanding of the "twist" as the introduction of other personalities and perspectives they must reconcile with. It frames the diversity of a team not as a problem, but as a new reality that each student must find harmony with to reach a goal. Figure 5.2 (page 121) is a graphic organizer to help a student plan for this type of story.

Standards	Initiating	Developing	Achieving	Advancing
Exchanging ideas (paraphrasing, responding, and offering insights and ideas) I can exchange ideas. This means I can build on the ideas that others offer by using their words or paraphrasing their ideas before I add my own. When I add my own ideas, I can qualify what I mean and justify that I am accurate by using the evidence from outside sources to show that I am connected to the quality work of other experts.	• Responds when prompted • Contributes, but ideas are disconnected or loosely connected to the general flow of the conversation	• Paraphrases are stilted or clumsy, often copying the exact words of the previous speaker • Offers ideas but minimal support for them • Engages mostly by listening; personal contributions are minimal	• Paraphrases to clarify, build on, or challenge another • Paraphrases previous responses smoothly so the listener feels heard but not parroted • Validates personal responses using sufficient support for ideas (like examples and clarifying terminology) • Prompts continued civil discourse with open-minded, logical answers • Shares personal beliefs and ideas in a respectful and inviting way that welcomes input from others	• Paraphrases based on the emerging themes from the overall conversation (not just the words of the previous speaker) • Synthesizes and articulates insights emerging from the collective wisdom of the group • Embeds ideas in references from multiple sources to lend credence to ideas
Referencing background preparation (paraphrasing, quoting, and citing materials) I can come prepared. This means I can refer to the things I studied and materials I prepared for a discussion. I will read and research in advance of the discussion, and I will show my preparedness by citing the evidence that I encountered when I was preparing.	• May or may not be able to provide examples from background preparation if asked • May provide evidence, but it is insufficient or irrelevant for supporting the conversation	• Talks in general about evidence and examples to support the collaboration	• Uses evidence from background materials to rationalize personal thoughts and contributions • Easily and readily employs quotes and paraphrases from reference materials to support claims • Locates appropriate references to respond to questions or statements from peers	• Makes connections to materials that were provided during the planning phase, as well as materials from previous learning (for example, earlier units of study)

Source: Erkens et al., 2019.

FIGURE 5.1: Sample collaboration analytic rubric.

Kishōtenketsu	Essential Question	Your Response
Ki (Introduction)	What was the goal of your collaborative project?	We were designing a playground for our school using what we learned about geometry and measurement.
Shō (Development)	What personal strengths were you able to bring to this project?	I am a very clear speaker, so I was able to take the lead on presenting our ideas back to the class.
Ten (Twist)	How were you surprised by the work or ideas of a teammate?	Bryan had lots of ideas that didn't resemble any of the playgrounds I've ever seen. I didn't think they were very good ideas.
Ketsu (Reconciliation)	How did you reconcile with your teammate's approach? What did you learn?	I reconciled with Bryan by asking him to explain his ideas using geometry and measurement. Some of his ideas were supported with mathematics, and some weren't. I learned that math is important to ensure our playgrounds are safe for kids to use.

FIGURE 5.2: Sample graphic organizer using the Kishōtenketsu story structure to tell the story of a collaborative endeavor.

*Visit **go.SolutionTree.com/assessment** for a free reproducible version of this figure.*

An example of a story a student might tell of their collaboration using this structure would be to describe how they are working with a team to design a lesson for their peers on a specific figurative language device. They decide with their team that their goal is to create an engaging, hands-on lesson. With this shared goal in mind, the student offers to search for the facts about their device so they can share the information in an engaging PowerPoint presentation. All seems to be going well until the student researcher is surprised at how their teammate decided to put together the presentation. Their presenting teammate is passionate about public speaking, and they've learned that slides are most effective when they have only images rather than a block of text.

The student in question is a nervous presenter and prefers having notes on the slides so they can read directly from them, looking away from the audience. This moment is critical for this student's learning and growth, but also for the success of the team. Without knowledge of the story structure above, the student would likely perceive this moment as a conflict and try to challenge their peer so they can stay in their comfort zone. Or, worse yet, they will reach out to the teacher to solve it for them. However, if the student has this framework ahead of time and has discussed the mental harmony that comes with recalibration, they might see this as an opportunity to reset to a new reality. Should they choose harmony, they might find confidence in their ability to present as they realize that looking at the audience feels more like a conversation than a performance. The first step toward helping students walk down this path is helping them to imagine it. They need a new story.

Curricular Recalibration

In volatile times, it is important to adopt a new narrative structure to make sense of the events of our lives. If we fail to adopt a story structure grounded in harmony, we will continue to see the world through the lens of conflict, conquest, and crisis. It is interesting that the story structure of Kishōtenketsu originated in Japan, as it is a country that has a deep understanding of the need to continuously recalibrate in the face of disruption. As an island country, Japan is uniquely poised to experience tsunamis and earthquakes, leading the citizens to adopt a mindset of stoicism in the face of imminent disaster. It's not a matter of *if* they will need to rebuild, but *when*. Stoicism threads language. Often heard are words like *gaman* (n.d.), a Japanese term of Zen Buddhist origin that means enduring the seemingly unbearable with patience and dignity. It would benefit those in the West to adopt a Japanese story structure that honors this value.

But how might students learn this story structure as a means of assessing course content? Consider the following suggestions arranged by content area.

- **History:** In history class, most of the curriculum centers on conflict and conquest. How might the story of recalibration help students to experience their world today with more acceptance? How might viewing life as the continuous adaptation to a new element give them a mental model that makes it feel less like things are constantly falling apart? For example, students may reimagine the story of the Great Depression by taking a more expansive view than the hardship and suffering people experienced over that fateful decade after the stock market crash of 1929. See figure 5.3 for a sample of how a student might tell this story.

- **Science:** When students learn the scientific method, it is typically as a step-by-step process that leaves little room for surprise. However, so many of the greatest discoveries throughout history were the result of things not going according to plan. Telling these stories can help young scientists

Kishōtenketsu	Essential Question	Your Response
Ki (Introduction)	What was the setting for the event?	The Great Depression (1929–1939) happened mostly in the United States but affected countries all over the world. It started after the stock market crash in 1929, leading to huge problems like unemployment, failing businesses, and banks running out of money. In farming areas, there was also the Dust Bowl, where severe drought made life even harder.
Shō (Development)	Who were the characters involved?	The main people involved were: * Regular citizens: Farmers, workers, and families who lost jobs and struggled to survive * Leaders: Herbert Hoover, the U.S. president when it started, and Franklin D. Roosevelt, who created the New Deal to help fix the economy * Institutions: Banks, factories, and government agencies that played roles in either causing or fixing the crisis * Other countries: Nations that relied on U.S. trade and loans were also affected
Ten (Twist)	What unprecedented event happened?	The stock market crashed in October 1929, which caused banks to fail and businesses to shut down. Millions of people lost their jobs, and in farming areas the Dust Bowl made things worse by destroying farmland and forcing people to move.
Ketsu (Reconciliation)	How did both the setting and characters recalibrate following the event to find a new normal?	The U.S. economy started to recover through Roosevelt's New Deal, which created programs like Social Security, bank protections, and job opportunities through public works projects. Farmers got help through conservation programs, and many moved to other places to start over. People adjusted by working together to survive tough times, relying on government support and learning how to save money and manage better. New laws and government programs were put in place to prevent another Great Depression, helping create a more stable economy.

FIGURE 5.3: A graphic organizer applying the Kishōtenketsu story structure to the Great Depression.

see the value in being wrong about a hypothesis and find harmony through observing and accepting unexpected evidence. The discovery of penicillin is a perfect example of this narrative. After returning from a holiday, Alexander Fleming found that the mold growing on a petri dish was preventing bacteria from growing. Figure 5.4 is an example of how a student might tell the story of this event using a graphic organizer.

- **Physical education:** Experiencing an injury or illness can be devastating. The experience often occurs without warning and demands that we recalibrate our activity to avoid further harm and ensure we can heal. Students need to understand the stories of people who have overcome such injuries and regained their former abilities so they can tell the stories of their own health journeys. Students may capture their understanding of this important lesson after hearing from a guest speaker like Mike Shaw, a Canadian skier who broke his neck after a fateful jump and slowly had to learn to walk again. Figure 5.5 (page 126) demonstrates how a middle school student might tell the story of recalibrating following a devastating injury after listening to Mike speak to their school.

Ecosystems Documentary Project

Now we turn to an example of telling the story of a return to harmony in a macro, interdisciplinary way through an ecosystems documentary project. Ecosystems, by their nature, are harmonious systems, meaning the interactions between the diverse organisms create a certain stability. However, human activities are a twist to this balance, forcing these systems to recalibrate in all types of ways, some of which are proving disastrous for biodiversity. The World Health Organization's Millennium Ecosystem Assessment (2005) reports the following:

> Over the past 50 years, humans have changed ecosystems more rapidly and extensively than in any comparable period of time in human history, largely to meet rapidly growing demands for food, fresh water, timber, fiber, and fuel. This has resulted in a substantial and largely irreversible loss in the diversity of life on Earth. (p. 1)

Story offers a deeper way for students to make meaning about this critical truth than memorizing facts for a traditional test. This deeper learning is critical to our future as students mature into future policymakers.

When Natalie was working as an instructional coach, she codesigned a nature documentary project with middle school science teacher Jaclyn Colville so students

Harmony Through Story

Kishōtenketsu	Essential Question	Your Response
Ki (Introduction)	Who was the main character of the story?	The main character was Alexander Fleming, a bacteriologist working at St. Mary's Hospital in London. He was known for his research on bacteria and infections.
Shō (Development)	What was the context of this accidental discovery?	In 1928, Fleming was studying staphylococcal bacteria in his lab. He was trying to find ways to kill harmful bacteria, but his lab was famously untidy. He left some petri dishes with bacteria uncovered while he went on vacation.
Ten (Twist)	What was an unanticipated twist?	When Fleming returned, he found that a mold, later identified as penicillium notatum, had grown on one of the petri dishes. What was surprising was that the bacteria around the mold had been killed, which no one had ever seen before. This was an accidental but groundbreaking discovery.
Ketsu (Reconciliation)	How did the characters and setting recalibrate to this twist? What can we learn about science from this story?	Fleming realized the mold produced a substance that could kill bacteria, which he named penicillin. Although he discovered it, he couldn't figure out how to produce it in large amounts. Later, scientists like Howard Florey and Ernst Chain took Fleming's work further by mass-producing penicillin, making it one of the most important medical breakthroughs in history. This recalibration saved millions of lives and changed the way infections were treated forever. Fleming's story shows that science often relies on curiosity and noticing unexpected results. His discovery of penicillin was accidental, but paying attention led to a major breakthrough. It also highlights the importance of teamwork, as others helped develop his finding into a life-saving medicine. Science thrives on observation, openness, and collaboration.

FIGURE 5.4: A graphic organizer applying the Kishōtenketsu story structure to the accidental discovery of penicillin.

Kishōtenketsu	Essential Question	Your Response
Ki (Introduction)	What was the setting for the event?	The story happened on December 16, 2013, in Colorado, at a ski hill where Mike Shaw was coaching freestyle skiing.
Shō (Development)	Who were the characters involved?	The main character was Mike Shaw, a Canadian freestyle skiing coach. The other people involved were the athletes he was coaching and the medical staff who helped him after his accident.
Ten (Twist)	What unprecedented twist of events happened?	While demonstrating a trick called a Nose Butter 720, Mike landed wrong in soft snow. This caused a serious neck injury, leaving him paralyzed from the neck down. It was a life-changing and unexpected accident.
Ketsu (Reconciliation)	How did both the setting and characters recalibrate following the event to find a new normal? What can we learn about overcoming a serious injury?	Mike faced his recovery with a positive attitude and determination. In less than four months, he was able to walk out of the hospital, and within a year, he was back skiing. He also became an inspirational speaker and wrote a book about his experience. The new normal for Mike was using his story to motivate others to overcome challenges, while the ski community saw him as an example of resilience and hope. From Mike Shaw's story, we can learn that overcoming a serious injury takes determination, a positive attitude, and support from others. Even when things seem impossible, staying focused on small goals can make a big difference. Mike didn't give up and he showed that a strong mindset and hard work can help you recover and find new ways to live a meaningful life. His story also teaches us to be grateful for what we can do and to inspire others with our challenges.

FIGURE 5.5: A graphic organizer applying the Kishōtenketsu story structure to analyze how to overcome a serious injury.

Harmony Through Story

could step inside an ecosystem and construct meaning through story. It was an interdisciplinary project that met science and ELA standards as students also had to build a sophisticated understanding of visual literacy, including planning through storyboarding. Teachers can replicate and remix this project using the following four major milestones through the four-act structure of Kishōtenketsu.

1. **Ki (introduction):** Introduce students to the different elements of an ecosystem (producers, consumers, and so on), provide practice to build their confidence and fluency with the information, and invite them to apply this information by designing an imagined ecosystem with a partner.

2. **Shō (development):** Continuing to work with their ecosystem elements, students build a physical model of their ecosystem.

3. **Ten (twist):** Once students build their ecosystems, have them draw a human activities card from a deck. They must complete a collaborative constructed response by working with their partner to describe how the elements of their ecosystem would have to adapt to the activity on the card, for better or worse. Some examples of human activities include the following.

    a. Agriculture
    b. Destruction of wildlife
    c. Deforestation
    d. Overpopulation
    e. Overconsumption
    f. Plastic production
    g. Greenhouse gas emissions
    h. Draining rivers or streams
    i. Overhunting
    j. Genetic modifications
    k. Invasive species

4. **Ketsu (reconciliation):** After learning about different visual literacy techniques, students create a documentary that consolidates everything they have learned so far. The documentary should cover the elements of their ecosystem, the human impact, and the resulting adaptations. Students use their built ecosystems as the set and film clips on their iPads, to which they may add voiceovers.

Most importantly, this four-part design allows a teacher to implement four formative benchmarks so they can ensure all students are ready for an uptick in cognitive rigor at each stage of the story. As discussed in chapter 2 (page 35), some assessment methods are better matches for certain types of thinking than others. Once a teacher has assessed students' understanding of ecosystem elements through a selected-response format, they can determine if students are ready for the increased complexity in thinking required in a constructed response. Though the idea of creative projects (like building a physical ecosystem) is nothing new, the added layer of assessment literacy is a departure from the norm. It ensures the project doesn't fall into the trap of being hands-on but shallow in thinking. The four-act story structure of Kishōtenketsu can be a helpful frame to conceptualize the critical benchmarks we must attend to in our assessment planning if we hope to maintain the integrity of teaching at a high level of cognitive rigor.

The Story of How I'm Learning

Life is unpredictable, and sometimes in the process of learning, we all experience unanticipated twists that cause a personal recalibration. As learning (and life) unfolds, the awareness of one's internal narrative, and potentially how to revise it through others' perspectives, allows students to reflect on how they learn and the ways their internal stories help (or hurt) their progress. The stormy first draft, the sailboat metaphor, and the user manual are three activities students can use for this purpose.

Stormy First Draft

When things in our life go wrong, our storytelling brain jumps to conclusions. We derive a sense of calm and false harmony from having a "complete" understanding of what just happened, even when that understanding is wildly inaccurate and based on limited facts. For instance, imagine a teacher pitching an idea for a new initiative to their district leadership team on Zoom. While they are in the middle of the pitch, their superintendent seems to look disgusted. With only this limited observation, that teacher tells themselves that their senior leader hates their idea and is going to shut it down. By believing this story, the teacher starts to stumble on their words, becomes defensive, and bombs the rest of their presentation. Meanwhile, the superintendent only made that face because they caught a glimpse of their face on the camera and were horrified by how tired they appeared. As the example demonstrates, rather than be grounded in an expansive view of reality, the story we tell ourselves is often motivated by our fear and anxiety. When the unexpected happens, we want to return to a place of clarity about the world as quickly as possible, even when this hastily constructed story isn't accurate. It's human.

In her book *Rising Strong*, Brown (2015) calls this psychological reaction to unprecedented events an *SFD*. While she defines the *S* using colorful language, we refer to the abbreviation as a *stormy first draft*. This reaction is stormy because it is formed in a moment where the waters around our metaphorical sailboat have become rough and we are struggling to find our footing. And it's a first draft because it's often based on limited information and therefore incomplete. To return to a place of mental harmony, we need a reality check. Brown (2015) suggests saying to both ourselves and others, "The story I'm telling myself is . . ." (p. 91). For instance, the teacher in the previous example could have paused their presentation and said, "I just saw Laurie make what appeared to be a disgusted face, and the story I'm telling myself is that something I've just said really didn't land. Is that true?" Then, Laurie might have laughed as she shared her story of seeing herself in the camera and thinking about how she needs to get a better night's sleep tonight. Tension gone. Crisis averted. When students are taught to share their understanding of themselves or a situation with this phrase, it invites others to share their perspectives and helps them to take a tentative stance about what they currently believe to be true. It is a rehumanized way to ask for feedback.

This strategy works beautifully in tandem with another move that Brown (2018) suggests called a rumble. A *rumble* is when two people or a team decide to come together for an honest and vulnerable conversation about where things may be breaking down in their relationship. When students collaborate, the storming phase is inevitable, so inviting students to call for a rumble when they have a stormy first draft to share is a powerful conflict resolution strategy. Of course, sometimes a student's SFD might turn out to be true. In this case, the rumble is even more important to understand all perspectives and perhaps even have a conversation about healthy boundaries going forward.

For instance, while working on a collaborative project, two students may approach a teacher to tattle on one another, hoping the teacher will take their side and put the other student back in their place. The teacher had already introduced the idea of an SFD to students as they reflected on their learning in previous units. Now, she returns to this idea with the two students locked in conflict. After sending them away with the sentence starter, "The story I'm telling myself is . . ." she invites them both to an honest conversation to listen to each other's stories. She reinforces previous instruction on why we use the word *story* to share our perspective. She coaches them to listen to understand, rather than reply, by asking questions and paraphrasing (more on this in chapter 9, page 211). This conversation is a rumble. She asks both students to explore a third alternative together that they might compromise on, offering suggestions if necessary.

If we view this scenario through an assessment lens, the teacher was able to elicit authentic evidence of each student's learning, support the offering of peer feedback, co-construct an instructional response, and consolidate learning through reflection. This is formative assessment in practice.

The Sailboat Metaphor

To return to the beginning of this chapter, if we understand knowledge through the metaphor of a raft or a boat, we can also use that metaphor as a proxy for our students' mental harmony or well-being. Overwhelmed students struggle to pull the pieces together. When they tell the story of their current state using the metaphor of a sailboat, specifically, we can elicit evidence of their sense of direction, personal values, strengths, weaknesses, and influential relationships, letting us reflect that information back to them to increase their self-awareness.

Psychologist Hugo Alberts (2016) designed a psychological framework around eight elements of a sailboat that students of all ages can use to increase their understanding of the many different aspects of themselves and their surroundings that influence how they act and feel daily. Figure 5.6 illustrates these eight elements.

Just like we need to shift away from Western story structures grounded in conflict to explore harmony and recalibration, so too must we shift away from clinical psychology toward *positive psychology* to get the most out of this metaphor. The biggest aim in the field of positive psychology is to increase autonomy and resilience, to help the client become the "captain" of their own boat rather than someone needing intervention. Teachers work with students at a time in their lives when they're starting to make sense of themselves and their place in the world. Therefore, we must help students increase self-awareness, an important facet of any social-emotional learning program.

To better understand how these elements interact and how we might coach learners to construct a deeper understanding for themselves, let's explore each element in turn. Note that some elements are inside the self (steering wheel, destination, leak, sails, and compass) while others are outside the self (water, other boats, and weather).

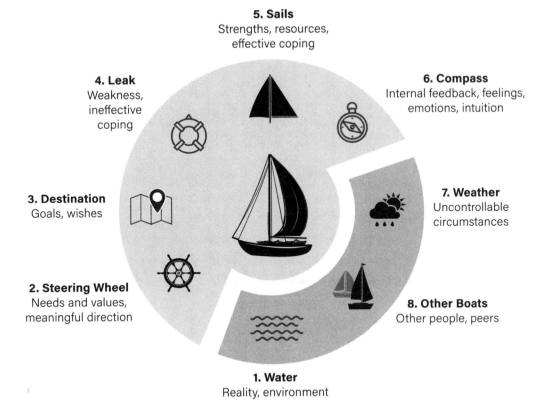

Source: Alberts, 2016.

FIGURE 5.6: Eight elements of the sailboat metaphor.

1. **Water:** Water represents students' direct *physical environment*, including their class, school, house, geographical location, and so on. As humans, when we get uncomfortable, we often want to change our environment. However, the deeper issues, or leak, will persist in the new environment if we have not addressed it.

2. **Steering wheel:** The steering wheel communicates our *values*, which provide the direction and sense of alignment for our actions. Helping students to clarify their own values is integral to helping them determine their success criteria for the decisions they must make in life.

3. **Destination:** The destination represents the specific *goal* that a student, or a team, has for themselves. These goals are a means of making values concrete.

4. **Leak:** The leak symbolizes the *weaknesses* that get in the way of value alignment and goal achievement. There is a tendency to want to focus solely on fixing weakness; however, we must understand that

this action will not directly increase well-being. For instance, if we do not hoist our sails to catch the wind, plugging the leak will not move us forward.

5. **Sails:** The sails represent *strengths* and help to accelerate value alignment and goal achievement. They are energizing aspects of our functioning that are either mindsets or activities that enable optimal functioning, development, and performance (Linley, 2008).

6. **Compass:** The compass represents our *emotions*, which provide important information about whether we are aligned with our values and on track. Though we have both positive and negative emotions, we shouldn't view them as good and bad, but rather as signposts that give us information about our values and goals. For instance, for many students, fear could mean that they are stepping outside of their comfort zone and living in alignment with their value of learning.

7. **Weather:** Weather represents all the *uncontrollable circumstances* in our students' lives. This could include the loss of a loved one, world events like a pandemic, or accidental injury. These events are a natural part of life, so teaching students to lean on their strengths to navigate a storm is key.

8. **Other boats:** This represents *other people* in our students' social network. These boats might be the members of their team, or they might represent family and friends. What's important to make sense of here is whether these boats are having a positive or a negative influence.

Now that we have made sense of the elements of the sailboat metaphor, how can we successfully use it in the classroom? Obviously, we are not psychologists sitting with one client over the course of an hour unpacking the interactions of these elements to uncover insights. To help both individual students and teams get the most out of this metaphor, we can leverage self-reflection and peer feedback through dialogue. The graphic organizer in figure 5.7 can help students prepare to tell their story to a peer or in a story circle; however, the teacher must provide the context for their responses. For instance, we can ask students to describe how things are going in a specific class, like English language arts, or in school in general if we have them in homeroom. Alternatively, a teacher might have teams respond to these prompts as a team at a midpoint in a collaborative project to figure out how they might optimize their journey.

Harmony Through Story

Element	Questions	Response	Peer Probing Questions	Peer Notes During Discussion
Water	What is the water like around your sailboat?		What in your environment is making the water rough? What do you think it would take to reach calm seas?	
Steering wheel	What values are steering your boat?		How well are you using your values to steer? What decisions have you made to align with your values?	
Destination	Where are you going? What goals are you trying to achieve?		Where else might you go? Would it be a better destination?	
Leak	What is something you are struggling with?		How might you plug the leak?	
Sails	Where do you feel strong?		What other strengths are putting wind in your sails?	
Compass	What emotions are you feeling? What do they reveal?		Name a recent emotion you experienced. What did it teach you about your values?	
Weather	What is the weather like?		Do you feel equipped to handle stormy seas? How might you increase your ability to navigate them?	
Other boats	How are other boats impacting your journey?		How might you better navigate other boats?	

FIGURE 5.7: Graphic organizer to support peer dialogue around the sailboat metaphor.

*Visit **go.SolutionTree.com/assessment** for a free reproducible version of this figure.*

Though we may not be able to provide coaching for every student, a quick read through student responses on the graphic organizer will tell us who is currently at risk, leading us to prioritize a conversation with these students. The ultimate goal is to shift their focus away from external blame to internal accountability. As the student describes their sailboat in more depth, the teacher can respond in ways that achieve the following.

- Highlighting possibilities and pitfalls of different directions and destinations
- Maintaining the student's autonomy to determine their own values
- Serving to increase the independence of the student
- Increasing the student's self-awareness of the internal and external factors influencing their actions

User Manual

For students to show up in a collaborative team, they need a way to tell the story of the individual role they might play *prior* to the collaboration occurring. The truth is, we all have prosocial and antisocial defaults when we work in a group. For instance, many of us in education are notorious dominators who would rather do all the work ourselves than let our peers impact our grade, so to speak. Whether you see that example as prosocial or antisocial is for you to decide. One way to tell the story of who we are when we work with others is to create a user manual, which is a practical handbook we create about ourselves that explains how to best work with us.

On their podcast *Brave New Work*, organizational change experts Aaron Dignan and Rodney Evans (2023) discuss user manuals in depth as they often use this practice when consulting companies who are seeking better collaboration among employees. One story of transformation they tell is unforgettable. In a company they worked with, the CEO was known as being exceptionally hard to please. Whenever employees presented to him, he would sit with his arms crossed, leaning back in his chair with a sour look on his face. Of course, this led to teams not doing their best as they felt fear take hold. However, the stormy first draft they were telling themselves—the story that he was annoyed with his employees and dissatisfied with their work—was shattered when he completed his user manual. In it, he explained to teams that he had a serious back injury that made it painful for him to sit for long periods. The only way he could relieve that pain was to lean back and cross his arms to stretch. This is another classic case of needing to recalibrate our stories. Let this be your warning to make a user manual for yourself and share it with both your students *and* peers.

To unlock deeper collaboration in the classroom, students must be empowered to tell the story of themselves as collaborators. Not every user manual needs to be the same, as each student is different. Consider the following non-negotiable prompts all students must respond to as well as some optional prompts students can choose from to best tell their story as a teammate.

- Non-negotiable prompts include the following.
  - I add value to teams by . . .
  - Something you might find challenging about me is . . .
  - My preferred communication style and tools are . . .
  - The way that I most like to receive feedback is . . .
  - My values include . . .
- Student choice prompts include the following.
  - My personality type is . . . This means that . . . (Include a link to a student-friendly online personality quiz.)
  - You'll convince me to get on board by . . .
  - The environments in which I thrive have . . .
  - I'm really passionate about . . .
  - The time I do my best work is . . .
  - I don't have patience for . . .
  - You can help me by . . .
  - Things I do that annoy other people include . . .
  - People gain (or lose) my trust when they . . .
  - My style as a collaborator is . . .
  - I view success as . . .
  - The best team I ever worked with was . . .
  - One fun fact about me is . . .

There are many places where students can store and update their user manual over time. For example, they may complete a template their teacher prepares for them as a page on Google Sites and store it in their personal website as a part of their digital portfolio. Or, they may create a physical document that lives in a file the teacher returns to them at the start of every collaborative activity. Whatever format a teacher uses, the important thing is that every student feels they *own* their manual. They should be allowed to make it their own and add personal touches and style; that way, they're more likely to want to share it with others. The possibilities are endless for making these manuals accessible (in physical or digital form) to all students so they can learn more about their peers before responding when seeking reconciliation.

Summary

We must learn to find harmony in disharmony. We must learn to see unprecedented events as not a loss to our sense of normalcy, but a facet of it. To pull from the field of epistemology, it's helpful to view our mental models as a raft or a boat that carries us through rough waters, rather than a pyramid prone to collapse. As we encounter evidence that counters our beliefs, we may replace a log on our raft here or there while remaining afloat. However, there is also space on our metaphorical boat to hold seemingly contrasting beliefs at once—such as the need for both individualism and collectivism, and the validity of both written and oral traditions.

Kishōtenketsu is an Asian story structure that can help us cultivate more mental and cultural harmony. In four acts, it tells the story of recalibration and reconciliation. We can use this structure to help students reframe their experience as authentic collaborators, and to reframe their understanding of curricular content as a story of adaptation, be it historical events, physical injuries, or ecosystems. As we hold space for students to tell the story of themselves as learners, they can learn to navigate mental disharmony by telling a stormy first draft to calibrate with the perspectives of others. Then, using the metaphor of a sailboat helps empower students to be active agents in their school experience. Finally, creating a user manual can help students tell the story of themselves as collaborators to navigate the inevitable storming phase they will encounter when working with a diverse team. If we can hold space for these stories in our classrooms, imagine the possibilities for our future society to navigate the stormy seas of the many challenges our world faces.

Chapter 5 Discussion Questions for Learning Teams

Journal your response to the following prompts in the space provided. Share your thoughts during team discussion.

1. What quote or passage encapsulates your biggest takeaway from this chapter? What immediate action (small, medium, or large) will you take because of this takeaway? Explain both to your team.

2. To what extent do you believe your students see unprecedented events as an opportunity for expansion rather than a loss?

3. Where do you see potential to use Kishōtenketsu's four-act structure as a constructed-response method of assessment in your content area?

Page 1 of 2

Rehumanizing Assessment © 2025 Solution Tree Press • SolutionTree.com
Visit **go.SolutionTree.com/assessment** to download this free reproducible.

REPRODUCIBLE

4. Where do you see potential to use Kishōtenketsu as a structure to plan an integrated project with four milestones that demonstrates an intentional increase in cognitive rigor?

5. How might teaching students about a stormy first draft support conflict resolution?

6. What concerns or challenges arise when you think about using the sailboat metaphor in the classroom? What suggestions can you think of as a team to address them?

7. What steps might you take as a team to support implementing user manuals schoolwide so students might update them from year to year?

Page 2 of 2

Rehumanizing Assessment © 2025 Solution Tree Press • SolutionTree.com
Visit **go.SolutionTree.com/assessment** to download this free reproducible.

Chapter 6

REFLECTION THROUGH STORY

The idiom that hindsight is 20/20 is often accurate. It is usually through reflection that we gain clarity. However, reflection in schools can easily toggle between being a deep, meaningful process and a superficial compliance exercise. Though it can be challenging to make self-reflection habitual, intentional practice can go a long way to help students reflect on *what* they are learning and *how* they learn. This can be revealing about both where they are now and what they need next to keep growing.

This chapter guides teachers to understand why they must foster student self-reflection and shows how story is a helpful tool for accomplishing this. It suggests thinking backward, using an end-beginning-middle structure to craft a story of what they've learned. The chapter concludes by offering three strategies students can use to tell the story of how they're learning: (1) profile of a learner, (2) learning journey map, and (3) real-time reflections.

The Big Idea

Sometimes the real story is not truly clear until we view it through reflection. During learning, the outcome is often incomplete and emotional swings can skew our judgments. While learning is never truly final, pausing to reflect at certain intervals can make space for students to take inventory of both what they learned and what next steps they can take. In the following sections, we examine why reflection is necessary, how reflection is challenging, and why reflection requires specificity.

Reflection Is Necessary

Most teachers inherently understand the power of and the need for student reflection, but time pressures often lead teachers to cut reflection out of their routines. Too many standards, too many disruptions, and too little predictability often leave teachers scrambling to get through all that needs to be done. It is in reflection, however, especially metacognitive reflection, where some of the most effective learning takes place.

In his now-legendary 1910 book *How We Think*, John Dewey asserts that reflection is a critical component of a holistic and meaningful learning experience. Consider the following takeaways.

- *Learning as a social process* means student reflection should focus on their learning experience within the social context of the classroom, and teachers should create opportunities for students to learn collaboratively.

- *Integration of learning* means students learn best when they can apply what they've learned to real-world circumstances, which means student reflections are most effective and impactful when they connect what they learn to their everyday lives.

- *Learning should be continuous, active, and experiential,* which leads to reflection being dynamic rather than a stagnant event, as well as a bridge between students' concrete experiences and the meaning they derive from them.

Dewey, in many ways, was far ahead of his time as so many of the concepts in *How We Think* are readily applicable and relevant in a 21st century classroom.

Information literacy is the ability to find, critique, organize, and use information in a variety of formats. Both information literacy and metacognition are essential skills for success since these skills improve individuals' ability to handle complexity (Denke, Jarson, & Sinno, 2020). Researcher Derek Cavilla (2017) studied the effects of reflection as a tool for improving metacognitive practices and effectively enhancing overall academic motivation and performance. He finds that not only is reflection important for students academically, but reflection also has "the transformative power . . . to fundamentally change the way students think and perceive their effort, motivation, and ability to complete novel and familiar tasks" (p. 4). Cavilla (2017) offers the following conclusion, which fully encapsulates the need for reflection and metacognition, and how critical those skills are for students as they transition into adulthood:

> [Student reflection] should be implemented in a well-structured, intentional manner with purposeful fidelity throughout the course of a student's academic career so that it becomes ingrained within the very way that he or she approaches the complex issues of intellectual and social-emotional growth throughout his or her life experience. If this task is accomplished, we have fulfilled our mission as educators because our students deserve more than a curriculum and instruction that teaches them concepts and facts; they are entitled to the exposure of skills and tactics that will allow them to develop into their full and utmost potential as an individual. (p. 12)

Students who are explicitly taught metacognitive activities tend to be more highly engaged (McCormick, Dimmitt, & Sullivan, 2013) and develop increased self-knowledge (Rusche & Jason, 2011). It is through reflection that lifelong learning takes place (Colley, Bilics, & Lerch, 2012). Telling the story through reflection can't be a one-off "fun" activity. It must be well-structured, intentional, and purposeful so students reap the substantive benefits of the process. As Cavilla (2017) states, "There is a clear rationale for the integration of reflection in the classroom" (p. 4).

Reflection Is Challenging

Revealing things about oneself—whether positive or negative—is challenging for students. Revealing positive outcomes (for example, "I'm really good at determining theme") comes with the risk that other students will see that as bragging, which may come with negative comments or negative social implications. On the other hand, revealing negative outcomes (for example, "I'm really struggling when we're learning in groups") comes with the risk of ridicule and feelings of being less than one's peers. The degree of risk is contingent on how supportive the classroom culture is, but the risks are there, nonetheless.

Introspection illusion (as mentioned in chapter 2, page 53) can significantly impact student reflections as well. Despite having instant access to one's own thoughts at any time, people don't always see themselves in the most accurate light. Therefore, students might think they're competent when they are not; or they might think their skills are lacking when they're not. It may take time for students to be completely honest about what they're learning and how they learn as both require a level of vulnerability that many students are initially reluctant to accept. Personal comfort with the process, especially when sharing reflections with the class, could be another barrier. Additionally, students may not value the practice and process of self-reflection; they may see it as just another task that takes up more of their time and energy. Making students aware of the benefits of self-reflection may shift their perception to see it as a valuable part of an enhanced learning experience.

It can be challenging for teachers to engineer opportunities for students to self-reflect since some may feel ill-equipped to implement and assess student self-reflection. Barriers may include lack of familiarity with the practice, insufficient time, or external pressure to raise academic achievement. These barriers can result in teachers finding student self-reflection challenging to habituate.

Reflection Requires Specificity

The irony is that teachers can't afford to eliminate student self-reflection and metacognition if academic achievement is truly the goal. However, to have an impact, self-reflection requires a level of specificity that begins with intentionality. The more intentional a teacher is in creating the prompts and guides for students to reflect on both what and how they learn, the more specific the output will be. Figure 6.1 provides some examples from different educational levels that illustrate the contrast between loose and tight prompts. *Loose* prompts are broad, open-ended questions with little connection to specific outcomes, while *tight* prompts are clear, targeted questions or criteria, aligned with specific learning outcomes, to guide students' reflection. The tighter the prompt, the more impact self-reflection will have. Loose prompts lack specificity and will likely result in an unhelpful range of responses. Given the value and impact of self-reflection on student achievement, teachers would be wise to develop more specific prompts, as figure 6.1 demonstrates.

Being intentional with the *input* (that is, the prompt) will lead to greater clarity on the *output.* Specificity leads to clarity, which allows students to identify their specific strengths and the areas in need of strengthening, both with *what* and *how* they learn. Superficial prompts (such as "How well did you do?") will lead to superficial responses (such as "I did pretty well"), so while there might occasionally be a place for more holistic or general self-reflections, specificity is better. *Doing* self-reflection is good, but *using* self-reflection is better. What serves as the bridge between the doing and the using is the clarity of information about themselves that students gain through the exercise.

Intentionality and clarity lead to action, as long as teachers provide enough time and space for students to act. The whole point is for students to increase their proficiency when reflecting on what they are learning and become more personally competent as they reflect on how they learn. They can only do that when given the time

Level	Loose	Tight
Elementary School	How well do you collaborate?	What parts of working in a collaborative team do you find most challenging? Is there something you and your group could do to address that challenge?
Middle School	Reread your writing and self-assess using the rubric.	Which of the three styles of writing (informational, narrative, or argumentative) is the strongest for you as a writer? Try to highlight specifically why that style is so aligned with who you are, both as a learner and as a person.
High School	How well do you understand cell division?	How confident are you in your understanding of how inherited genetic traits can and do vary? What signs or cues along the way helped you realize that you were understanding or struggling with this concept?

FIGURE 6.1: Examples of loose and tight prompts.

*Visit **go.SolutionTree.com/assessment** for a free reproducible version of this figure.*

to act. Again, overall time restraints (real or perceived) can lead to self-reflection being one of the first things teachers cut or marginalize. However, students' responsive actions could lead to more efficiency elsewhere. Knowing how students learn most effectively could lead teachers and students to make more efficient decisions as they set up and participate in learning experiences. When teachers know students' strengths and the areas they need to strengthen, they can make more efficient instructional adjustments. Self-reflection and metacognition are not just add-ons; they are an essential part of accelerating both what and how students learn.

Cultural Connection

While the traditional story structure is predominantly a beginning-middle-end sequence, some stories begin with the end and create an end-beginning-middle sequence that places an emphasis on reflection. Stories that begin with the end allow us to better understand the process involved in meeting an outcome.

Reordering the Story

Formalism is a mode of literary criticism founded in Russia in the early part of the 20th century that structured the analysis of literature. Vladimir Propp and

Viktor Shklovsky, two Russian formalists, coined the terms *fabula* (Propp, 1968) and *syuzhet* (Shklovsky, 1965) in the early 20th century. *Fabula* refers to the content of the story while *syuzhet* refers to the chronology of the story. This distinction in storytelling is important because what's being told (fabula) and how it's being told (syuzhet) can operate independently. The content or sequence of events has one chronology that is non-negotiable; everything happens according to time. However, the way those events are relayed to an audience need not follow the exact same chronology.

Earlier you read that Aristotle's *Poetics*—the earliest surviving work of Greek drama and literary theory—established that plots need to have a beginning, middle, and end. This led to most classical literature having synchronous fabula and syuzhet; the story was told in the exact same order in which it occurred. Formalism illustrated that the fabula and syuzhet could be treated separately, establishing an asynchronous relationship between the content of a story and the order in which it's presented. This can lead to more dramatic and impactful storytelling, especially in the case where surprise, mystery, or intrigue is at the heart of the story. This asynchronous relationship between the fabula and syuzhet is all over pop culture.

Let's look at an example. In the opening scene of the film *John Wick* (Stahelski, 2014), the title character crashes an SUV into a wall. He staggers out of the vehicle, puts pressure on a wound to his stomach, crawls to the side, takes out his phone, and watches a video of his wife on the beach. He then slumps over and shuts his eyes. The audience quickly learns this opening scene is actually near the *end* of the story as Wick is grieving the death of his wife. As his wife appears throughout the movie, the audience understands the fabula-syuzhet relationship is asynchronous. Highly acclaimed TV show *Breaking Bad* (Gilligan, 2008–2013) used this asynchronous relationship to open the series with an RV getaway scene that is clearly not the beginning of the story. Flashbacks strategically placed throughout a story also provide a creative way to tell that story. In fact, it seems rare these days that the fabula-syuzhet relationship is synchronous. As students share both what and how they are learning, they can begin with the end (for example, "I am a more focused learner than I was at the beginning of the school year") and then explain how they got to that outcome: end, beginning, middle.

Grind culture has taken over so many aspects of our lives. With twenty-four-hour news and a never-ending social media feed, we can easily feel as if everyone else is doing more than we are. It's tempting to feel we have to keep pace and keep moving! Pausing to reflect, therefore, can feel like a waste of time; after all, time is money. Teachers can feel the same pressure, as it seems there is never enough time to cover all that needs to be covered. However, coverage without learning is also a waste of time as it attempts to create the false division between teaching and learning. The "I taught it, they didn't learn it" false dichotomy centers the teachers' input over the students' output.

If learning is the goal, then we must make time for student reflection, as the learning and metacognitive reflection are how students grow. Reflecting on what and how they learn provides students a moment to take inventory of what they have achieved so far, what's next in service of continual growth, and how to get there more effectively and efficiently. Reflection is an essential part of how we learn, so it is a paradox (and even somewhat backward) to suggest there isn't enough time for reflection because we are too focused on student learning.

Navigating Our Blind Spots

Everyone has blind spots and implicit bias. Student reflections can help teachers ensure the culture of the classroom is fair and equitable. Teachers should ask themselves, "Is my approach to instruction consistently (even if inadvertently) prioritizing one group over another?" (Revisit the cultural archetypes discussed in chapter 2, page 41, as needed.)

Students have blind spots too. Their stories live inside them and can, at times, consume them, even when those stories may not be entirely true. If all self-reflection remains private, students may not have the chance to monitor their own thinking and test it against the realities established by the collective. Students (and adults for that matter) can easily underreact or overreact given the internal illusions or looping narratives that can warp their sense of reality. Venturing outside of ourselves and sharing our stories allows for a more objective reality check.

One way to unearth these potential illusions or looping narratives is to create more opportunities for oral reflection within a collaborative group. The default for student reflection is often a written format, which of course can be shared with others, but it provides less immediate feedback. When sharing their stories orally, students can instantly check their illusions against the perception of the small group or whole class. When handled with finesse and care, these collective reality checks can create a real-time conversation that brings the student's view of themselves closer to the truth. This can also help teachers recognize whether anything within the instructional or reflective experiences is inadvertently contributing to the revealed inaccuracies.

Competency Connection

To self-reflect is to think critically about oneself. The acts of *analysis*, *synthesis*, *critique*, and *prediction* (to name a few) are embedded throughout the self-reflective process. Self-reflective students are developing and using their critical thinking skills and dispositions, even though the focus of that critical thinking is themselves. The following sections explore critical thinking about the self and about the collective as well as critical thinking within the collective.

Critical Thinking About the Self

Reflection through story is ultimately critical thinking about what one is learning and how they are learning. Reflecting on the story of what students are learning embeds critical thinking into the process. Students will *analyze* and *critique* their strengths and areas in which they need strengthening, *synthesize* a potential action plan, and *predict* (through goal setting) the potential impact of that plan. Additionally, telling the story of how they are learning has students thinking critically about themselves as learners. They will examine how they learn to determine the optimal conditions to succeed, coping strategies to use when conditions are less than favorable, and ways they can grow to become more self-regulatory about their learning. The addition of storytelling allows students to create a narrative that navigates the connection between the individual ideas of *what* they have learned and the loss of accomplishments in *how* they learn. Students could also potentially narrate the connection between what and how they learn, since their level of engagement with the particular learning goals could quite easily impact their approach to learning. No list of bullet points will show that.

Critical Thinking About the Collective

Students can also reflect (that is, think critically) about the collective, which adds *collaboration* as another competency that the reflection process authentically addresses and develops. Students can analyze how they work together and the degree to which they support one another. Are they functioning as a collective (working with and for one another) or a group of individuals (working for themselves with just the appearance of a collective)? Reflective opportunities emerge when students are asked to consider how they respond when a classmate is struggling or whether they share tips and strategies that overcome obstacles. By sharing their stories, they contribute to the collective and participate in creating an inclusive classroom. The conversation among students is a collective and collaborative effort that gives each student the opportunity to share their observations, critique (not criticize) what others have to say, resolve any conflicts that may emerge, and form consensus about what's next as a whole.

Critical Thinking Within the Collective

Finally, students can think critically about themselves within the collective by reflecting on how they act and operate as an important part of the whole. This is the bridge between the *me* and *we*. Students can tell the story of how their contributions impact the collective's performance and progress, of whether they effectively communicate their needs to the team and add to the collective thinking, of what strengths they bring to the team, and of whether those strengths are being maximized. When students tell this story, they must be specific and substantive, referencing a specific time when their identified strengths and contributions were actively in play. Also, students can tell the story of how they had to adapt their collaborative style so they could make a more significant contribution to the team. Our collaborators influence the team's overall effectiveness, so students can reflect on whether they are consistently a positive influence in their collaborative efforts.

The Story of What I'm Learning

Reflection is a pivot point in the learning process as it can be a look back at what was and a look to what's next. Teachers must disrupt the frenzy of continual coverage to create opportunities for students to reflect on what they have learned. Defense of learning and grading conferences are two ways to accomplish this.

Defense of Learning

An effective way for students to reflect on their accomplishments is a defense of learning, which can be a powerful way to celebrate student achievement, promote accountability, and foster a culture of reflective learning. A *defense of learning* is a forum where students demonstrate their understanding, justify their learning choices, and explain how their knowledge applies to authentic contexts or personal growth. A defense of learning can occur at the end of the unit, semester, or school year. By providing students with the opportunity to showcase their accomplishments, engage in meaningful discussions, and receive feedback, defense of learning can help students tell the story of their learning. The structures and routines surrounding a defense of learning can vary, so teachers (or schools) should clearly articulate the specifics of how it will play out in their context.

Start by defining the purpose of the defense of learning; this is an essential first step. If the defense is to showcase individual student growth, then the student stories will focus on their individual trajectories from start to finish. However, if the purpose is to tell the story of proficiency, then the focus will be on student learning against the success criteria for the standards.

Next, clearly establish the format of the defense of learning, whether that be tight or loose. It could take the form of an oral presentation, a poster session, a digital presentation, or even a performance (depending on the topic), so it should be clear whether there is a specific required format or students have a choice. Ideally, the defense of learning would maximize student choice but there could be specific circumstances (for example, in a physical education class) where certain formats are more conducive to storytelling. Other considerations could include whether students will tell their story through a portfolio, lead workshops with their peers, receive feedback through peer review, solicit community involvement, or set goals as a result.

To prepare for the defense of learning, students could use an asynchronous fabulasyuzhet relationship; beginning with the end can be an effective way to grab an audience's attention. Provide students with the chart in figure 6.2 to help them plan their defense of learning. They can ultimately decide the order for telling the story of what they have learned, but the planning process gives their initial thoughts some structure.

This reflection planning tool is just one way for students to organize their thoughts; it's not mandatory, and students should have the freedom to plan in their way since it is *their* story. Also, this reflection can be as formal or informal as is warranted so they have flexibility in how they tell their story.

An example of a more formal structure comes from the New Media Academy at Hollywood High School in Los Angeles, California. There, all seniors are required to participate in a defense of learning process to demonstrate their academic and career technical learning. This process includes three components: (1) an academic research paper on a topic of their choice, (2) a service-learning project documented through time-lapse videos, and (3) a defense in front of a panel of community and industry partners. It's a chance for students not only to document and reflect on what they have learned, but also to document and share that journey with outside partners and experts. For more about the New Media Academy's defense of learning process, see the ConnectEd (2017) entry in the References and Resources section at the end of this book for information about a video demonstrating the defense of learning process.

Reflection Through Story

What is the headline of what you have learned?	
"The Green Machine: How Plants Power the Planet"	
What background knowledge did you already have? * I knew the definition. * I knew the role of sunlight and water in the process. * I had some basic understanding of plant anatomy.	What was your level of interest when we started? My level of interest was in the middle. I have always been more interested in human biology than plants.
What were the most challenging aspects of this topic and how did you try to overcome them? The most challenging aspect was understanding the difference between light-dependent and light-independent reactions, especially the complex biochemical steps and how they interconnect. I tried to overcome this by watching a few YouTube videos that showed animations of the processes. I also tried to make real-world connections with global issues as well as daily life, with things like gardening.	
Were any peers helpful to you along the way? Yes, my classmates sitting in our small group were helpful. We actually supported each other as we were trying to learn.	Were there any outside resources that helped you? Not too many. I used a couple of YouTube videos, as mentioned above.
Sketch out an **end-beginning-middle** story. End: Plants grow and provide us with food and oxygen, helping all living things survive. Life on Earth depends on this process. Beginning: It all starts with sunlight hitting the leaves. The green stuff in the leaves, called chlorophyll, soaks up the light. Middle: Inside the plant, water and air (carbon dioxide) mix with the sunlight's energy. The plant makes food (glucose) to grow and releases oxygen for us to breathe.	

FIGURE 6.2: Sample reflection planning activity to prepare for defense of learning.

*Visit **go.SolutionTree.com/assessment** for a free reproducible version of this figure.*

Grading Conferences

Teachers can set up a grading conference where students reflect and report the degree to which they've met the standards. The grading conference could be set up for a particular unit of study or specific competencies being learned, a predetermined interval (for example, a quarter), or the entire span of the subject (that is, a semester or school year). A grading conference would not just be about students articulating what grade they have earned—it can also be a valuable opportunity to discuss student performance, provide feedback, and set goals for going forward.

If a grading conference is going to be a pivotal reflection point, it has to be more than a question of what grade students think they deserve.

Once the teacher has scheduled the grading conference, students should prepare by gathering substantive information through reflection. Figure 6.3 offers an example of the questions students could use to prepare. This process need not result in the filling out of a form, though it could; the point is to make sure students go through the process and consider all questions and can speak about the process as well as the outcome.

Using the asynchronous relationship between the fabula and syuzhet during a grading conference can create a natural flow since the students could begin with the end (here's the level or degree to which I've met the learning goals), then go back to the beginning (here's where I started), and close with the middle (this is what my journey entailed). Teachers should encourage students to not just hit the highlights, as important as they are, but also articulate the challenges and roadblocks they overcame to reach their determined level of success.

The underpinning of any grading conference is, of course, accuracy; it's not a productive experience if students are inaccurate in their self-assessments. Lay the groundwork for this by establishing criteria and ensuring students are clear on what each level of success looks like. Randomly deciding on a grading conference at the last minute may not be wise as students won't have the opportunity to prepare along the way. The most productive grading conferences likely include planning in advance of any learning cycle.

END (Self-reflection on performance)

What aspects of my work do I feel particularly proud of in this assignment or course?

Can I identify specific examples where I demonstrated strong skills or understanding?

What level of proficiency have I reached?

BEGINNING (What was I thinking and feeling when we started this learning?)

What were my initial goals for this assignment or course?

How confident was I at the beginning?

To what extent do I believe I achieved these goals, and how did my goals evolve throughout the process?

MIDDLE (Challenges)

What was the story of the journey along the way?

Were there any specific challenges or difficulties I encountered during the assignment or course?

How did I navigate these challenges and what support did I seek?

Would I do anything differently if I had the chance to do it over?

MIDDLE (Approach to learning)

What is the story of how I approached this learning?

Was my approach to this learning consistent or were there times I was inconsistent?

If consistent, is that something I could replicate going forward?

If inconsistent, what could I do to make sure that inconsistency doesn't become a habit?

MIDDLE (Feedback)

Have I reviewed the feedback provided on my assignments?

How well did I use the feedback I received?

Was there a specific piece of feedback that was particularly helpful along the way?

Are there any comments or suggestions from the feedback that I would like to discuss or seek clarification on?

FIGURE 6.3: Grading conference preparation form.

*Visit **go.SolutionTree.com/assessment** for a free reproducible version of this figure.*

The goal of a grading conference is not only to discuss grades but also to foster a positive and supportive learning environment. While it would be ideal to tailor the approach based on students' needs, teachers can consider the following general guidelines to get started with grading conferences.

- **Schedule in advance:** Inform students in advance about the grading conference. This allows both the teacher and the student to come prepared.

- **Communicate the purpose:** Clearly communicate that the purpose of the grading conference is to discuss the student's achievement, provide feedback, and collaborate on strategies for improvement.
- **Prepare feedback:** Prepare specific feedback by highlighting strengths and areas that need strengthening. Give specific examples.
- **Critique rather than criticize:** When discussing areas for improvement, *critique* by offering specific suggestions or solutions for how the student can enhance their performance. Criticism only focuses on what's wrong.
- **Set an agenda:** Create an agenda to keep the discussion focused. Include items such as reviewing specific assignments, discussing overall performance, setting goals, and addressing concerns the student may have.
- **Discuss goal setting:** Work collaboratively with the student to set *stretch*, yet achievable, goals. These goals should be specific, be measurable, and have a clear timeline.
- **Encourage questions:** Create an open dialogue by encouraging students to ask questions and express their thoughts. This helps ensure that the conference is a two-way communication process.

There are numerous ways teachers can structure grading conferences; however, to ensure the experience is an authentic opportunity for deeper reflection, create a substantive process that goes beyond ascribing an overall grade.

The Story of How I'm Learning

Telling the story through reflection on a macrolevel can involve overt storytelling. That story emerges after a longer process, in which a student can use a reflective lens to document and tell the complete story of growth. However, it can also involve more micro processes where short-term reflections continually shape the story in real time. The following sections explore three of these micro processes: (1) profile of a learner, (2) learning journey map, and (3) real-time reflections.

Profile of a Learner

The macro view of a student reflecting on their learning is likely to fall under the umbrella of a profile of a learner. A *profile of a learner* is most often a combination of cognitive, metacognitive, motivational, and social characteristics that contribute to a student's ability to learn. The cognitive characteristics often focus on critical competencies (for example, critical thinking, collaboration) rather than specific learner goals or standards. While there is no universal set of characteristics that make up the profile of a learner a school chooses to adopt, there is often significant overlap between schools since the core characteristics of effective learners are often cross-cultural.

Examples of a profile of a learner are plentiful. The International Baccalaureate (IB) program identifies a collection of ten capacities and responsibilities guiding their commitment to "develop internationally minded people who, recognizing their common humanity and shared guardianship of the planet, help to create a better and more peaceful world" (International Baccalaureate Organization, n.d.). The ten capacities and responsibilities are as follows.

1. Inquirers
2. Knowledgeable
3. Thinkers
4. Communicators
5. Principled
6. Open-minded
7. Caring
8. Risk-takers
9. Balanced
10. Reflective

Visit www.ibo.org/benefits/learner-profile for more information on the IB learner profile.

The Evergreen School District (n.d.), a transitional kindergarten (TK)–8 district in San Jose, California, states the following on their website:

> The knowledge, skills, and attributes our students will need to pursue individual dreams and positively impact the world are defined in our Profile of a Learner. As a *Learner, Communicator, Collaborator, Critical Thinker, Innovator,* and *Advocate,* our profile includes outcomes and learning targets we want all our students to achieve during their school years in Evergreen School District.

This approach is more directly rooted in the critical competencies, and yet there is much overlap between the Evergreen School District's and IB's profiles of a learner.

The First Nations Education Steering Committee Principles of Learning briefly discussed in chapter 3 (page 57) are worth returning to here more expansively. All items in the list of principles are, in fact, competencies in their own right, but "represent an attempt to identify common elements in the varied teaching and learning approaches that prevail within particular First Nations societies" (FNESC, n.d.). The complete list, as FNESC (n.d.) presents on its website, is as follows:

> Learning ultimately supports the well-being of the self, the family, the community, the land, the spirits, and the ancestors.
>
> Learning is holistic, reflexive, reflective, experiential, and relational (focused on connectedness, on reciprocal relationships, and a sense of place).
>
> Learning involves recognizing the consequences of one's actions.
>
> Learning involves generational roles and responsibilities.
>
> Learning recognizes the role of Indigenous knowledge.
>
> Learning is embedded in memory, history, and story.
>
> Learning involves patience and time.
>
> Learning requires exploration of one's identity.
>
> Learning involves recognizing that some knowledge is sacred and only shared with permission or in certain situations.

Given the diversity present on most campuses, school faculty would be wise to cast the widest net possible to land on characteristics and competencies in a profile of a learner that are culturally expansive, relevant, and transferable for students in the future. Then, the real work of supporting students to gather evidence and defend their learning against this profile can begin.

Learning Journey Map

Sarah Stein Greenberg (2021), executive director of the Hasso Plattner Institute of Design at Stanford University, advocates using a learning journey map, which can do the following:

> [A learning journey map] helps you literally chart your own experience over time and identify the moments when you soared effortlessly and when you ran into challenges. It helps you take something that's usually internal and invisible—your own learning—and bring it outside yourself, where you can examine it more objectively, discover your strengths, and identify and work through your challenge areas.

While her focus is on the *what I'm learning* paradigm, the same idea can apply seamlessly to *how I'm learning*. Figure 6.4 is an example of a learning journey map.

Students can use the learning journey map to reflect on how they're learning by tracking not only their growth with competencies and habits of learning, but also the emotions they feel at certain checkpoints. The connection between their levels of success or frustration and the emotions they experience will allow for a more authentic telling of their story. In figure 6.4, you can follow the simultaneous journey of competency development and the accompanying emotions as the

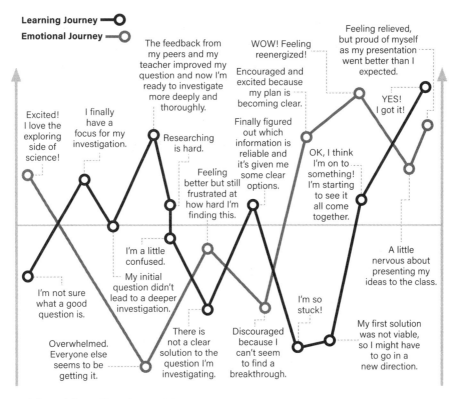

Source: Adapted from Greenberg, 2021.
FIGURE 6.4: Learning journey map.

mapmaker becomes more collaborative. What began as uncertainty and emotional unrest became assertiveness and self-efficacy.

Real-Time Reflections

Within shorter (or even daily) intervals, students can use reflection to tell the story of how they're learning in real time. Coming out of any experience, teachers can provide students the space to consider both their competency development and the corresponding emotional experience. For example, a teacher might ask students to reflect using the question, "What was the most meaningful idea you contributed to the collaborative problem-solving effort?" or "How did it feel when the team rallied around the solution you suggested?" Of course, not all experiences will be seamless or positive, so a teacher can include questions that address less-than-favorable experiences too, such as, "Did you feel any frustration during the problem-solving exercise?" or "How did you manage your emotions when you felt your contributions were not being accepted?"

To facilitate this, teachers could either provide a bank of prompts that students can use or provide a more generic prompt that allows students to capture the essence of what they experienced. Consider the following list (by no means exhaustive) of some sample prompts a teacher could use to facilitate student reflection of how they're learning.

- What was the most dominant emotion you felt completing this assignment? Did this emotion help or hinder your progress toward completion? Would you want more or less of that emotion next time, and what strategy could you use to accomplish that?

- Do you feel you were an active, fully contributing member of the collaborative team today? Were there aspects before or during the collaboration that contributed to your level of contribution? Is there anything you would do next time to enhance your contribution to the team?

- What, if any, connection do you notice between how you feel and how you learn? Is that something you are aware of ahead of time or is it something you don't notice until you are in the midst of learning?

The key for teachers is to create prompts that engage students in metacognitive, self-regulatory reflection that facilitates the telling of their story.

Students can tell the story of how they learned either privately or publicly. Students can keep their thoughts private by journaling. Over time, they can see how their competencies and emotions have progressed and regulated. Whether teachers read the journals (or listen to the recordings) depends on a student's level of trust. Most students trust their teachers on at least a surface level, but a deeper level of trust is needed if students are going to share their honest reflections. This is something for teachers to pay attention to, and teachers would be wise to ask students whether they are comfortable sharing and receiving support rather than require them to share.

Publicly, students could share their reflection stories with a trusted partner or group. Being able to have honest and authentic conversations with trusted peers can be invaluable when students know their peers will be supportive and not judgmental about the inevitable ebb and flow of how they learn. Again, trust is the key, so while a teacher may rotate groupings or seating assignments throughout the school year, the trusted partner or group with whom the students share their stories could remain constant.

Summary

While reflection is an essential part of learning, it can be challenging for teachers to find or make the time to engage students in meaningful ways. Often, reflection is the first practice teachers marginalize (or eliminate) because they may perceive it as an inefficient use of time given the pace some teachers believe they must keep to cover their curricular standards. However, coverage is overrated when the pace is so relentless that learning is compromised. Reflective metacognitive processes help students understand for themselves how far they've come and what's next going forward.

Reflection through story, since it happens *after,* allows students to play with the fabula (the content) and the syuzhet (the order) when sharing with others. Using an end-beginning-middle structure brings the outcome to the forefront and paves the way for a kind of collective curiosity about how they got there. In this way, students ask, "What was the contrast from end to beginning?" and "Was the middle smooth or messy or both?" This reversal of order is not necessary, but there is an element of creativity within the storytelling when this is done since, like many Hollywood films, the suspense rests within the process rather than the outcome.

Reflection through story also seamlessly creates a competency connection since reflection represents critical thinking about oneself, whether that be a reflection on what or how students are learning. Also, reflection could be a collaborative effort about a team's collective strengths and stretches in terms of how they work together and what each individual contributes to the greater good. The possibilities are limitless as the foundation of practice could be as formal (like defense of learning or grading conference) or informal (like daily or weekly reflection routines) as desired.

Chapter 6 Discussion Questions for Learning Teams

Journal your response to the following prompts in the space provided. Share your thoughts during team discussion.

1. What quote or passage encapsulates your biggest takeaway from this chapter? What immediate action (small, medium, or large) will you take because of this takeaway? Explain both to your team.

2. Describe a few of your most successful experiences with implementing student reflection. What specifically made those experiences successful? Are those elements you could enhance going forward? How would you do so?

3. Describe a few of your most challenging experiences with implementing student reflection. What specifically made those experiences challenging? How might you mitigate those challenges going forward?

Page 1 of 2

Rehumanizing Assessment © 2025 Solution Tree Press • SolutionTree.com
Visit **go.SolutionTree.com/assessment** to download this free reproducible.

REPRODUCIBLE | 159

4. What other factors, besides student competence and confidence, do you think are important to remember, establish, or mitigate when adding *reflection through story* to your classroom routines? What degree of confidence do you have that you can do that?

5. Could you envision facilitating a reflection on the collective? What coaching would your students need? Could that be a productive experience for your students, given the right parameters?

6. Would a defense of learning or a grading conference be more seamlessly implemented schoolwide? Is there an alternative to those two that you think would better fit your context? Explain your thoughts from the perspective of the faculty, students, and parents.

7. Would your students benefit more from real-time reflections on what or how they are learning? What are some of your favorite real-time reflection prompts that you have used in the past? What made them your favorites?

Page 2 of 2

Rehumanizing Assessment © 2025 Solution Tree Press • SolutionTree.com
Visit **go.SolutionTree.com/assessment** to download this free reproducible.

Chapter 7
PERSPECTIVE THROUGH STORY

Perspective permeates how we construct meaning and interpret events; nothing is purely objective. Our lived experiences filter how we respond to past circumstances, to current conditions, and to future possibilities. Educators often emphasize the so-called objectivity of the third-person perspective, whether they are writing academically or narrating a student's achievements. This gives the illusion of distance and objectivity. However, honoring the first-person perspective reveals the more nuanced complexities of any event, situation, or circumstance.

This chapter calls us to admit that objectivity is an illusion and that each person views reality through their perspective. Perspective is both simple and complex, and students must learn to check their perspective against external validation to ensure they're able to see themselves accurately. Teachers can help students recognize their perspective and value diverse perspectives that differ from theirs. The chapter concludes by examining three elements of perspective that support students in telling the story of how they're learning: the (1) forethought, (2) performance, and (3) self-reflection phases.

The Big Idea

In storytelling, there is no pure objectivity. Yes, there are irrefutable facts within some fields; however, within our human experiences, perspective will always shape the story of what happened and how we interpreted it. The following sections explore three illusions that affect perspective: (1) the illusion of objectivity, (2) introspection illusion, and (3) extrospection illusion.

The Illusion of Objectivity

In August 2006, the International Astronomical Union (IAU) downgraded Pluto to a dwarf planet. Since 1930, astronomers considered Pluto a planet . . . until they didn't. The most interesting part of the Pluto demotion is that not all scientists agree. To be considered a planet, according to the IAU (n.d.), an object must meet the three following criteria:

1. It must orbit around the sun.
2. It must be round or nearly round.
3. It must be gravitationally dominant (that is, it is not under any other objects' gravitational influence).

The argument in 2006 was that Pluto did not meet the third condition since its mass is less than the combined mass of the objects in its orbit. At least that's according to the IAU resolution, which only 5 percent of the world's astronomers voted for, and therein lies the controversy: not everyone agrees. Prior to August 2006, there would have been unanimous agreement—pure objectivity—that Pluto was a planet, and yet, now it's debatable.

We find the same illusion in assessment, especially with the use of multiple-choice questions as well as percentage-based grading. Multiple choice feels objective since there is one correct answer. However, teachers make many choices as they develop questions, including the phrasing of the question stem and the clarity or confusion that could emerge from the provided answer options. Rather than the judgment coming after the fact, it comes before in the many choices a teacher makes designing a multiple-choice test. Additionally, percentage-based grades *seem* objective and yet there are so many situations where an identical score could be the result of dissimilar circumstances. Imagine two students score a 75 percent (15 out of 20) on a mathematics assessment. One of the students left five questions blank (having no idea how to answer them) while the other answered all twenty questions but made five simple mistakes. Simply counting right and wrong has them both land at 75 percent, although it is clear that one of the students has a deeper understanding of the content than the other.

When teachers use their professional judgment to make indirect scoring inferences (for example, when assessing writing), it gets worse. Over one hundred years of research shows that when teachers make an indirect scoring inference of quality and assign a 0–100 percent score, the margin of error among teachers is plus or minus 5 to 6 points (Guskey & Brookhart, 2019). This constitutes a

10-to-12-point window, which means three English teachers could read the same essay and one might determine it's a 72 percent, another determines it's a 78 percent, and the third determines it's an 84 percent. Therefore, while on the surface it might feel precise, research disagrees. Even when there are fewer choices (such as 0 to 4), there will still be some subjectivity within the decisions teachers make, though the discrepancies will be dramatically reduced.

The point here is that we as assessors must lean into subjectivity because it represents using professional judgment and making decisions. It's not that anything goes or there are no facts, but often the perspectives of even the most factual event can vary. Rain, for example, could be welcomed by a farmer and lamented by a baseball team. Both views of the same event are valid, so while both sides agree that it's raining, their perspectives on that event would be dramatically different, or subjective.

Introspection Illusion

Let's take a deep dive into introspection illusion. *Introspection* is when any human being looks inward to examine their own thoughts, feelings, motives, and intentions. Because we all have access to our innermost thoughts, one might think that our views of self are most reliable. However, psychologist Emily Pronin (2009) disagrees:

> Advances in cognitive and social psychology have questioned the degree to which introspection can uncover the sources of our judgments and actions. . . . People's introspective access to their conscious intentions, emotions, prescient thoughts, and salient attitudes all can mislead them in their efforts at self-understanding. In short, introspection often is not a valid and reliable method for assessing the self. (pp. 2–3)

This creates a kind of internal irony that we have to constantly wrestle with. The irony of introspection illusion is that no one knows our own thoughts, feelings, and intentions better than we do, and yet our introspection may not be reliable. According to Pronin (2009), *introspection illusion* "involves people's treatment of their introspections as a sovereign (or, at least, uniquely valuable) source of information about themselves. People tend not to show this heavy introspective weighting when considering the introspections of others" (pp. 4–5). The irony—and where the illusion lies—is that we see ourselves as the most reliable judge of self but don't extend that same reliability when others are judging themselves. The dilemma is that we can tend to want our perspective to be unchallenged while remaining skeptical or dismissive of others' perspectives.

The answer to this dilemma is that all introspections and perceptions should, as much as possible, be verified externally. Imagine that one person is offended by something another person said or did. The offender might say, "That wasn't my intent." That could be true in their mind, but the introspection of not being offensive has to be judged against the other person's external verification. In this case, it can't be because they were offended. Someone else is always at fault. We all have blind spots and biases that we have to check, so having some kind of external validation for our perspective is most helpful. We may not eliminate our biases, but we can dramatically reduce them with outsourced verification.

Extrospection Illusion

While not widely recognized in the field of psychology, the term *extrospection illusion* can be defined by the sum of its parts, with *extrospection* meaning the observation of external reality and *illusion* meaning a misperception. Therefore, *extrospection illusion* is where individuals misread or misinterpret external events since they have limited information. This illusion can lead people to overestimate their ability to empathize with and understand the perspectives of others. This is somewhat ironic. We often think we know ourselves better than anyone else does (introspection illusion) and yet we can also, at times, think we have greater insight about others since they must suffer from introspection illusion.

An example of extrospection illusion is assuming that a person who appears happy on the outside must be content and satisfied in their life, neglecting the possibility of hidden struggles or internal conflicts. Another manifestation occurs when individuals judge someone's intelligence solely based on their appearance, overlooking the potential for depth and complexity within the person's mind. In interpersonal relationships, people may believe they can accurately gauge the feelings of others by observing body language, leading to misunderstanding and conflicts (as discussed in chapter 4, page 83). How many arguments begin when one person believes the other person is angry, even when they're not? The one person keeps insisting the other is angry until the other becomes angry, not because they were angry in the first place, but because the other person kept pushing.

Cultural differences can exacerbate the extrospection illusion, as individuals may use their own cultural norms and assumptions to interpret the behavior of people from different cultural backgrounds. Cultural variations in communication styles, nonverbal cues, and expressions of emotion can contribute to the illusion, as individuals may mistakenly attribute meaning to what others say and do based on their own cultural framework. Stereotypes and preconceived notions about different cultures can also interfere with accurately understanding others. Failing to recognize the influence of cultural differences is usually problematic. Increased awareness and cross-cultural competence are how we will mitigate the impact of the extrospection illusion in diverse social environments. The extrospection illusion highlights the importance of recognizing the limitations of our external observations and why a more nuanced understanding of others' internal experiences is critical. Luckily, we can access these internal experiences through story.

Cultural Connection

Culture is a shared perspective. Most cultures emerge when groups of people have a like-mindedness about how they view the world, how they interact with one another, and how they internally interpret the events of their lives. Though human beings are not a monolith, even within the same culture, there are cultural experiences that shape like-minded attitudes or points of view. In the following sections, we examine two such cultural experiences and issue a call for curiosity.

The Entomophagy Divide

Some people eat insects. Reading that sentence may have elicited a strong internal reaction for you, but not everyone has the same reaction: that's perspective. *Entomophagy*—the eating of insects—generally divides people into two perspectives: those who believe insects are a viable source of nutrition and those who couldn't even imagine it. According to entomologist and author Jun Mitsuhashi (2004), "In ancient times, when humans first appeared on the earth, insects might have been important foods for them, because they had neither the tools to hunt large animals, nor techniques for agriculture" (p. 786). Entomophagy has been a part of human history and is still a viable food source in many parts of the world. Researchers Marianna Olivadese and Maria Luisa Dindo (2023) explain the following:

> Insects such as crickets, grasshoppers, and ants have been eaten for centuries and are still considered a delicacy in many parts of the world, especially in Africa, Asia, Latin America, and Oceania. Entomophagy has, thus, been a part of human history for thousands of years and continues to be an important food habit for many people around the world.

Whether we personally like it or not, the consumption of insects is here to stay.

Your reaction to the topic of entomophagy reveals a lot about your cultural foundation and perspective. While some are repulsed by the idea, others see entomophagy as perfectly normal. Some may even hypothesize entomophagy to be a potential solution to food scarcity around the world. While the eating of insects is not the sole measure on which we reveal cultural norms, the polarized reactions to this practice certainly serve as a way of revealing one's culture through their perspective.

The thought of eating insects usually makes one disgusted or hungry; again, that's perspective. There is always a truth, and yet that truth is always calibrated through our perspective. How we see things, people, and circumstances is often underpinned by our cultural norms. We are conditioned by our culture and that leads us to have a certain perspective that serves as what's at least our initial lens of interpretation.

The Rashomon Effect

The internationally popular Japanese film *Rashomon* (Kurosawa, 1950) has given its name to a particular story structure. According to blogger Sam Azgor (2021), the "Rashomon effect" is "where people give significantly different but equally believable details of the same event. It describes a situation where the people involved in the same incident give conflicting interpretations or descriptions, while everyone's interpretation seems plausible." Our perspective, shaped by both our internal thoughts and external circumstances, leads us to our personal interpretations.

The Rashomon effect has been a common storytelling structure ever since the film with the same name. The American movie *Gone Girl* (2014), about a wife who has gone missing and her husband becoming the prime suspect, is another example of this structure. The first half of the narrative is told from the husband's perspective and the second half is told from the wife's. Another example is the 1994 movie *Pulp Fiction*, where different character perspectives are interweaved throughout. Sometimes whole scenes occur out of nowhere, but ultimately, all the characters come together at the end. There are countless examples of films that tell the same story from the perspectives of multiple characters, which allows audiences to gain a greater breadth of understanding of the story itself.

The dichotomy is that we appreciate it when others see things from our perspective, but we sometimes fail to offer the same in return, or we are dismissive of others' perspectives since they don't align with our own. We see it now in politics where dismissing (rather than understanding) the other side's perspective is the norm. Rather than debating ideas, some politicians would rather use words like "dangerous," "crazy," or "radical" to neutralize their political rival's perspective on meaningful issues that require a more nuanced approach.

A Call for Curiosity

The Rashomon effect is more than just a fun story structure; it might be the most authentic representation of life in popular culture. There are facts but the interpretation of those facts (events, circumstances, and even people) is vetted through our perspective. This is what makes life so interesting and simultaneously so challenging. One student might find getting a C grade on an assignment as a disappointment while another might see it as a triumph. While this is not an endorsement of alternative facts, the Rashomon effect does highlight the subjectivity of human truth and the idea that different people can perceive the same event in dramatically different ways. This mirrors the authentic experiences where individuals bring their own perspectives, biases, and emotions to any given situation, which shapes their understanding of what happened.

There is always more to the story, which should make us more curious, not less. In the polarized political climate of the early 21st century, others' perspectives are often unwelcome and those with different views or interpretations are easily branded as "harmful," "crazy," or even "dangerous." Rather than being curious as to how or why someone has a different perspective, many in society today retreat to their social media echo chambers to cast shame on anyone who doesn't agree with their worldview. Rather than finding common ground, many just double down, taking an uncompromising and disinterested stance. It feels that bipartisanism, which was once seen as a sign of strength, is now seen as compromising one's principles, which implies that one's own perspective is the correct perspective. No one has a monopoly on how to view the world, but so many act as if they do.

The solution to this is to embrace the multidimensionality of perspective, to become curious about ourselves and others. We know we have our own perspectives, biases, and emotions. Have you ever been curious as to why they are what they are, how they developed, and why you are so unwavering in those stances? Have you ever asked others the same questions? Students can be just as susceptible to this, since the groupthink of social media, peer groups, and even some inadvertent modeling from adults (for example, political conversations at the dinner table) make for an irresistible echo chamber.

Curiosity is also how we can avoid the binary bias in education. For instance, the so-called *math wars* (Boyd, 2012) unnecessarily pit mathematics reformers against traditionalists. The reformers advocate for a more inquiry-based approach in which students are exposed to real-world problems that help them develop fluency in number sense, reasoning, and problem-solving skills, with the idea that they learn the thinking that underpins the mathematics. Traditionalists maintain that students must first develop computational skills before they can understand concepts of mathematics. They argue that students should memorize and practice these skills using time-tested traditional methods until they become automatic. Rather than creating a war and bunkering down in foxholes, each side could be curious about the other and try to seek common ground. As in the movie *Rashomon*, the mathematics reformers have a perspective and so do the traditionalists. Understanding and empathizing with the story of each side is how we find common ground.

Competency Connection

We explored social competence in chapter 4 (page 83) in the context of conflict through story, but social competence is also the driving competency embedded in perspective. The competence to see *me*, *you*, and *us* is how we gain an understanding of and honor all perspectives. While perspectives may never truly align, it is essential that all perspectives be heard and appreciated, which is the lens through which we will revisit this competency. The following sections examine the need for intrapersonal and interpersonal skills in respecting multiple perspectives.

Intrapersonal Skills

While everyone has a perspective, the essence of perspective is being able to combat introspection illusion by filtering thoughts through the right questions. Developing the right skills and practices to filter one's perspective is important to ensure our perspective is not erroneous or misguided. Some perspectives are inconsequential. Our perspective about who is the greatest basketball player or pop star of all time is of no consequence to anything or anyone. On the other hand, there are times when our perspective is consequential. Our perspective on whether it's acceptable to keep a twenty-dollar bill found on the floor of a restaurant is one example. One's perspective does not provide a default cover where anything goes because it's their perspective. Asking ourselves the right questions is a competency that provides an effective filter for substantiating our perspective. Students and adults can consider the following questions when examining (that is, thinking critically about) their perspective.

- What experiences have shaped my beliefs?
- Who or what has influenced my thinking?
- How has my perspective evolved over time?
- What are my assumptions or biases?
- How do my emotions impact my perspectives?
- Am I open to alternative viewpoints?
- What values are most important to me?
- Have I sought out diverse experiences?
- What role does fear play in my perspectives?
- Do I engage in self-censorship?
- Am I willing to challenge my own beliefs?
- What evidence would prove that I am wrong?

Being socially competent begins with us not just knowing our perspective but also authentically understanding where it came from and how it has evolved over time.

One way teachers can help students develop these intrapersonal skills is to create opportunities for self-reflection. This can help students become more aware of their strengths and areas in need of strengthening, and can foster self-awareness and self-regulation. Whether they're focusing on learning experiences, behaviors, or emotions, students can self-reflect through journaling, discussions, or personal goal setting. Over time, the hope is that self-reflection becomes habitual.

Interpersonal Skills

Strong interpersonal skills are necessary for us to understand others' perspectives. It begins with empathy and active listening. Active listening is the key interpersonal skill that leads to empathy, which is essential to understanding others' perspectives. Once again, the interconnected nature of the critical competencies is revealed. Active listening involves focusing on what the person is saying, avoiding interruptions, and providing feedback to demonstrate understanding. This leads to being able to put yourself in someone else's shoes and appreciate their emotions and experiences. Open-mindedness and respect underpin both active listening and empathy, helping us resist the temptation to immediately dismiss any perspective or opinion that is different from ours.

Additionally, self-awareness is another important disposition of interpersonal skills. While this might seem more *intra-* than *inter-*, it is essential that we be aware of our own biases, beliefs, and emotions as we approach conversations with others. When we recognize that our own perspectives may be limited or biased, we can understand how we might be reacting to others as they share their perspective. Cultural awareness also matters since understanding and appreciating cultural uniqueness are important for empathizing with diverse perspectives, which includes recognizing that an individual's cultural background is likely a heavy influence on their viewpoints. Culture runs deep, so being aware of—and honoring—cultural lenses will make it easier to empathize.

Interacting with others to understand their perspectives requires mutual patience, adaptability, and a commitment to constructively resolving conflict. Students (and people in general) need the patience to deeply build an understanding of another's perspective and have the adaptability to navigate the ebbs and flows of an ever-evolving conversation where a continual evaluation (and possible adjustment) of their approach occurs. Within those ebbs and flows of trying to understand others' perspectives, conflict could arise as understandings and misunderstandings emerge. Constructively resolving that conflict is essential as we find common ground with people we might not entirely agree with.

One way for teachers to help students develop interpersonal skills is to provide collaborative learning activities where students must work together toward a common goal. This structure encourages communication, active listening, and the respect for others' ideas. It can be advantageous to begin this process with a low-stakes opportunity to teach students how to productively talk (and listen) to each other without any risk to the gradebook. Working in teams ideally helps students recognize and appreciate differences in perspectives and how to navigate those differences.

Multiple Perspectives

It is undoubtedly challenging to recognize that multiple perspectives can be true. Many of us were taught there is the *Truth* and then there's everything else, yet perspective reveals that there can be multiple viewpoints to the same event or circumstances. Whether it's superficial (for example, best fast food restaurant) or substantive (for example, where to trim the school district budget), we can often be convinced that our perspective is right and everyone else's is wrong.

This is where social competence through critical thinking comes in. If we can think critically within social situations where multiple perspectives are conveyed, we will have a greater chance of navigating the complexities of believing that multiple perspectives are true. The social part of social competence is the emotional side of the ledger, while critical thinking is the technical side. In substantive conversations involving multiple perspectives (for example, political discourse), our emotions tend to rule the day, which makes being open-minded and empathetic challenging. When emotions run high, we tend to lose perspective and get locked into our opinions, often because we are convinced that we are right and everyone else is wrong (Durnová & Karell, 2023).

Recalibrating the truth in the middle is how we gain our perspective back. If we can bring some of the technical side into the discourse, the critical thinking, we can find ways to *analyze* the position another person asserts and the substance that supports it without making it personal. We can *critique* (not criticize) without undercutting relationships and we can *synthesize* their positions authentically without getting defensive. We will never remove emotion when multiple perspectives are on the table, but we can be more thoughtful in finding ways to interact that are productive and supportive rather than divisive.

The Story of What I'm Learning

Perspective permeates all learning. Many historical events, scientific breakthroughs, literary works, or even innovative solutions discovered through inquiry have multiple perspectives. Also, it is through the telling of those stories that we can reveal our own perspectives. The following sections explore the differences between telling a perspective, taking a perspective, and sharing a perspective and indicate how each approach uniquely supports students' growth.

Telling a Perspective

Telling a perspective is likely the simplest assessment format, as students tell the story of what they are learning. Whether examining the past, the present, or even the future, telling the story through a particular perspective is arguably the most accessible to learners. All the intra- and interpersonal skills previously discussed still apply, only students are applying them to people and situations they've studied rather than know firsthand. Considering Newton's third law, which states that for every action in nature there is an equal and opposite reaction, could be a way for students to begin seeing the other side of everything, since nothing happens in a vacuum.

Providing students a simple structure and process to follow can help them formulate their thoughts on gaining a perspective on what they are studying. Figure 7.1 provides a structure for students to follow in order to gain an understanding of the perspective they are telling. Admittedly, the figure is somewhat generic, so it's important not to get locked into any particular process, which means teachers have the freedom to adapt and adjust this process to fit the context of their particular subject. Better yet, involve students by asking them, "Are there any adjustments to the process you think are important to add with this particular learning?" The students' age and maturity will impact the degree to which they can contribute to analyzing that process, but they can contribute in some small, medium, or large way.

Process	Directions
Introduction	Set the context and clearly articulate the perspective within that context that you are taking.
Background	Provide a brief overview of the situation or people you are examining, looking specifically for any causes and triggers that are significant.
Impact	Present a timeline of events and assess the short- and long-term impact.
Perspective	Tell the story from the perspective you have chosen. Be sure to acknowledge and address other perspectives that others might have.
Conclusion	Summarize main points and emphasize why the particular perspective you've taken is valid and reasonable.

FIGURE 7.1: Choosing a perspective.

*Visit **go.SolutionTree.com/assessment** for a free reproducible version of this figure.*

There are many opportunities within multiple subject areas to take a perspective, whether past or present. Students could take a perspective on the American Revolution (history), the onset of AI in society (science), or the most effective approach to living a healthy lifestyle. Middle and high school students could share a perspective on the impact that social media have on society. Elementary students could give a perspective on how a certain animal receives different types of information through their senses, processes the information in their brain, and responds to the information in different ways. Teachers need only look for opportunities where there are multiple perspectives for students to go deeper with.

Taking a Perspective

While *telling* a perspective is a third-person account, *taking* a perspective is a first-person one. This is where students put themselves in the shoes of the person they are examining and try to empathize with their views. The opportunities are endless, with historical figures, scientists on two sides of an issue, individuals debating points of social tension in society, someone lost in a foreign city with limited language skills, a physicist solving a complex problem, or a person deciding what the best approach to fitness would be considering their body type and genetic makeup. Students may still use the same process outlined in figure 7.1, but now it's a first-person account that could include a more intimate discussion of some of the emotions *they* would feel in a particular situation.

There is also the opportunity for students to use their imagination in taking another's perspective. They can imagine they were the main character of a novel and make an alternate decision from the one in the story. In mathematics, students can explore the perspectives different societies or cultures have brought to mathematics throughout history, which can help them appreciate the diversity of mathematical thought throughout the world. Additionally, any problems that authentically allow multiple solution pathways promote a deeper understanding of the underlying concepts and help students appreciate that there can be more than one valid approach to solving many problems.

Taking a perspective allows for the authentic integration of cultural perspectives, which could begin with the foundation of the cultural archetypes mentioned in chapter 2 (page 35). Culture is certainly more nuanced than the archetypes, but the archetypes (written versus oral and individual versus collective) are a good place to start. Here is where the underpinnings of multiple perspectives can be revealed.

As students see the multiple perspectives unfold in any given situation, they can understand those multiple perspectives more intimately against the backdrop of their cultural nurturing. At times, there may be no reconciliation or alignment possible when multiple perspectives are rooted in culture; however, the point is not to reconcile but to accept and appreciate others' perspectives.

Sharing My Perspective

Yet another level to perspective is the opportunity for students to provide their own perspective, which they can do in traditional or nontraditional ways. Traditionally, verbal or written communication has always been a way for students to reveal their perspective. Verbally, through presentation or debate, students can express their perspective. In writing, students express their perspective through an essay, a journal entry, op-ed pieces, or even a blog entry or series. Perspective would be not just the expression of an opinion but a substantive account of why they view the situation, circumstances, or thing (for example, a work of art or fiction) the way they do. In short, students must tell the story of their perspective rather than simply follow the five-paragraph essay format.

Literacy expert Thomas Newkirk (2014) describes traditional essays as an *extractive* model of teaching argumentation that is silent and impersonal. Essay writing also demands that students engage in selective reading, whereby they choose information from a source and drop it into a "tightly contained form, tyrannized by a thesis, the stern father who sits at the head of the table and rules over all" (p. 49). By doing so, he suggests that we are working against our human biology for storytelling and alienating students from learning.

Instead, he suggests a style of informational writing that is highly personal and maintains a voice for the reader to be with. This voice must tell a story in the form of antecedent and consequence, or an "arousing fulfillment of desire" (Burke, 1968, p. 124) that invites the reader to join in the writer's journey. The writer can achieve this through crafting a title that builds anticipatory tension, finding an "itch to scratch," determining the players and how they are in conflict, sharing the moves of their mind, and creating a need for a thesis and writing toward it.

A practical example of this reimagining of the argumentative academic essay is *The Story of My Thinking: Expository Writing Activities for 13 Teaching Situations* by educators Gretchen Bernabei and Dorothy Hall (2012) as they demonstrate the power of story to structure writing as an inquiry in and of itself.

1. Describe a scene or situation that unearths an interesting question.

2. What is the question?

3. What are some possible answers?

4. What is the most compelling answer?

5. How does this new understanding help you understand other parts of the book?

Thinking nontraditionally, teachers can provide students with opportunities to share their perspective through artistic expression, where students tell the story of their perspective by creating a work of visual art, such as a drawing, painting, or photograph. The artistic expression could also be a performance through dance, music, or theater. This is not restricted to only those subject areas, but we're not suggesting that all classroom teachers would create opportunities for artistic expression every week. The idea is to be strategic about creating seamless opportunities for students to artistically express their perspective. Students could do this by taking inspiration from current events or even people from the past. Imagery is a powerful medium that stirs emotions and clarifies a student's perspective. An important assessment reminder here is that teachers are not assessing the artistic expression; they are still assessing the learning that the students' expression of their perspective reveals. That's why the establishment of clear criteria on *what* they are learning is critical.

Our modern digital platforms also allow space for students to share their personal perspectives. Students could create video content or podcasts that give them a more longitudinal space to share their perspective and, potentially, to share how their perspective is evolving. Clearly some guidelines and safeguards would need to be put in place if these videos or podcasts were to be shared with the general public, but they wouldn't have to be shared that widely; they could be contained within the classroom. Online discussions or even social media *could* be spaces where older students express themselves, but again, the appropriate safeguards and guidelines would need to be in place. The opportunities are endless, both within what they are learning and the media through which students can express their perspectives.

The Story of How I'm Learning

Students telling the story of how they're learning through perspective is at the heart of being a self-regulatory learner. As mentioned in chapter 2 (page 35), the self-regulatory phases align perfectly with the three questions that drive the self-assessment cycle as students monitor their own learning. While self-assessment centers on what students are learning, the self-examination of how they're learning through perspective asks *why* they took the approach they did. The following sections outline three phases of the process: (1) the forethought phase, (2) the performance phase, and (3) the self-reflection phase.

The Forethought Phase

During the forethought phase, students will analyze the task to set goals and make plans as to how they are going to meet the established learning goals. Teachers could ask students to offer their perspective as to why they set the goal they did and why their plan is the most effective way to reach their goal. From their perspective, what previous performances did they base their goals on, what degree of challenge do they anticipate, and how might they overcome any small or large challenges should they arise? Rather than the teacher simply judging the degree of challenge of the goal, the students should offer their perspective, providing further insight into what they believe is possible (and reasonable) for them.

The forethought phase also includes students examining their self-motivation beliefs, where they evaluate their level of efficacy toward reaching their goals. Their perspective as to why they do or do not believe the expectations are plausible provides the teacher with insight as to how confident the student is and what supports or redirection might be needed. Admittedly, there is much overlap between reflection and perspective, but a focus on perspective gives the teacher some understanding of students' thought processes as they approach any learning goal. A teacher may uncover a disconnect between their perspective of the students and the students' perspective on themselves.

A grade 4 student could, for example, engage in both purposeful goal setting (for example, "My goal is to write a story that makes readers feel like they are really there") and motivational self-talk to build their confidence (for example, "If I get stuck this time, I'll just take a deep breath and focus on just one part of the story at a time"). The intent here is for students to have a clear purpose for the task as well as for managing how they learn. In addition, students could consider the environment within which they are completing the task (for example, "What will help me focus?") to ensure they don't get distracted.

Ultimately, the focus during the forethought phase is about students' outcome expectancies. What do they expect to accomplish and why do they believe that?

What is the root of that expectation and how might the teacher shift the students' perspectives (if expectations are unreasonably minimal) by reminding them of past successes and revealing the current growth trajectory they are on? Goals that are challenging, yet reasonable, will push learners to reach new depths of understanding, so when those expectations are misaligned, it is important to have the students' perspective as to why.

The Performance Phase

While they are learning, students will exercise strategies for self-control, which, again, are about self-management. Students thus gain perspective as to what's working to maintain their focus or what might be interfering with their ability to stay consistently engaged. The student's perspective would allow the teacher to suggest any enhancements or alternatives for the student to try. Could the student, for example, find more relevance within the inquiry project to increase engagement? Are there any visual or auditory reminders the student recognizes could help them stay focused? Is there a list of questions they could ask themselves when they are stuck? Students' perspectives on what would be effective or ineffective are invaluable in helping them become more aware of themselves as learners.

Becoming more aware is about students using metacognition to understand their habits and strengths as learners. The following list contains examples of some questions students could consider; adaptations for younger children are offered in parentheses.

- Am I focused or distracted? If distracted, what will get me back on track? (Am I focused or distracted? If I'm distracted, what can I do to help myself pay attention again?)
- What do I do (and how do I feel) when I encounter a challenging problem or question? Does that help or hurt my chances of overcoming the challenge? (What do I do when something is really hard for me? How do I feel about it? Does what I do help me figure it out?)
- Do I find myself procrastinating, and if so, why? (Do I wait too long to start my work sometimes? If I do, why do I think I do that?)
- What learning environment works best for me? Why? (What kind of spaces or places help me do my best work? Why do they help me?)
- Am I taking breaks when needed or am I pushing myself too hard? Why or why not? (Do I stop to take breaks when I need them, or do I try to keep working even when I'm too tired? Why?)

- Was my previously set goal realistic or a little too much? Why? (Was the goal I picked something I could do, or was it a little too hard? How can I tell?)

- Do I ask questions when I don't understand or do I stay silent? Why? (When I don't understand something, do I ask for help, or do I keep quiet? Why do I do that?)

- What habits contribute to my success in learning and which ones hinder my progress? Why? (What things do I do that help me learn, and what things make it harder for me to learn? Why do I think that happens?)

Not every question in this list applies to every learning situation, so teachers would be wise to choose specific questions that match the situation, especially early on when trying to establish the metacognitive habit. If it's a short-term activity, then questions about taking breaks will not apply, but certainly questions about being distracted or procrastinating would. Again, the focus of the questions has to be on *why*. Why are you continually distracted or why do you keep setting unrealistic goals that set you up for disappointment, even though what you are achieving is still significant?

The Self-Reflection Phase

The self-reflection phase is all about students gaining perspective on how they learned. It begins with self-evaluation, where students assess their performance. While students are self-assessing the degree to which they met the learning goals academically, they can also evaluate themselves as learners. A student might reflect on two questions: "What will I do differently in my next inquiry project to improve my results?" and "Did my emotions during the project influence my persistence? If so, what can I do next time to prevent this?" This allows the teacher to gain the student's perspective on whether they would approach things differently given another chance, what they learned about themselves that could carry forward, and how they can give themselves a better chance to succeed.

Another aspect of the self-reflection phase is causal attribution, which asks students what they attribute their success or lack thereof to. For example, a grade 10 science student might ask themselves after a successful inquiry-based learning experience, "Did my success depend on following a detailed plan, or were there other factors, like luck or teacher support, that caused my success?" Again, when students tell the story of their perspective, they provide insight into how their beliefs and the teacher's beliefs might be at odds. Ideally, students would disproportionately attribute their successes to what they did—that success came from within and they have significant control over their outcomes. External causation is unreliable, so it's important to redirect students whose perspective is that other people or circumstances are responsible for this success (for example, my teacher made an easy test). It is quite possible for students' perspectives on success to be skewed, so having them tell their story will help teachers provide any redirection or correction. We want to honor students' perspectives, and yet we are also aware of the introspection illusion that can shape that perspective.

The self-reflection part is also of interest as the students' perspectives on their level of satisfaction of the outcome will provide a potentially interesting contrast between the goals set in the forethought phase and the end result. If students are not satisfied with their results, redirecting them back to their goals could be a way for them to gain their own perspective on how they set challenging yet reasonable goals for themselves. Their adaptive responses at this phase will help them as they cycle back to the forethought phase the next time around.

Perspective through the story of how students learn reveals the root causes of both successes and challenges. Teachers can (and often do) use their experience to infer why a student has or has not been successful. Having students tell their own stories of success or lack thereof, however, gets them actively examining their own thinking and provides teachers an opportunity to check their inferences to see how accurate they are. The inferences teachers draw may be assumptions that are misplaced or misguided given the students' perspective on what happened.

Summary

Objectivity is an illusion. There are facts, but then there is the interpretation of those facts, which is what perspective is. We all have a perspective, but our perspective should be checked against external verification since we can suffer from introspection illusion and fail to see ourselves accurately. We may also make assumptions about others based on superficial signals. Perspective is both simple and complex. It's simple because we know everyone can articulate a perspective; it's complex because accepting others' perspectives, especially when they differ from ours, is not always straightforward.

Revealing our own perspectives requires the intrapersonal skills to ask ourselves the right questions to understand how our perspectives developed, what biases we might carry, and what underpins the specific perspectives we hold. Asking ourselves some tough questions will ensure that we appropriately scrutinize our perspectives.

Empathizing with others' perspectives requires interpersonal skills of open-mindedness and patience. Suspending our preconceived ideas is easier said than done, but it is necessary if we are to accept and embrace diverse perspectives that can often be culturally nurtured and uniquely established.

Students' perspectives on *what* they are learning can be shaped as they tell a perspective (third person) or take a perspective (first person). Investigating or revealing multiple perspectives deepens the learning as there is rarely one clear way to see things. Students' perspectives on *how* they learn come from metacognitive monitoring as they experience the instructional process. A student's perspective helps the teacher verify their inferences about the learner. It also provides the student with a more intimate understanding of self, the ability to navigate the inevitable challenges along the pathway to proficiency, and clarity about why their default dispositions and responses may or may not be helpful.

Chapter 7 Discussion Questions for Learning Teams

Journal your response to the following prompts in the space provided. Share your thoughts during team discussion.

1. What quote or passage encapsulates your biggest takeaway from this chapter? What immediate action (small, medium, or large) will you take because of this takeaway? Explain both to your team.

2. To what degree do you notice introspection illusion in your students? Are there situations or circumstances that increase or decrease this illusion?

3. When are you susceptible to extrospection illusion with your students? Are there times when you make assumptions about students based on superficial or limited information? How can you mitigate that tendency?

REPRODUCIBLE

4. Has your school been purposeful about teaching students the intrapersonal skills needed to fully understand the root of their perspectives? What more needs to be done?

5. Has your school been purposeful about teaching students the interpersonal skills needed to fully appreciate others' perspectives? What more needs to be done?

6. When you think about perspective through story within your grade level or subject, what topic or concept do you feel is most applicable? Would the *telling*, *taking*, or *sharing of* perspective approach be most seamless to implement?

7. When you think of examining the students' perspectives as related to how students are learning, what aspect do you feel or find is the easiest (even if not easy) to implement? What aspect do you feel or find is the most challenging?

Rehumanizing Assessment © 2025 Solution Tree Press • SolutionTree.com
Visit **go.SolutionTree.com/assessment** to download this free reproducible.

Chapter 8
IMAGINATION THROUGH STORY

Without imagination, we would not have the many innovations that continue to shape our society and the critical hope grounded in empathy required to carry us into a future of ecological and social well-being. Imagination helps students answer the age-old question, "So what?" as they learn course content and envision practical applications of knowledge. Our human capacity for imagination is also necessary for students to tell the story of how they are learning, as it plays a critical role in both the creative process and goal setting.

This chapter explores the role imagination plays in knowledge, inspiration, and freedom. Though students become adept at identifying a story's intended meaning, they must also become empowered to make their own meaning of a story by engaging with its symbols and emotions. This ability is intimately connected to the creative process itself, and teachers must support students to become aware of their creative process and understand its phases. Students must become creators to thrive in a fast-growing economy and meet future challenges. The chapter concludes with three strategies students can use to tell the story of how they're learning: (1) imagining goals, (2) the ninety-day letter, and (3) a creative fuel playlist.

The Big Idea

Imagination is the pathway to unlocking new knowledge through the inspiration to create and act. When applied on a societal scale, it is the necessary precursor to creating a more inclusive culture that upholds freedom for all. The following sections explore imagination and knowledge, imagination as inspiration, and imagination as freedom.

Imagination and Knowledge

It might be tempting to view knowledge and imagination as a dichotomy, with knowledge as *fact* and imagination as *fiction*. This dichotomy is manifested in our schools; standards related to knowledge and understanding increase as students move up through the grades, whereas standards related to exploration remain relegated (and often restricted) to the primary years, especially kindergarten. Imagination is seen as belonging to the young and naive. However, we must reject this dichotomy, which organizes knowledge and imagination into separate silos and a false hierarchy. In truth, these mental constructs are deeply interconnected. All knowledge was once imagined, and all imagination is born out of knowledge.

Albert Einstein once said, "I am enough of the artist to draw freely upon my imagination. Imagination is more important than knowledge. Knowledge is limited. Imagination encircles the world" (Viereck, 1929, p. 117). Einstein, credited with many scientific discoveries in our repertoire of knowledge, offers authority on this topic. There is a distinct need for imagination to lead to the generation of new knowledge. In fact, many discoveries and epiphanies were born of spontaneous imaginings triggered by stimulus in the environment. After watching an apple fall to the ground, Isaac Newton wondered why it happened to fall straight down, rather than sideways or upward, and imagined some type of force at work on the apple. Through subsequent experiments, this imagining was later refined into the knowledge of gravitational theory. However, it wasn't just the image of an apple falling downward that led to this discovery, but rather the breadth of knowledge that Newton already possessed about mathematics and calculus. These provided the mental structures he needed to run his thought experiment before conducting a real one.

We can see this interplay between imagination and knowledge at work for both competent and novice learners. A learner who has developed competence in his after-school theater program may suggest to his teacher that he meet the criteria for argumentative writing by reading a slam poem, imagining the moment when he performs for his peers, earning their accolades and awe. By contrast, a novice learner in that same class may manifest their lack of background knowledge in argumentative writing with resistance to initiating the task, loudly proclaiming for all to hear that this essay is pointless. In this case, they must be invited to imagine possibilities by exploring mentor texts to build a foundation to start writing.

Across each of these examples, we can see that imagination not only has an important relationship with knowledge, but it is also an integral catalyst to agency.

Imagination as Inspiration

There's something mystical about imagination. Sometimes, inspiration can spark our imagination out of nowhere. In her best-selling book *Big Magic: Creative Living Beyond Fear*, Elizabeth Gilbert (2015) offers a perspective on inspiration she personally disclaims as "unscientific" but that is grounded in her professional experience as a writer. She describes the moment a new idea arrives to her "as if I was falling in love, or just heard alarming news, or I was looking over the precipice at something beautiful and mesmerizing, but dangerous" (p. 33). Alluding to the title of the book, Gilbert describes the moment an idea appears in our imagination as *magic*. She describes ideas as entities that exist outside of us, floating through the universe until they try to divert our attention away from our phones, our anxieties, our current dramas, and our duties so that we might partner with them to bring them into reality. Our job, then, is to hold the space for them to become known to us.

Of course, inspiration is not all magic. In his book *The Science of Storytelling: Why Stories Make Us Human and How to Tell Them Better*, Will Storr (2019) suggests a rather practical purpose for all the stories we tell as humans: to inspire strategy learning. He argues that by observing other people engage in actions in their life, we find the inspiration to take steps in our own. The people around us—especially those in whom we are most likely to see ourselves—plant the seeds of inspiration in our imagination. For instance, when someone aligns with our social identities in some way, we can see a model for how the choices they've made might play out in our own life.

When we see someone who both represents us and has achieved an outcome we seek, our ability to imagine ourselves in their shoes inspires us to take the first step. Since we already want to be in their shoes, it's easy to imagine ourselves stepping into them. By listening to how they have navigated their journey, we begin to see a clearer image of how we might approach our own path. As they share about an impactful opportunity they are currently undertaking, or a breathtaking level of success they are experiencing, we have two options: to become intimidated and recoil in self-doubt, or to become inspired to imagine the possibilities for our own life. When we choose the latter, we begin to see a fuller picture of where we'd be living, who would be beside us, and perhaps even exactly what we would be wearing as we step into these same opportunities. When we receive more information about how to navigate our journey toward a desired outcome, everything else in our life opens to the possibility of change as well.

Imagination as Freedom

In their work to determine a taxonomy of imagination, researchers Amy Kind and Peter Kung (2016) differentiate between imagination that is *instructive*, meaning to make sense of the world as it is, and imagination that is *transcendent*, meaning that it moves away from the world as it is. They explain the complex interplay between these two purposes, like the relationship between knowledge and imagination. They explain that we must understand the world as it is to dream of what is possible, and alternatively, to see a vision of a better future to fully interrogate the limitations of the present.

If we hope to understand the present to build a better future for all, we must start by imagining our own identity as an iceberg. There are many tropes and stereotypes that limit our collective imagination and, therefore, our freedom to be fully known; they prevent us from telling accurate stories of who we are. Most of an iceberg exists below the waterline, and so too do all the experiences, values, relationships, and beliefs that make up each of us and how we interact with the world. What exists above the waterline is what others can easily see or perceive, such as our physical appearance, accent, or mannerisms, and we know that this is only a small fraction of what makes us who we are. We have all been in situations where others have unfairly assessed us based on a trait above the waterline. Perhaps we have even done the same to others, only to stand corrected once we came to know them better. If we can recognize this truth about our own identity, we are equipped to imagine the same is true for everyone around us, despite what stereotypes might have us believe. Figure 8.1 demonstrates this metaphor of an iceberg to help students imagine the multifaceted nature of identity.

A more nuanced understanding of identity as traits we mostly cannot see and can only imagine better equips us to understand social problems as structural in nature rather than the result of the inherent shortcomings of a particular gender, race, ethnicity, sexuality, or other identity marker. Two examples include the idea that women simply don't desire leadership, and a certain race is inherently lazy or ignorant, leading to a lower socioeconomic status. The complex diversity of each person outside of a single, observable trait makes such assumptions inaccurate. There are simply too many variables below the waterline for observers to make an accurate assessment. Therefore, we must turn our attention to questioning and reimagining the shared social structures that we all coexist within, and which are leading to inequitable experiences for people based on a single facet of their identity. This is *social imagination*, the ability to connect "the problems of individuals to that of broader society" (Nickerson, n.d.), which critical pedagogy scholar Henry Giroux (2022) describes as an important facet of a pluralistic and democratic society.

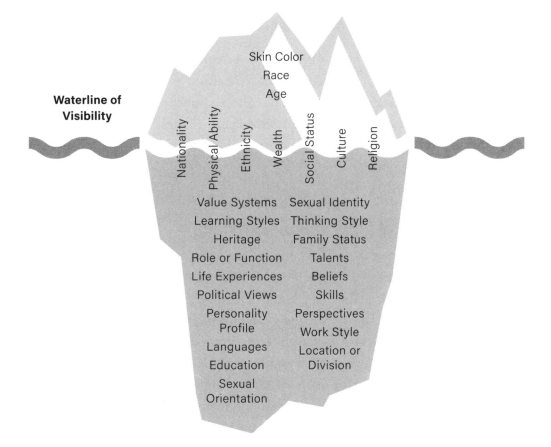

FIGURE 8.1: Iceberg metaphor representing observable and nonobservable facets of identity.

Giroux (2022) argues that political extremists threaten our capacity for social imagination by using education as a tool for domination rather than liberation. He cites as examples the policies in many states that range from banning books to policing the words educators are allowed to use, specifically as they relate to gender and sexual orientation. He views these actions as an attack on our willingness to think critically, question, and imagine so as to actively engage in democratic politics and liberal society. Giroux (2022) argues:

> If educators are going to develop a politics capable of awakening our critical, imaginative and historical sensibilities, it is crucial for us to remember education as a project of individual and collective empowerment—a project based on the search for truth, an enlarging of the imagination and the practice of freedom.

We must never lose sight of the most important role of imagination, which is to see ourselves and each other more clearly and continuously build a more humane society.

Cultural Connection

Some stories are intentionally unstructured and dreamlike, inviting personalized meaning. While our information-rich modern culture has made us intolerant of ambiguity and this lack of structure, it has also reawakened a search for answers that makes structureless stories relevant once again. The following sections examine how audiences make meaning of story without structure, how insisting on instant clarity blocks imagination, and how we can reclaim imagination by creating meaning within.

Make Meaning of Story Without Structure

The unfettered nature of imagination is reflected in three types of stories without structure: dreams, song lyrics, and oneiric films. Humans have always been fascinated by the function of dreams. Though the images are nonsensical in nature, the act of making sense of the seemingly random images has value. For instance, cognitive neuroscientist Antti Revonsuo (2000) proposes what he calls the threat simulation theory of dreams, in which we run mental "fire drills" of the things we most fear. This leads to one of the most fascinating facets of dreams: that we all experience the same stories again and again, no matter what culture we are from. For instance, the most widely cited dream across cultures is the story of losing our teeth, which some people interpret as a fear of saying the wrong thing or of bodily degradation. When we take the time to reflect on a dream such as this in our conscious mind, we can untangle some of the deeper fear that sparks the dream in the first place and acts as a barrier to our agency. The less this threat impacts our psyche, the less common the dream becomes.

The lyrics of many pop songs often lack logical sequence or narrative and are more often deeply tied to expressing an emotion the songwriter was feeling than telling a story. Though there may be images or fleeting moments of clarity within the lyrics, the process of writing a song often has more to do with fully processing the pain of a breakup, anger toward society, or the beauty of nostalgia. And yet, though the creator was living in their own imaginative space at the time of writing, those of us who consume music will find endless ways that the combination of words, chords, and layers holds personal meaning for us.

In film theory, the abstract, dreamlike lack of structure that a filmmaker might use is a style referred to as *oneiric*. Filmmakers use an oneiric style to create a cinematic experience similar to the randomness of a dream, leaving the viewer to make sense of the details through the lens of their own experiences and reflections. Oneiric films are meant to provoke thinking, not provide direction. This approach is said to stem from a wider belief by film critics that the human mind is fallible when it comes to interpreting story, so a filmmaker might as well leave the entire narrative up to interpretation (Filmmaking Lifestyle, n.d.). Mainstream films such as *Vanilla Sky* (Crowe, 2001) and *The Tree of Life* (Malick, 2011) follow such a structureless style and have won critical acclaim, though audiences sometimes resist the invitation to make meaning of the film on their own.

Modern Insistence on Instant Clarity

Perhaps one of the biggest barriers to our ability to daydream and tap into the explorative power of the imagination is that we are living in a culture of now. Widespread access to the internet and supercharged search engines that can process millions of pieces of information has made it so that we can find the answers to our questions instantly. When faced with a global pandemic, we no longer need to wait for the reasoned advice of health officials when we can find a more compelling answer in a viral podcast episode. This access to instant "clarity" means many of us avoid the discomfort that comes from ambiguity, especially if life with the internet is all that we have ever known, such as is the case with our students. However, a tolerance of ambiguity is necessary to find reliable answers to the complex questions of our time.

Giroux (2022) describes the technological disruption in our culture as *disimagination machines*. These machines, he argues, are leading to a culture of immediacy through the increase of social isolation and information overflow that has more to do with stoking consumer glut than building a capacity for thinking. As he explains, "A culture of immediacy, coupled with a fear of history and 24/7 flow of information, now wages war on historical consciousness, attention spans, and the conditions necessary to think, contemplate, and arrive at sound judgements." In short, our imagination is under attack.

In our culture of *now*, there is a rush to have the first opinion on a topic rather than a commitment to be accurate and grounded in imagining multiple perspectives and ideas—to be viral rather than valid. This has led to many looking to follow others rather than trust their own thinking. Our imaginations are being hijacked by the loudest voices, leading people into fairy tales of conspiracy and corruption. That's the thing about our imagination; it can go either way. It can be used to engage in wonder and curiosity about a growing body of knowledge and explore possibilities to make ourselves and society better. Or it can work overtime to convince us everything is going wrong and lead us into despair. How might we help our students, consumers who have never known life before social media, use their imagination for more of the former and less of the latter? In this chapter, we propose assessing the creative process to do just that.

It's not all doom and gloom in our modern world since the internet, though. The insistence on instant clarity can find its counterargument with a perennial human need to create meaning within. In particular, the rise in popularity of tarot card readings in the early 2020s might be evidence of this need (Bailey, 2021).

Create Meaning Within

It is no surprise that tarot card readings are once again trending in the early 2020s. In 2021, the editorial and communications director for U.S. Games Systems reported that sales of the card decks doubled in the past five years, following a huge spike in sales during the 2008 financial crisis (Bailey, 2021). Let's first unpack what exactly tarot cards are to understand why this might be happening and how it reveals a need for story without structure amid a culture of immediacy.

Tarot cards were originally created in 14th century Italy as a deck of playing cards for a wide variety of games. The deck includes seventy-eight cards that feature many different images and symbols that have been tropes in stories throughout human history. For instance, in the widely popular *Rider-Waite Tarot Deck* (Waite & Smith, n.d.), the fool features a young character with a bundle on a stick standing at the edge of a cliff. This image calls to mind optimism, new beginnings, and adventure. The empress card depicts a regal woman sitting on a throne surrounded by lush greenery, symbolizing creativity, fertility, and abundance. While tarot began as simply a deck of playing cards, they took on a new purpose at the end of the 18th century when French occultists made claims about their history and meanings. This led to the practice of reading the cards to better understand one's own, or someone else's, past, present, and future. Often, a reader flips cards over, one by one, and offers vague descriptions of the cards' meaning, inviting the person receiving the reading to draw connections to their life. The act of flipping symbolic cards simply creates the space for the person being read to accept what they already know to be true.

So, why is this antiquated practice of tarot reading trending again in the 21st century? Sarah Pulliam Bailey (2021) of *The Washington Post* notes that sales surged twice during the 21st century: the 2008 financial crash and the COVID-19 pandemic. Both events led many to become consumed with fear and anxiety, and the habit of picking up one's phone only made the feelings worse as voices shouted from all corners of the internet, offering polarizing and hyperbolic perspectives on what was happening. Perhaps the oneiric nature of tarot is the antidote to our culture of immediacy, as more and more are craving a deeper meaning about themselves and the world from within.

Competency Connection

Imagination is the engine of the creative process, a process that has become essential in our rapidly changing world. However, we must think big to start small. Applying the creative process to improve society begins with building confidence in gaining feedback on novel ideas. The following sections examine creativity as a process, creativity as the new normal, and creativity in the classroom context.

Creativity as a Process

If we can understand imagination as being grounded in knowledge and inspiration, allowing us to dream of a better world, then creativity is how we make our ideas a reality. Imagination is integral to the creative process. However, like imagination, creativity is tricky to clearly define and even more challenging to assess. For this reason, creativity is the least likely of all the critical competencies to be taught by educators.

In *Growing Tomorrow's Citizens in Today's Classrooms*, Erkens and colleagues (2019) challenge the myth that creativity is unteachable. They argue that assessing creativity without stifling it is possible when educators assess students' creative process rather than the final product, as "it's more prudent for the learner to evaluate [their] own final product" (p. 162) to determine its level of creativity. Any attempts by a single educator to evaluate the creativity of a product will be limited by their own bias as they lack the wider perspective required to judge the value in the creative work. Instead, they should assess the *process* of creativity by offering reflective prompts and dialoguing with learners to help them to determine their strengths and weaknesses and continue to grow as creators.

Consider the following process for teaching and assessing creativity (Runco, 2007, 2014; Sawyer, 2006; Wallas, 2014).

- **Preparation:** Identify an area of curiosity or a problem for further investigation.

- **Incubation:** Ponder ideas by exploring intuition, synthesizing concepts, imagining possibilities, and constructing preliminary possible products, processes, or solutions.
- **Illumination:** Develop realizations, insights, epiphanies, and inspiration.
- **Verification:** Seek feedback and validation during the formative phase for whether potential solutions are worth pursuing, assessing, and making personal decisions regarding next steps.
- **Implementation:** Move ideas from concept to reality by producing the product, process, or solution to share with others.

While these phases follow a logical sequence, there is an interdependence between them whereby a learner might move from illumination to verification, only to find verification unsuccessful, leading them back to preparation as they determine a new direction altogether. Later in this chapter, we will provide practical ways to help students tell the story of how they are learning the incubation and illumination phases as they tap into the power of imagination.

Creativity as the New Normal

Humans in the 21st century face ecological collapse and technological disruption. As a result of these problems, we are living through unprecedented times marked by volatility and rapid change. In *21 Lessons for the 21st Century*, renowned world history professor Yuval Noah Harari (2018) writes:

> We are consequently left with the task of creating an updated story for the world. Just as the upheavals of the Industrial Revolution gave birth to novel ideologies of the twentieth century, so the coming revolutions in biotechnology and information technology are likely to require fresh visions. The next decades might therefore be characterized by intense soul-searching and by the formulation of new social and political models. (p. 34)

We can take this to mean that the "way we've always done it" is over and we now must reimagine everything. Creativity, therefore, must no longer be seen as a pastime relegated to the arts, but a critical competency required for survival in the future. With this in mind, we must recognize the close relationship between creativity and innovation, whereby thinking with creative intent can spark the design of solutions to the many problems inherent in societal disruption. As described by educational authors and consultants James Bellanca, Robin Fogarty, and Brian Pete (2012), "Innovation and creativity are inextricably linked. It has been said that innovation is imagination realized, and only when the creative thought is put into action does innovation occur" (p. 39). But the link between creativity and innovation goes beyond just thinking and action; it also explains not only how we might achieve a new normal when we break from the norm, but also how we might create a new *and better* normal that taps into the collective imagination for freedom.

Because of this fact, creativity and innovation have become integral to the bottom line of companies both large and small (Sawyer, 2006). Corporate success in the 21st century belongs to those who can adapt and evolve the fastest, considering the constant upheaval we are living through. For example, animated film studio Pixar encourages the practice of "plussing" to speed innovation, whereby all employees must seek to advance the ideas of their colleagues rather than block them. GE Appliances' FirstBuild approach means the company embraces an open innovation mindset that allows creators to keep the patent to their designs in exchange for GE having the advantage of getting it to market fastest. A 2021 analysis by Deloitte indicates that the creative economy is growing faster than all the other economies analyzed and is projected to experience a 40 percent growth in size by 2030. Creativity has fully emerged as our new normal. Therefore, it must become a critical component of every educator's intended learning outcomes for students, regardless of whether it is explicitly included in already outdated curriculum documents.

Creativity in the Classroom Context

To expand our understanding of creativity outside of both a process and a necessity in our modern economy, we must also explore the scope and time creativity requires to effectively develop and assess it in the classroom.

When it comes to scope, the main takeaway is this: not all creative works are going to be of significant value to society. In fact, most of what students create in the classroom is not the type of creative output that would earn them an influencer contract on social media. Creativity researchers James C. Kaufman and Ronald Beghetto (2009) developed a "Four C" model to help us better conceptualize the scope of this competency as it intersects with expertise. They define each of the developmental stages, which can span in individual lifetime, as follows.

- **Mini-c level:** This is the type of creativity inherent in learning. Anytime we attempt something new, we are engaging in mini-c creativity. Though what we create will not likely have value to anyone else, it is a meaningful and novel experience for us.

- **Little-c level:** With more practice and through a couple feedback loops with others, we are starting to get better at what was once new to us, increasing the value of what we create to others.

- **Pro-c level:** At this level, we might be able to produce work at a professional level and may even make a living from our creative pursuit. This level requires many years of intentional practice and formal training.

- **Big-C level:** This is the type of creativity that makes the history books. Here, we might be cited for the impact of our work across our career and be compared to others who have made considerable contributions to the field. Think of Steve Jobs or Albert Einstein.

In the classroom, our emphasis is likely to be little-c creativity, involving practice and formative feedback. This is an important scope to recognize as it ensures that students aren't being held to standards outside their reach or compared to others at a professional level in their field.

Other than recognizing the appropriate scope of creativity, we must also recognize the necessity for ample time in the classroom. The creative process's phases of preparation, incubation, illumination, verification, and implementation take time. In particular, the early phases that tap into students' imagination require much more time than they typically receive in the school setting. As R. Keith Sawyer (2006) discusses, students must have a relaxed state of mind to allow for the *default mode network* to become activated below the level of conscious awareness. Have you ever had an epiphany in the shower? This is because the subconscious brain is activated when the conscious brain is focused on another rote task, like showering, taking a walk, listening to music, or driving. This is the default mode network. Therefore, "it's necessary for teachers to create the required time and space for learners to experience relaxed thinking and much-desired epiphanies" (Erkens et al., 2019, p. 158).

The Story of What I'm Learning

According to Shen-yi Liao and Tamar Szabó Gendler (2020), *imagination* is the ability to "represent possibilities outside the actual, represent times other than the present, and represent perspectives other than one's own." This represents a structure that teachers can use when thinking about how students can tell the story of curricular content using their imagination. Teachers can guide students to explore possibilities outside the actual, times outside the present, and metaphors and analogies—concepts explored more fully in the following sections.

Possibilities Outside the Actual

As students deepen their knowledge about a historical event, a book, a mathematical process, or a scientific law, they build the capacity to activate their imagination. Knowledge and imagination are interconnected, so challenging students to use their knowledge to describe imagined stories of alternative possibilities will demonstrate their ability to apply imagination in a plausible way. Using knowledge to imagine beyond what was taught elicits evidence of an extended or sophisticated understanding, the highest level possible on most proficiency scales.

To activate students' imaginations to tell the story of what they are learning, we ask, "What if . . . ?" Once students finish reading *To Kill a Mockingbird*, for example, teachers can ask them, "What if Atticus had managed to gain an innocent verdict for Tom Robinson? How would that have impacted the other characters' reactions?" Or, while studying the water cycle in science class, a teacher could ask students to imagine, "What if there were no evaporation in the cycle? How would humans have to adapt to that reality to ensure our survival?" In a mathematics class, students could explore possibilities outside of the familiar base 10 number system (meaning having ten symbols, 0–9) by a teacher asking, "What if our number system only had seven symbols, from zero to seven? How would you solve these simple addition questions?" Finally, a band teacher might invite students to explore the nature of music by asking, "What if AI created all our music instead of human beings? Would we be able to tell the difference? What loss would that be for humanity?"

To use this evidence as a summative assessment of sophisticated learning, we must provide formative feedback to support all students in producing insightful and plausible stories using their imagination. As always, we can lighten our load as teachers when we enlist the support of the students themselves, providing opportunities for them to work together to expand their perspectives before generating an individual answer.

Times Outside the Present

One of the most important times outside of the present we must ask students to explore is the future. In our world today, describing events as "unprecedented" has become, well, the precedent. This may lead us to conclude that the future has officially become unimaginable; futurists would beg to differ, though. Futurist Jane McGonigal applies her PhD in game theory to design future simulations to improve the lives of people and solve challenging problems of our times. In her book *Imaginable: How to See the Future Coming and Feel Ready for Anything—Even Things That Seem Impossible Today*, McGonigal (2022) writes, "The most important work of a future simulation is to prepare our minds and stretch our collective imagination so we are more flexible, adaptable, agile and resilient when the 'unthinkable' happens" (p. 14).

Throughout the book, McGonigal (2022) lays out a tangible strategy to help anyone, even young students, effectively imagine the future to awaken their creative capacity today. Once they've engaged in a subject of study for an extended time, students can take the first step: a game called "one hundred ways anything can be different in the future." This game draws on Dator's Law, one many futurists adhere to, which states, "Any useful statement about the future should at first seem ridiculous" (Forchheimer, 2022). To set up this game, first determine a topic. It might be broader (school), more specific (mathematics), or granular to a unit of study (number sense). Then, pose the challenge to students to work collectively to determine twenty things they know to be true about that topic (or challenge students to come up with one hundred things as a collective).

Now, here's the fun part that will plant some powerful seeds for the imagination. Challenge students to go through each of the statements and determine how the opposite might be true instead. The more strange or alternative it seems, the better. Tell them to go for it. For instance, "Mathematics knowledge is measured through a test" might become "Mathematics knowledge is measured through play." Then, in the real stretch for the imagination, students work in teams to answer the question, "What might lead to this change?" The task is to come up with a convincing explanation, no matter how absurd the statement seems at first. Encourage students to use the internet to find factual evidence to support the case that this change is already occurring.

This is a powerhouse formative assessment strategy under one condition: each team must share their arguments to the class. If the goal of formative assessment is to provide information that will enhance learning, then the alternate possibilities are the perfect feedback to do just that. Amid an ethos of play, students will come to see a course, content, and themselves in a new light that opens a space for freedom, creativity, and deeper understanding. After sharing their ideas, invite students to choose one to explore more fully in a constructed response. You can use this evidence of students' sophisticated understanding of course content as a summative assessment.

Metaphors and Analogies

Another way students can tell the story of what they are learning is to embrace using images to make meaning, just like the oneiric film structure or tarot card readings. The images themselves are meaningless, so we must use them to seek meaning within.

In their book *Visible Learning for Literacy*, authors Douglas Fisher, Nancy Frey, and John Hattie (2016) unpack practical strategies for eliciting evidence of learning during three phases of learning: surface, deep, and transfer. The most challenging of these phases for teachers to track is *transfer*, or the application of knowledge to novel situations. Teachers are excellent at eliciting surface-level knowledge through selected-response methods like matching, fill-in-the-blanks, and multiple-choice questions. They can elicit deeper learning through constructed-response methods like short answer questions. Transfer, however, eludes most teachers. Inviting students to tell the story of what they are learning through the imagery of metaphor and analogy is one strategy teachers can use to accomplish this.

A *metaphor* is a figurative language device where we compare two unlike things by saying one thing is another. For instance, many popular song lyrics use metaphors, such as when Pat Benatar compares love to a battlefield. It's a potent strategy to associate an image (and therefore emotion) with a concept, which makes it sticky in students' long-term memory. *Analogy* is a similar figurative device where we draw a connection between two seemingly unlike things for comparison. For instance, "A sword is to a warrior what a pen is to a writer." In this example, students see the pen of a writer as a powerful weapon, recognizing the significant impact of words.

Students should be invited to create a metaphor or analogy only after they have demonstrated a deeper understanding of course content. A metaphor is a slightly less complex task for a learner, so the teacher might introduce both metaphors and analogies and let students choose their level of challenge. Consider the following ideas for making this a meaningful assessment exercise.

- Co-create success criteria for a high-quality original metaphor or analogy.
- Allow students to choose concepts they are most comfortable with.

- Increase complexity by providing random images and inviting students to find a connection to course content.

- Invite students to trade metaphors or analogies and explain someone else's thinking to enhance the spread of ideas across the class.

- Use this high-complexity, low-effort task for a student who wants to move from a 3 to a 4 on a proficiency scale and asks for extra-credit work.

For example, a teacher who has just finished a lesson on adding and subtracting integers may ask students to create a metaphor to transfer their understanding. The teacher assigns each student a random image taken from the royalty-free image website Unsplash. The teacher knows that the hardest part about adding and subtracting integers is subtracting a negative integer from a negative integer, turning it into an addition situation. One student receives an image of a vehicle driving during a winter snowstorm. The student creates the following metaphor:

> *Adding and subtracting integers is driving a car in winter because sometimes things aren't what they seem, like when a driver has to slow down and be more careful due to the icy conditions. This is like when you subtract a negative from a negative, and you have to think carefully to remember to add these numbers together because you are on the left of the number line.*

All students then upload their metaphors into the class portfolio. At the start of class the next day, each student reads through their peers' metaphors to choose one to comment on, explaining how it helped them understand the concept.

In the next section, we explore how to turn inward, supporting students to set their own goals and hold space for epiphanies during the creative process.

The Story of How I'm Learning

Goal setting is imagination based. Teachers tap into learners' imaginations when they support students setting meaningful goals and hold space for them to find inspiration through their default mode network. Imagining a more successful future (and the pathway to get there) taps into an internal creativity. Teachers can support students to do this using goals, the ninety-day letter, and a creative fuel playlist.

Imagining Goals

The importance of personal goal setting to raise achievement of a variety of outcomes is well documented in the research (Black & Wiliam, 1998; Burns, Martin, & Collie, 2018; Gregory, Cameron, & Kearney, 2011; Hattie & Donoghue, 2016; OECD, 2017; Ross, 2006). Every teacher wants their students to create and execute better goals for themselves, yet most still overlook the critical role of imagination in this process.

The late Maxine Greene was an American philosopher, author, social activist, and teacher who was a pioneer for women in education. She fought to be included in many male-dominated spaces, including presenting at educational philosophy conferences and serving in senior leadership positions in the Philosophy of Education Society and the American Educational Research Association. Greene understood firsthand the importance of imagination to exercise freedom by setting goals that would help her seize opportunities that society did not yet offer. Greene (2000) writes, "Of all our cognitive capacities, imagination is the one that permits us to give credence to alternative realities. It allows us to break with the taken for granted, to set aside familiar definitions and distinctions" (p. 3). She goes on to say, "It takes imagination on the part of young people to perceive openings through which they can move" (p. 14). Students must tap into their imagination to set goals as a precursor to agency. Or, as assessment expert and author Katie White (2021) writes, "By inviting students to set their own goals, we are building independence, decision making, and investment in learning experiences. . . . We are also communicating a belief in students as agents of change and as important people in the learning relationship" (p. 73).

White suggests three "inspirational tools" for the imaginative practice of goal setting: exemplars, samples, and mentor texts.

1. **Exemplars:** Providing models of past student work that demonstrates a level of excellence is essential for students to co-create criteria for a product outcome. These criteria provide an important scaffold for students to set a personal goal as they embark on the product creation for themselves.

2. **Samples:** Providing works in progress or samples of work that do not meet the standard of excellence is a way to engage students in a conversation about next steps or opportunities for improvement in their own and each other's work.

3. **Mentor texts:** Providing examples of products created by experts in the field, such as novelists or scientific researchers, helps students to notice and name their moves and expand the field of possibilities for their own work as they find inspiration in the folks demonstrating pro-c or even big-C creativity.

The timing of goal setting, both short term and long term, offers a symbiotic relationship for learning. When we pair a long-term vision with short-term action steps, it's a potent recipe for success. Educational researchers Alexandra Usher and Nancy Kober (2012a) reiterate this idea in a study where they demonstrated that short-term goal setting that increased students' perceptions of abilities had a positive effect over time. We will provide a tangible strategy for using the emotion of story to activate a long-term vision in the next section, but for now, we offer the following practical considerations for short-term goal setting.

- **Create predictable routines:** Goal setting is an important first phase in the cycle of self-regulated learning, which also includes performance monitoring and reflection (Panadero, 2017). A natural way for students to experience this cycle of learning is to set a goal on Monday and reflect on Friday. Within that weekly goal, students can set daily targets to monitor their performance.

- **Ensure student ownership:** The temptation is strong to set group goals on behalf of students, but students must set their own goals if they are to experience agency and grow as learners.

- **Focus on self-regulated learning strategies:** While long-term goal setting is best associated with the essential standards teachers have identified in a given course, short-term goal setting with an intentional focus on self-regulated learning strategies will have the greatest impact on academic achievement (Butler, Schnellert, & Perry, 2016).

Figure 8.2 includes several areas within self-regulated learning in which students may choose a short-term goal.

Ninety-Day Letter

A powerful practice to help students set long-term goals in a way that taps into their imagination and natural abilities as a storyteller is a ninety-day letter. In this activity, students write their future selves a letter ninety days from when writing, as if they have already achieved their goals. This practice is especially powerful because

Environment	I choose to complete work in a location that minimizes distractions.
	I independently access necessary resources for each task.
Behavior	I consistently follow class expectations.
	I follow the established routines throughout the duration of class.
Emotions	I effectively name and cope with my emotions (frustrations, overexcitement, anger, boredom, and so on) to ensure they do not interfere with my learning.
Motivation	I confidently tackle challenging tasks, even if it means I may make some mistakes along the way.
Strategic Actions	I interpret a task, make a clear plan, enact strategies, and adjust as necessary to maximize success.
	I use effective problem-solving strategies.
Cognition	I can evaluate information to arrive at my own conclusions that are consistent, reasonable, and valid.
Relationships	I effectively collaborate with peers and teachers to extend learning through feedback.

FIGURE 8.2: Aspects of self-regulated learning to scaffold student goal setting.

Visit ***go.SolutionTree.com/assessment*** *for a free reproducible version of this figure.*

it supports students in imagining how achieving their goals will make them feel and taps into the research that demonstrates how tangible outcomes become a reality through belief and mindset (Lipton, 2016).

First, explain to students the purpose of the letter and the power of their thoughts and emotions in influencing their behavior. Then invite them to respond to the following prompts.

- If you could achieve one of our essential learning goals in (course name) in the next ninety days, what would it be? Why is that goal important to you?

- What do you want your report card comments to say?

- Are there any projects you need to complete in the next ninety days?

- How do you want your relationships with your peers to improve in the next ninety days?

- How do you want to improve your relationships with your teachers in the next ninety days?

- What are you desiring more of in this class right now?

- What do you want less of in this class right now?

- What does the ideal (course name) class look like to you, from the minute you arrive to the minute you leave?

Now that students have written answers to the prompts, invite them to read back over their answers and write an annotation beside each one describing how they want to feel. You can offer them the following prompts.

- Because it will make me feel _____.

- Because it will make me feel like a _____.

Finally, invite students to write their letters. Provide them with some heavy-duty craft paper, because they are going to be looking at these letters often, rereading them to motivate themselves. The goal is to write the letter to themselves as if ninety days have already passed and they have achieved all the goals and emotional outcomes they hoped for. Coach students to write the letter in a supportive and celebratory tone as if they were talking to their best friend. Providing a model letter of your own can help students see what this looks like. In fact, this is a practice you might even enjoy taking up in your own life. Consider the following example:

Dear Natalie,

Wow! The research around goal setting was bang on ... this practice is a GAME CHANGER for learning. You've committed to your own personal goal to support your students to tap into their imagination and set personally meaningful goals. You must feel so proud of your planning and commitment to see it through. The agency you are witnessing in your classroom as a result is stunning. Students are finding relevance and purpose in their work and developing as self-regulating learners. I know you were unsure at first whether this strategy would be worth the time it would take away from direct instruction, but it's accelerated learning of everything else. You must truly feel like an educator and partner in your students' learning as you've shared your journey with your goal as they work toward their own.

Enjoy this well-deserved feeling of accomplishment; you've earned it!

Sincerely,

Nat

The final step left in this process is to fold the letter up and write on the front the date exactly ninety days from the current one. Then, over those ninety days, the goal is to keep it close and reread it often. For students, it perhaps becomes an independent reading bookmark, or lives in a specifically marked place in the room. The beauty of setting goals over a ninety-day period is there is ample time if students get off track to find their way back again. Then, after ninety days, invite students to reflect on how accurate their letter was, then use those reflections to repeat the process all over again!

Creative Fuel Playlist

There is a well-known adage that says, "When words fail, music speaks." With these words in mind, how might we use music as a tool to activate learners' imaginations?

The incubation and illumination phases of the creative thinking process are the most challenging for teachers to elicit evidence of since they both take time and because they are internal. However, if we allow students to get lost in music within school time, that expansive and explorative space can activate their mind in ways that spark an epiphany. The evidence we seek of these two phases will come when students tell the story of what they imagined after receiving time and space to listen to music with intention.

Of course, there is always the worry of wasted time. Yet, what if providing this "free" space to explore during school hours sparked a moment of inspiration for students on a creative project they are undertaking in class? This type of inspiration motivates them to snap out of their reverie and rush to grab a pencil to record their idea before it disappears. What if other students could see that moment of inspiration and feel motivated to find their own? Most teachers can agree they want their students to be creative thinkers, but we cannot reap that reward without playing in this ambiguous and "unproductive" space of imagination. We can't experience something new without an uncomfortable break from the norm.

To begin curating a creative fuel playlist, open a conversation about how music can spark imagination. Tell the story of a song that makes you get lost in your thoughts and ask students if they've had that experience. Add their songs to the board. Then, invite students to open the digital music player of their choice. Create a new playlist titled "Creative Fuel" and allow them to add songs to this list they can use for future incubation and illumination sessions. Once each student begins to populate their own list, invite them to join in opportunities to listen and activate their imagination. Consider the following examples of how students might engage with their playlist.

- Allow students to listen to a song as they settle into class and doodle in their notebooks as their minds drift.
- Turn the lights low after lunch and invite a meditative moment where students find a comfortable position to settle their minds and bodies into a dreamlike state.
- Fully engage the default mode network by asking students to bring their devices with them as the class takes a walk around campus while consuming some creative fuel.

Encourage students to apply this practice to their lives outside of school and continue to populate the list on their own.

As students become practiced at curating a playlist and listening to prompt inspiration, we can ask them, "What did you imagine as you were listening?" This question will elicit the evidence we seek of the creative process. Students may begin by sharing with a partner in a low-stakes way as the teacher wanders the room to listen. Or, if students are working through a creative project with a team, they might immediately share ideas and discuss with their group. Use the following questions to spark storytelling following an imagination session with the creative fuel playlist.

- What did you imagine as you were listening?
- Why do you think those images came to mind for you?
- Is there anything you saw that you might make a reality in this class?
- What did your imagination reveal about you as a person?
- Do you think your daydream was realistic? Or was it purely fantasy?
- What work should we take up in this class to help make your ideas a reality?

Figure 8.3 illustrates how a teacher might use success criteria to note "grows" and "glows" from student responses, gather evidence for formative purposes, and decide on a response to support all students toward the next stages of the creative process—namely, verification and implementation.

Grows	Success Criteria	Glows
Student routinely begins their playlist from the beginning, rarely listening to new songs. Student appears distracted by peers and often makes overtures to get their attention while listening. Student expresses limiting beliefs about how listening to music in class is wasted time. Student demonstrates tense body language signaling anxiety.	**Incubation:** Pondering ideas by exploring intuition, synthesizing concepts, imagining possibilities, and preliminarily constructing possible products, processes, or solutions	Student intentionally chooses songs to further explore certain ideas or questions. Student shows evidence of pulling together ideas learned from other contexts. Student emerges with practical ideas they can use in their work.
Student only uses songs that others suggest but doesn't seem moved by them. Student tells stories to entertain peers rather than to expose their inner self. Student expresses limiting beliefs about not being creative and having no ideas.	**Illumination:** Developing realizations, insights, epiphanies, and inspiration	Student speaks with animation and excitement as they share their new idea. Student rushes to grab a pencil or type on their computer to capture an idea while listening. Student talks through their imagined ideas in a way that reveals deeper insights about themselves.

FIGURE 8.3: A single-point rubric for two phases of the creative process with possible student responses.

*Visit **go.SolutionTree.com/assessment** for a free reproducible version of this figure.*

Of course, students who *glow* in these phases of the creative process will determine their own extension activities as their inspiration naturally sparks their next steps. It's the students who struggle to engage as creative thinkers who will require intervention to successfully move into the verification and implementation phases. Consider the following possible interventions to respond to those students who consistently fall in the "grows" category.

- **Engage in a one-on-one conference to address limiting beliefs:**
  Talking to a student individually is the perfect opportunity to help

open their mind to the possibility that they can expand their creativity, a skill everyone can develop. Working with this student on their own is important, because there is a social desirability bias that can emerge in front of peers, especially as being creative is often gendered as feminine. Asking questions such as, "How might imagination and creativity help someone be successful?" will allow the student to generate their own perspective and open their mind to new possibilities.

- **Anticipate behavioral barriers:** Students who struggle with this type of activity are likely facing behavioral barriers such as wanting to engage with their peers to use stories to entertain rather than illuminate. This is completely predictable and therefore avoidable behavior. Think strategically about where students are sitting for listening sessions or ensure pairings for storytelling that will provide models of prosocial behavior for students who need it. There will always be a small group of students who test boundaries and struggle in this more unstructured scenario. In that case, increase structure by setting short-term goals with them or providing alternative options for what they can do while listening, such as using a fidget toy.

- **Couple visual curation with listening:** For students who struggle to see mental images that inspire them, allow them the choice to use their computers to find images to spark their thinking or provide them curated images related to the creative project at hand. Students can use Pinterest to curate images by searching key terms and adding images they enjoy to boards of their own creation.

- **Amplify the stories of inspiration to increase hope for all learners:** Allow students to share their epiphanies with the group. Asking them questions publicly will help to reveal their cognitive processes and provide a model for others, and their excitement will increase the hope that someone else's moment is next.

Summary

Imagination is the foundation of knowledge, inspiration, and the pursuit of freedom through positive social change. While most stories follow a predictable structure to support meaning making, our imagination often tells stories devoid of structure, appearing to us through random images and emotional associations.

We must embrace our unfettered imagination as an antidote to society's culture of now, fueled by 24/7 internet access, which often rewards instant clarity over deeper contemplation. Our culture also demands that we develop students as creative thinkers since innovation is the norm amid the accelerated rate of change. We must recognize that creativity is a process rather than a product. By sharing this process with students and clarifying what each phase entails, we build the context for rich feedback dialogues about how students are becoming creators, a critical skill in a fast-growing economy.

Students can explore possibilities outside the actual and times outside the present to communicate their imagination through story. Open-ended questions beginning with "What if?" are one way for students to sort through the knowledge they have acquired in a unit of study and analyze it from a different perspective. A playful game such as "one hundred ways anything can be different in the future" is another helpful way students can think like a futurist. Additionally, metaphors and analogies allow students to use their imagination to support knowledge transfer. Finally, goal setting is a critical function of the imagination and will amplify self-regulated learning when students are supported to creatively visualize what they hope to achieve.

Chapter 8 Discussion Questions for Learning Teams

Journal your response to the following prompts in the space provided. Share your thoughts during team discussion.

1. What quote or passage encapsulates your biggest takeaway from this chapter? What immediate action (small, medium, or large) will you take because of this takeaway? Explain both to your team.

2. Why do you believe it is critical for students to develop their imaginations in your specific subject or grade level?

3. How do you currently develop the creative process in your classroom? How did the ideas in the chapter affirm your practices? How might the ideas in this chapter extend your practices?

REPRODUCIBLE | 209

4. How might you reorganize an upcoming unit so that students can tap into their imaginations to deepen their understanding of course content? What traditional assessments might you replace?

5. What challenges are you running into when it comes to student goal setting? How might you mutually support others on your team to navigate these challenges?

6. One of the biggest barriers to developing imagination in schools is the need for "unproductive" time. Do you believe this time might be critical to deeper learning of course content? Why or why not?

7. What first steps can you commit to as a team to develop your students' imaginations?

Page 2 of 2

Rehumanizing Assessment © 2025 Solution Tree Press • SolutionTree.com
Visit **go.SolutionTree.com/assessment** to download this free reproducible.

Chapter 9

CRAFT THROUGH STORY

Craft relates to the refinement and finesse that emerge as students develop proficiency, rather than a shallow demonstration like when students engage in "arts and crafts." When students engage in arts and crafts, they are often simply cutting and gluing predetermined pieces into a heavily teacher-guided project, which has some therapeutic outcomes but does little for deeper learning. Students demonstrate authentic craft when they engage in performance assessments that blend oral, visual, and written formats, such as digital storytelling. Students can also explore craft as they tell the story of how they are learning by recognizing the importance of feedback to enhance the artistry of their work and effectiveness of their creative process.

This chapter explores the role craft plays in learning, encouraging teachers to inspire their students to create beautiful work. It uses the traditional Hawaiian hula dance as an example of craft in storytelling and calls on teachers to avoid cultural appropriation and ensure cognitive complexity in hands-on learning. This chapter also focuses on how important feedback is in supporting students to refine their craft. It concludes with three strategies students can use to tell the story of how they're learning: (1) the communication story circle, (2) improved feedback processes, and (3) the creator's commentary.

The Big Idea

Craft is not an elusive type of magic, but rather the practice of building a level of refinement or finesse in an area of study. Teachers can help students develop their craft within their discipline by creating beautiful work that invites students to use knowledge rather than simply regurgitate it. In a standards-based learning paradigm, craft is how teachers and students can answer the age-old question, "What does exemplary learning look like?" The following sections examine what cultivating craft, moving toward refinement and finesse, and constructing beautiful work look like.

Cultivating Craft

In 1995, David S. Moore received an award for distinguished college-level mathematics teaching when he was a professor at Purdue University. He made considerable contributions to his field by serving on boards, acting as a director of notable mathematics associations and foundations, and writing many theories on statistics. As anyone who has attended university knows, though, a breadth of expertise in a field does not always make for an effective teacher. Here's how Moore (1995) defines the craft of teaching:

> A craft is a collection of learned skills accompanied by experienced judgment. The great advantage of thinking of teaching as a craft is the recognition that anyone can learn it. Competent teaching requires no special gift, no actor's personality, no divine spark. And if anyone can learn to be a competent teacher, then all who are employed to teach have the obligation to learn. (p. 6)

The word *craft* often conjures images of magic, and this confuses the definition of the word. Therefore, the craft of a great teacher is seen as an untouchable phenomenon, just as the artistry of a great painter is considered a highly personal and private space. This couldn't be further from the truth. The Merriam-Webster online dictionary defines *craft* (n.d.) as "skill in planning, making, or executing," no mention of magic whatsoever. However, we would like to extend this definition by also recognizing Moore's (1995) assertion that craft goes beyond just a set of learned skills, to include "experienced judgment." In the field of teaching, we refer to this as *professional judgment*, defined by the ability to make executive decisions based on a body of evidence. For instance, a teacher uses professional judgment when they decide to remove old evidence from the gradebook from earlier in the year once a student has demonstrated proficiency. This professional judgment arises from the instructional skill of unpacking proficiency in the curricular standards, as well as a deep respect for learners and the learning process. It is not an elusive practice, but one that emerges from a depth of knowledge and skill.

When we tap into craft, it is a liberating feeling. Reaching a depth of knowledge and skill that allows us to exercise reasoned judgment produces one of the most important byproducts of learning: joy. Being empowered to act in executive ways, as if we are the CEO of our own practice, feels like we are breaking some unwritten code. For students in the school space, where they often feel disempowered and are told to comply rather than create, holding space for them to cultivate craft is the ultimate show of respect.

Moving Toward Refinement and Finesse

There's a big difference between following a recipe and cooking. For one of the authors of this book, this learning journey dominated much of her twenties. When she graduated university, the only meal she could prepare independently was nachos. However, as a third-year teacher, she discovered something that changed this reality: a meal-kit service. For three years, she received the dinners in prepackaged bags with recipe cards that walked her step by step, with pictures, through the basics of cooking. Soon, after repetition with the same tactics, skills like roasting vegetables or preparing meat became second nature. It was only after years of scaffolded practice that cooking a meal according to personal preferences and making executive decisions along the way became second nature.

The shift from following recipes to becoming a chef is mirrored in myriad academic domains when students are supported to develop individualized refinement and finesse in their practice. We can see this when teachers give young writers the space and coaching to hone their voice following direct instruction on basic skills. As the adage goes, "You have to know the rules before you can break them." Young mathematicians must learn their basic facts before they can craft an elegant proof. Of course, this progression is not a lockstep sequence, but instead, one that can develop simultaneously. Learning is rarely a perfect progression. Many teachers might feel they can't teach craft as it's the untouchable nature of the subject, but if students are never given the opportunity to tell the story of how they are developing, they are less likely to experience the joy of the discipline as when they are empowered to make executive decisions.

The number-one question both of us receive when leading professional development on the shift to standards-based grading is, "What differentiates a 3 and a 4?" While the research is clear that fewer, more clearly distinguishable levels are key to minimizing our margin of error when grading (Guskey & Brookhart, 2019), there is considerable disagreement in the field about what exactly distinguishes these levels. Some would say that a 4 means exceeding expectations, or that students are beginning to work at the next grade level. However, we are not of this camp.

We believe that a 4 must reflect exemplary work due to a level of refinement and finesse with the standards of the current grade level of instruction. Think of it as going from good to great within the achievement of the standards. However, we strongly believe that a 4 is not a special opportunity limited to certain students identified as ready for enrichment. We clarify the criteria for a 4 so that we can align our instruction to it. Craft must be the goal for *all*, not just the chosen few. We must teach to a level of expertise to increase the number of students who rise to proficiency. While our students need a degree of competence to seek refinement, we are not gatekeepers to those whom we deem "low." A culturally affirming mind-set means adopting a pedagogy of confidence, approaching all learners as though they are in the gifted class, and disrupting the "cultural myth that the only way to close the gap is by focusing on weaknesses" (Jackson, 2011, p. 15).

Constructing Beautiful Work

Students have increased opportunities to develop their craft in every discipline when teachers explore the theory of constructionism. Not to be confused with the theory of constructivism that posits that learning is integrated into our prior knowledge within social contexts, the form of constructionism we advocate was developed by MIT professor Seymour Papert (2005) and suggests that deeper learning comes from making meaningful objects and artifacts as students connect knowledge by creating across media. In a 2005 article called "Teaching Children Thinking," Papert notes the important role of technology in this theory, but first warns us that "the phrase 'technology and education' usually means inventing new gadgets to teach the same old stuff in a thinly disguised version of the same old way." Papert (2005) goes on to explain that he sees the purpose of constructionism as follows:

> [I] present a grander vision of an educational system in which technology is used not in the form of machines for processing children, but as something the child himself will learn to manipulate, to extend, to apply to projects, thereby gaining a greater and more articulate mastery of the world, a sense of power of applied knowledge and a self-confidently realistic image of himself as an intellectual agent. Stated more simply, I believe, with Dewey, Montessori and Piaget, that children learn by doing and by thinking about what they do. And so the fundamental ingredients of educational innovation must be better things to do and better ways to think about oneself doing these things.

With this understanding of constructionism in mind, we can expand our understanding of craft to recognize it as both the development of reasoned judgment and the creation of authentic artifacts to deepen knowledge of both the discipline and self. Feedback plays a critical role in this dual purpose of craft. Ron Berger (2003) is a veteran teacher and professional development coach who has spent his career helping educators develop their capacity to teach craft, or as he calls it, *an ethic of excellence*. In many ways, this isn't innovation, but rather a return to the roots of education: mentorship, apprenticeship, and making. Berger (2003) argues the fundamental purpose of education is for students to produce beautiful work and for teachers and students to develop their capacity to provide high-quality feedback to support this goal.

In the video "Austin's Butterfly" (EL Education, 2016), Berger demonstrates the power of feedback to improve his students' scientific drawings of a butterfly. The video shows the butterfly go from a childlike scribble to a detailed and accurate capture worthy of professional standards. Critics of this task-based, granular feedback would cite research to say that this is not the route to long-term transfer (Hattie & Timperley, 2007). However, it is a powerful starting point to show students how the investment of effort in revision improves the outcome.

Berger (2003) describes three important conditions for fostering beautiful work in a school, one of which is directly tied to assessment.

1. A school culture anchored in purpose, value, and psychological safety

2. The wholesale rejection of shallow summative assessments in place of long-term deep work gathered in a portfolio and held to professional standards; a shift from coverage to deep reflection and feedback loops

3. A standard of excellence in the craft of teaching, specifically the ability to provide high-quality feedback, reflecting the deep and beautiful work that students are being asked to do

Deep work, deep reflection, and feedback loops are how students hone their craft and refine their skills.

Cultural Connection

Throughout history, the craft of any cultural expression outside the dominant culture is often misunderstood or even ridiculed. This is true both in the American treatment of the Hawaiian craft of hula (described in the next section) and also in the emergence of more authentic assessment formats in education. As consultants, we've heard countless teachers express the misunderstanding that more authentic assessment means a sacrifice of rigor. Just as Hawaiians have reclaimed the craft of hula as an act of cultural renaissance, many teachers are recognizing the craft of verbal and visual expressions amid the rise of TikTok and ChatGPT. The following sections explain why honoring cultural authenticity, ensuring cognitive complexity in hands-on learning, and incorporating oral and visual expressions of learning are key to cultivating students' craft.

Honoring Cultural Authenticity

A striking cultural example of our collective misconceptions about craft is the traditional Hawaiian hula dance. Most of us have a vague understanding of hula as a dance that originated in Hawaii and features women in dried grass skirts and bikini tops shaking their hips. However, this dance represents an important craft belonging to Hawaiian culture and is actually a form of storytelling. The training of the physical craft is akin to that of professional athletes. Young hula dancers work alongside a Kumu Hula, a master teacher, and also engage in the academic rigor of learning the nuanced history of their people. Young dancers become apprentices to their mentor and commit their life to their craft. They learn to skillfully blend the stories of their history with graceful, fluid movements to physically demonstrate the deep connection to the land (Ng, 2022).

Despite this, many still interpret this cultural form of storytelling as campy. If you've ever been to Hawaii, you've likely seen a luau where a drunken tourist hops onstage and imitates the dancers. This Western inability to recognize the cultural craft demonstrated in hula is tied to the history of marginalizing the oral tradition in favor of the written word.

The craft inherent in hula is more recognizable when we consider the near erasure of this storytelling tradition under colonization and the authentic revival of the craft starting in the 1970s (Ng, 2022). For hundreds of years before Hawaii experienced Western contact, hula was a sacred expression of storytelling. Inland cultures featured loud, bombastic dances that reflected volcanoes, while people closer to the sea used calm, melodic moves like the ocean. Everything changed when Christian missionaries began arriving in the 19th century. The sacred dance was outlawed as a lewd pagan ritual and barely survived as a practice done in secret to ensure it was not totally forgotten. In 1915, hula made it to the mainland of the United States during the Panama-Pacific exposition in San Francisco and was whitewashed and sexualized. Sultry hula girls became the lure of Hawaiian tourism.

However, everything changed following the civil rights movement in the United States. That fight for freedom inspired the Hawaiian Renaissance of the 1970s, which saw the Hawaiian language made one of the official languages and schools teaching the cultural history and practice of hula as an act of reconciliation. Now, hula is honored throughout the islands, even at large resorts, as performances have become educational opportunities. Or, as Kumu Kamohoali'i states, "People are history seekers today. They want to know the truth, and they crave something more authentic" (Ng, 2022). This story about the reclaiming of the cultural relevance and depth of the hula dance connects with the shift we are seeing in schools around authentic assessment. In short, what could have previously been written off as something shallow and frivolous is now being recognized as something with more depth and cognitive rigor.

Ensuring Cognitive Complexity

The cultural appropriation of the hula is like our misunderstanding of performance assessment in schools today. There is bias among some educators that constructionist performance assessments are just exercises in arts and crafts or a frivolous handling of the content rather than an opportunity to develop craft in a discipline.

When popular education podcast host and blogger Jennifer Gonzalez (2016) was an instructional coach, she discovered this for herself. She was working with a new teacher, Jason (not his real name), to support his planning in grade 6 social studies. Working with his teaching team on a unit about ancient Greece, he was tasked with designing and teaching a week about culture. On the first day of the week, he had students read a section of the chapter to fill in vocabulary terms on a worksheet. For the next three days, he gathered materials to have them create papier-mâché urns, which students decorated with images that represented things they loved to do for fun. On the final day of the week, they completed a short quiz matching key terms to their definitions.

Of course, Jennifer had some concerns. The standard that the class was supposed to address was the following:

> Students will demonstrate an understanding of the complexity of culture by exploring cultural elements (e.g., beliefs, customs/traditions, languages, skills, literature, the arts) of diverse groups and explaining

> how culture served to define groups in world civilizations prior to 1500
> A.D. and resulted in unique perspectives. (South Carolina Department of
> Education, 2011)

Gonzalez (2016) asked Jason to explain how the week of instruction he had designed met this standard. He explained that his mentor teacher had given him the Grecian urn idea, telling him it's one that students always love. She took this as her cue to work with him to redesign the week, raising the cognitive complexity of the tasks that students were asked to do, including completing an extensive questionnaire as a particular person from ancient Greece, identifying (and sketching) artifacts that would be important to them, and comparing and contrasting them with artifacts from today (Gonzalez, 2016).

The moral of this story is that we can't assume there is cognitive rigor in hands-on learning. It is our job as learning designers to create the context for deeper thinking when inviting students to make something. Of course, there are times when a teacher just needs to give their students a fun activity, be it as a community-building exercise or as a brain break. However, if we want to create the conditions for students to tell the story of their craft, it is their reasoned judgment with curricular content that matters most.

Incorporating Oral and Visual Expressions of Learning

One of the biggest reasons that opportunities to create beautiful work in school fall short is the marginalization of the oral and visual formats in favor of the "rigor" of the written word. However, the rise of visual social media apps like Instagram or TikTok challenges this cultural belief. During the pandemic, TikTok became an international obsession as people learned viral dance routines to feel like they were still together, despite being socially distanced. While the app began as a form of escapism from the dread of the cultural moment we were living through, the platform's videos soon took on a more educational tone. Many creators began creating "talking head" videos in which they spoke directly to their audience, educating them about a wide range of topics from antiracism to managing relationships with parents.

Amid this shift, Natalie posted "Fact: TikTok videos are only 60 seconds in length. Also, fact: Explaining a complex concept accurately in 60 seconds shows a considerable depth of understanding. Ergo, I dare you to replace your next test with a TikTok challenge" (Vardabasso, 2021). The comments and reposts came flooding in, with educators finding inspiration in the challenge, embracing the idea, and sharing how they are already doing exactly this. One commenter shared how he was using this idea in a "TED Tok" he was having his sophomores complete at the end of the year. Many pointed out how the app FlipGrid was a school-safe way to do this, where students can post video responses and comment on their peers' ideas. Additionally, Cynthia Fey (2021) drew attention back to the cultural influence of the platform when she posted:

> TikTok is my university. Learned more about Black excellence, about toxic Whiteness, about culturally responsive teaching, about democratic classrooms, about decolonization, about the lives of my Indigenous sisters & brother [*sic*], about concrete action in the last year than EVER.

The introduction of ChatGPT may be the final cultural push we need to give oral and visual formats for sharing learning the equal credit they deserve in the classroom. In a 2023 episode of *The Daily* podcast created by the *New York Times*, host Michael Barbaro and producer Stella Tan (2023) explored the impact of this artificial intelligence software on schools. They interviewed a wide variety of students as well as Darren Hick, assistant professor of philosophy at Furman University. The dramatic irony was ripe as students described how they use the software for nearly every assignment while never getting caught, while the teacher felt certain he could sniff out those sneaky few trying to use the platform. Perhaps, rather than try to develop more sophisticated ways to catch students "cheating" with ChatGPT, we need to recognize the cultural shift that is afoot. If we have such tools to support writing, we can turn our attention to more human ways of communicating our learning in our own voices.

Competency Connection

Craft is developed in the verification and implementation stages of the creative process where students engage in feedback dialogues. To support this development, teachers must resist the urge to provide task-based feedback and instead offer process and self-regulation feedback opportunities. Providing criteria for effective listening will accelerate students' ability to provide feedback to one another. The following sections discuss navigating the verification and implementation phases of the creative process, providing effective feedback, and developing communicators.

Navigating the Verification and Implementation Phases

As we outlined in chapter 8 (page 183), creativity can be assessed as a process that includes five interconnected phases: (1) preparation, (2) incubation, (3) illumination, (4) verification, and (5) implementation. If we want to develop creative thinkers, it is imperative we provide opportunities for students to self-assess this process rather than assessing the product outcome for them. Craft lives in the final two phases as students make important decisions regarding next steps in their product creation and reflect on their process. Figure 9.1 provides an overview of different questions we can use as teachers to lead the verification and implementation phases of the creative process, as well as questions students can use to guide self-discovery.

Phase Defined	Questions to Lead the Process	Questions to Guide Learners' Self-Discovery
Verification: This phase involves seeking feedback and validation during the formative phase as to whether potential solutions are worth pursuing; self-assessing; and making personal decisions regarding final steps.	• What are your criteria for quality? • Where would feedback be most helpful to you? • Will others appreciate this idea or work? • Whom can you ask? • How can you get a range of perspectives so you're prepared for the final stage? • What will you do with feedback you don't like?	• What specific strategies did you use while verifying your ideas? • Did you get enough feedback? • Was the feedback you received helpful? • How are you responding to positive feedback? To negative feedback? • Are you clear about next steps? • How can you improve your efforts in this phase?
Implementation: This phase involves moving the idea from concept to reality by producing the product, process, or solution and sharing it with others.	• Is it finished? • Is it working? Is it pleasing? • Are you ready to share it? • Are others appreciating it? Understanding it? • How do you feel about it? • What makes you proud of it? • What would you do differently next time? • What have you learned? • What comes next?	• What specific strategies or actions did you employ while finishing? • What was hard or easy to do? • What (or who) helped you the most? • What slowed down your process? • How could you improve your efforts in this phase? • What have you learned about yourself?

Source: Adapted from Erkens et al., 2019.

FIGURE 9.1: Questions to guide the verification and implementation phases of the creative process.

*Visit **go.SolutionTree.com/assessment** for a free reproducible version of this figure.*

Two common misconceptions about creativity are that it's a skill bestowed on the chosen few, experienced in tortured isolation, and that it's purely the pursuit of an aesthetic outcome. These misconceptions contrast with Sawyer's (2006) research into creativity in the sciences, which demonstrates periods of "intensive social interaction" (pp. 269–270) where "top scientists realize that scientific creativity depends on conversation and they do all that they can to create more collaborative connections" across radically different disciplines (p. 276). This is the verification phase of creativity out in the real world. Of course, there is the benefit of therapeutic creativity, when we make something just for ourselves. However, for students to reap the full benefits of this competency in our world today, they must be supported through the process of seeking and receiving feedback from their teachers, peers, and perhaps even experts outside of the classroom. Both the expert and the audience have an important say in the value of the creative product, and students' navigating this feedback and deciding what to keep and what to discard are critical skills at the heart of the creative process.

In many ways, verification is like when a designer engages in prototyping. It's where learners are invited to decide what works. This critical review process is how creative thinkers develop finesse and refinement (Catmull & Wallace, 2014; Sawyer, 2006) and in turn makes them more creative. The most highly creative companies have hardwired this phase into their policies and structures, but it might not look like you would expect (for example, Pixar's internal "plussing" practice). Much of this comes from the practice of improv in theater, where the mindset is to advance every offer by thinking "yes, and." As anyone who has embarked on a creative endeavor knows, sometimes the hardest part of the process is finding an idea. The last thing a company would want to do in the verification process is squash a nascent idea entirely.

Providing Effective Feedback

For all the documented benefits of feedback on learning, it can be challenging to implement in the school context. Because of the deeply ingrained belief that everything students do demands a grade, feedback is reduced to an explanation of why points were lost. This experience creates a negative, deficit connotation of the word, which carries into the adult workplace. All you have to do is listen to your internal reaction when envisioning the following scene to know this is true. During your morning break, your direct supervisor pokes his head into your classroom and says, "Hey, I just got an email from one of your parents. Do you have a second for some feedback?" Any teacher in this situation would feel their stomach drop. It doesn't have to be this way. In fact, we are so accustomed to giving feedback on the wrong things or using it as a vehicle for criticism that we are missing its potential to amplify learning.

When it comes to understanding the research into feedback, there are many nuances to acknowledge. After all, we are talking about the complexity of human communication. An important insight from the research, however, is that nearly one-third of the time, feedback is an unproductive exercise, meaning it does not lead to increased learning (Hattie & Timperley, 2007). This goes against the cultural myth that all feedback is beneficial. Where we get it wrong is what we choose to give feedback on, which changes the manner in how we deliver it. In their meta-analysis of the research on feedback, John Hattie and Helen Timperley (2007) offer a helpful framework of four levels of feedback to understand its potential as a means of communication.

1. **Personal:** At this level, feedback is aimed directly at the person ("Wow, you're so smart!"), and it does very little to improve learning.

2. **Task:** As the name implies, feedback at this level is directly focused on the successful completion of a task ("Go back over your essay and fix your run-on sentences"). This is a complex level to interpret, because in a paradigm where everything is graded, entered into the gradebook, and calculated into an overall average, it can appear this raises achievement. However, it shows very little evidence of transfer, meaning students will repeat the same errors over and over, indicating little learning has occurred.

3. **Process:** At this level, we zoom out from the task to ask students questions about how they completed the task ("What is a common mistake you make when completing essays? How have you fixed it?"). This is where the thinking begins to shift from the teacher to the student, using questions that cause thinking and therefore deeper learning.

4. **Self-regulated:** At this level, the conditions are in place for students to become an assessor on their own behalf ("How has your practice as a writer changed over time?"). In short, to tap into the power of feedback, we need to shift from offering directions that guide performance toward asking questions that cause thinking.

In 2020, John Hattie returned to this well-known meta-analysis on feedback and offered a critical perspective for any teacher trying to tap into its power: students don't understand the vast majority of the feedback their teachers provide for them (Wisniewski, Zierer, & Hattie, 2020). We see this research as a nudge toward a solution to one of the most challenging aspects of the feedback puzzle: teachers drowning in it amid large class sizes. If students don't understand the vast majority of feedback from their teacher, hopefully that serves as a reminder that we need to recruit others who are closer to their level of understanding—namely their peers—to provide feedback. Of course, we can't just turn over feedback to students and expect it to be successful. Students first need to be able to tell a better story of feedback before they are recruited as allies in providing it. We will describe a protocol to do this in the following section as we discuss how to develop the critical competency of communication.

Developing Communicators

Due to the interconnected nature of the critical competencies, we cannot expect students to engage in sophisticated feedback exchanges if we don't also attend to their development as communicators. The competency of communication often becomes the container for one of the foundational outcomes of our public education system: literacy. However, too often, literacy is reduced to the reading and writing of print texts. This has been one of the most pervasive trickle-down impacts of the accountability movement, resulting in widespread standardized testing. This means that we often neglect the other four language arts—viewing, creating, speaking, and listening. If we don't attend to students' ability to send and receive messages orally and visually, any claim that we are developing their craft as writers, scientists, mathematicians, and historians becomes hollow. We need to update our understanding of literacy in light of today's new communication media, many of which are verbal and visual. Further, since developing craft depends on feedback, we need to teach students how to successfully speak and listen if they want to get the most out of this exchange.

When it comes to speaking and listening, the latter of the two is a challenge in Western culture. In a culture grounded in individualism, developing our distinct voice often takes precedent over being an empathetic listener. The explosion of social media has exacerbated this fact as it provides a platform to amplify each individual voice. As a result, listening feels less important than being heard. How we teach and assess listening in school can be an antidote to polarization and people becoming more concerned with their own perspective than with understanding diverse perspectives. Most attempts to assess listening place emphasis on active listening rather than understanding and empathy. This leads to criteria like eye contact, taking turns, nodding while listening, and being supportive—behaviors teachers can observe and check off a list without sufficient evidence that students have achieved understanding. Active listening skills are still necessary, but they are just novice skills on the pathway to sophisticated listening.

A proficiency scale for listening is a helpful tool to provide feedback on feedback. As students learn about how dialogue is better than monologue when it comes to feedback, they can learn to become attuned to not only *what* a peer says, but more importantly, *how* they say it. Giving and receiving feedback can be an emotionally charged exchange. It can even activate a threat response in students who have been told for years in school spaces that they are not good enough. As both teachers and peers ask questions to elicit responses from learners, we seek to understand their response and to observe their emotional state. An emotionally dysregulated mind cannot process information, so helping each other to regulate these responses becomes a sophisticated demonstration of listening. Consider the following proficiency scale, which may provide useful support on this learning journey.

- **Insufficient evidence (ignoring):** The learner is completely disengaged from opportunities to listen, showing overt signs of rejecting others' perspectives, interrupting frequently, and demonstrating unproductive nonverbal cues like rolling their eyes.

- **Novice (pretending):** The learner demonstrates active listening in the form of eye contact and taking turns, yet they are often just waiting for their chance to respond and share their perspective.

- **Developing (selective listening):** At times, it appears the learner is listening to understand through the aptness of the questions they ask and their ability to paraphrase. However, they revert to sharing their own perspective when they feel it is being challenged.

- **Proficient (attentive listening):** The learner puts aside their own perspective when engaged in listening opportunities and completely focuses their efforts on making the other person feel heard, seen, and valued by asking questions and checking their understanding.

- **Sophisticated (empathetic listening):** The learner not only seeks to deeply understand the perspective of others when listening but is also attuned to the emotional state of the speaker and makes an effort to notice and name these emotions and find common ground to help regulate the speaker.

This proficiency scale best serves as a continuum for growth rather than a grading tool. Sure, there might be times where this scale could be used to verify students' achievement of speaking and listening standards, but the primary purpose is for students to understand where they are and *what's next*.

The Story of What I'm Learning

For students to develop a level of refinement and finesse in the different areas of study, we must allow them to view craft in action as well as develop it. Think of this section as how to teach the literacy of craft by providing opportunities to both read and write the language of expertise. Students can explore and cultivate the craft of any discipline by co-creating success criteria, using mentor texts, and practicing digital storytelling.

Co-Creating the Criteria of Craft

Co-creation is a powerful vehicle for students to build the vocabulary needed to become storytellers in any specific discipline. If we hope to develop craft in a subject area, we must first define the subset of skills that make up expertise in that subject. In what areas will students be called to exercise reasoned judgment? These skills must be transferable from unit to unit so that there are limitless possibilities for students to reflect and tell the story of how they are developing in the study of different content topics. Luckily, we've already spent most of this book outlining such skills: the critical competencies that are relevant and transferable across units of study. Inviting students to be partners in naming the success criteria for these competencies pays off in their willingness to notice and name these criteria in their own learning. However, co-creating success criteria for competencies presents a challenge, as most students have little background knowledge with them and finding tangible models for them to analyze is tricky.

A solution to the dilemma of finding models for competency development comes from the Collaborative Lab School in Minneapolis. An initiative by the nonprofit organization ThriveED, the school was created in collaboration with a public high school with the vision of disrupting the traditional power hierarchy in schools through the values of relationship and co-design. To embody these values, teachers were rebranded as "engagement guides." Two of the founding guides,

Breana Jacques and Shannon Finnegan, developed a powerful protocol for co-designing the criteria for competency with their learners. First, they negotiated which competencies were essential with their learners and landed on fifteen areas for learning, which they organized into three categories: leadership, life, and literacy (Vardabasso, 2023). For instance, *leadership* included collaboration and communication, whereas *life* included global citizenship and social justice.

After creating the list of skills, students went through a process to activate their background knowledge. They shared their thoughts in words and images to unpack what they thought of when they heard terms like *collaboration*, *social justice*, *digital literacy*, and so on. Then, the engagement guides posed a question to learners: "Who has these skills and where are they important?" From that discussion, students were empowered to take the most important step of this process—inviting folks into the classroom to answer questions about how these skills show up in their personal and professional life. Guests spanned demographics including age, race, job, and sexuality, representing the rich diversity of the learners so they could see themselves in future competency development. In a speed-dating format, students met with these mentors in groups, asked questions, took notes, then consolidated their learning into robust rubrics to guide assessment.

Using Mentor Texts

As students demonstrate their craft as communicators across disciplines, it is important that they have mentors for their journey. Of course, their teacher is one of these mentors, but experts in the field have much to offer, considering they have dedicated their career to their craft. Even the most knowledgeable scientist recognizes that if they can't communicate their findings in a way that moves people, they are unlikely to have the positive impact they seek on the world. We can think of all of the ways that an author in any discipline seeks to impact their audience as their "moves." If we create the space for students to notice and name the moves that experts make when communicating, they can emulate those moves when they communicate their own learning. In short, they will be empowered to tell the story of how they crafted their communication with intention.

Many literacy experts and practitioners have explored the practice of using mentor texts to teach craft in writing (Culham, Blasingame, & Coutu, 2010; Gallagher, 2011; Kittle, 2022; Marchetti & O'Dell, 2021; Shubitz, 2016). Several key phases emerge in the process of scaffolding student learning toward how they can tell the story of their craft. First, we must gather a wide variety of communication samples that use a unique move to inspire and engage. These samples can be found organically while reading and viewing, or they may be found within curated spaces, like Penny Kittle's (2022) book *Micro Mentor Texts* or the *New York Times*'s online curation of mentor texts from across their publications (Mentor Texts, n.d.). Once we have a text in mind, the following sequence will scaffold student application of the moves they've studied into their own communication.

1. **Unpack key vocabulary and context:** Ensure comprehension is not a barrier to students' ability to discuss the impact of a particular move by providing definitions of tricky words and a description of the larger text the smaller sample was taken from.

2. **Take a first-lap reading:** Read the text aloud to students the first time, just for them to immerse themselves in it.

3. **Take a second-lap reading:** Have students read the text independently, taking note of words, phrases, or parts that stand out to them. Allow them a chance to discuss what stuck with them and why.

4. **Ask a question to direct close reading:** Ask a question to focus students' attention on the particular move at work in that text. For instance, "How does the creator make you want to read more in the first few sentences?"

5. **Describe the move and its impact:** Record notes on the board while students work to describe, as specifically as possible, what the author did. Prompt them for more details.

6. **Name the move:** Ask students to partner up and determine an appropriate name for the move, then share with the group. For instance, "Starting in the action!"

7. **Create an anchor chart:** Transfer the name of the move, description, and sample sentence to an anchor chart to be hung on the wall.

8. **Model using the moves:** Next time you think aloud while writing, use moves pulled from the anchor chart on the wall.

9. **Include criteria:** When students are communicating, have them include several moves in their piece. Assessment of these criteria can be asking students to underline them, or better yet, to create a written reflection where they describe what moves they chose and why, telling the story of their craft.

Though many of the publications about mentor texts focus solely on helping students become better writers, we would like to offer a reminder that communication also includes speaking and visual representation. In fact, the more students are supported to see craft moves across media, the better supported they are to become storytellers not just in school, but in our media-rich society. Therefore, the idea of a "text" must be expanded to include photography, drawings, short-form video, speeches, podcast interviews, social media posts, and of course, written media like articles, books, and blogs. For instance, a teacher doing a think-aloud as they work through a mathematics problem on the board is a text that students can analyze to notice the craft moves of the author (the teacher). Rather than telling students, once again, to *show their work*, include an assessment opportunity for students to tell the story of how they are developing their craft as a mathematics communicator. If you really want to ensure this skill is valued, include a category to grade it on your report card. We all want to be seen for our capacity to make reasoned judgments in our work, but sometimes we need help finding the language to tell that story.

Practicing Digital Storytelling

Digital storytelling is a short-form digital media production that allows anyone to share their story and experiences. In many ways, it is the amalgamation of our historical evolution toward multiple media for storytelling, to land in a place that blends the oral, written, and visual. Often, digital stories feature a voice-over with images and music intentionally chosen to support what is being described. Of course, we have many examples of digital stories with the explosion of TikTok into popular culture, but there are also many companies and organizations using communications technology to rehumanize their marketing efforts. For instance, Alberta Health Services (n.d.) has a section of their website dedicated to patient and family storytelling with the tagline "Real people. Real experiences. Real impact" to shed light on the necessity of the public healthcare system in this Canadian province. These stories are perhaps more professionally polished and vulnerable than what we might see on social media, though these platforms are quickly becoming spaces for more professionalism and authenticity as well.

The possibilities for digital storytelling in the classroom and school spaces are profound, especially when students are telling the story of what they are learning. When Natalie was a teacher, she worked closely with an instructional coach to develop a film festival project that they refined over multiple years. In the context of middle school English language arts, the project launch involved students receiving an invitation to a film festival in a month's time that promised to entertain, inspire, and dazzle. Students were required to dress up for the occasion, as they would be in a real theater. As students started asking excited questions about this field trip, their early excitement turned to shock when they realized that the short films they would be viewing were their own. Over the course of the month, they authentically inquired into the essential question, "Why would anyone want to hear *my* story?" as they developed a digital story about a meaningful moment in their life. Throughout the journey, Natalie was able to elicit rich evidence of standards related to writing, collaboration, speaking and listening, and digital literacy.

While this is an exclusively ELA example, there is interdisciplinary potential when the standards are paired with the exploration of content knowledge in science, history, or mathematics. Students might tell a digital story of a pivotal moment in history, a famous innovator in science or mathematics, or the arc of a character in English. When we approach digital storytelling in an interdisciplinary way, we are leaning into constructionism exactly as Papert (1972) intended—constructing a deeper understanding of the world by using technology to produce beautiful work.

One of the most popular frameworks for digital storytelling comes from Joe Lambert, founder of the StoryCenter. In his book *Digital Storytelling: Capturing Lives, Creating Community*, Lambert (2018) offers a seven-step approach that covers the essential steps during the writing and construction phases. The first four steps, all within the writing phase, are as follows.

1. **A point of view:** A powerful story starts with the first-person perspective. The writer must write using the *I* pronoun rather than the more distant "he/she/they." Students writing about curricular content must choose a perspective to step inside as they write.

2. **A dramatic question:** A digital story must ask a juicy question and build toward an eventual answer. This is what separates a true digital *story* from a TikTok video of an influencer providing an overview of the events of their day. Using story circles at the beginning of the writing process can help students get feedback on which questions are most intriguing to their peers.

3. **Emotional content:** The goal of the digital story is to evoke an emotion from the audience, be it joy, fear, sadness, or excitement. That is the feedback that lets the writer know the story worked.

Using digital stories as mentor texts and inviting students to name the emotion they evoked in them can teach them how this is done.

4. **Economy:** The challenge in writing is to remain in the strict parameter of a two-to-three-minute story. This challenges students to create a vignette focusing on a specific moment in the story and bringing it to life. Logistically, this ensures all student stories are viewable in a single sitting by an audience of peers and parents.

The final three steps, all within the construction phase, are as follows.

5. **Pacing:** As students revise their written story, they must make important decisions about when to slow down and when to speed up. This often means cutting out parts that aren't actually essential.

6. **The gift of your voice:** At this part in the process, students record themselves reading their story aloud. We cannot emphasize enough the necessity of providing instruction and practice on volume, tone, and pacing. Our voices hold power, so students must be supported to ensure this doesn't just become an exercise in reading aloud, but rather *storytelling*.

7. **Soundtrack:** The right music will underscore the emotional tone of the story and bring it to life. It's important students understand copyright parameters and choose instrumental tracks that are licensed for reuse. Two websites, Bensound (https://bensound.com) and Incompetech (https://incompetech.com), have many royalty-free soundtrack options.

The Story of How I'm Learning

The fuel for the learning journey to develop craft is students' ability to give and receive feedback, which in turn requires them to be competent speakers and listeners. The following sections discuss how teachers can support students to use communication story circles, improved feedback processes, and the creator's commentary.

Communication Story Circle

Just as with conflict resolution in chapter 4 (page 83), a story circle is an important protocol to create the space for students to reflect on significant moments of speaking and listening in their lives, learning from one another. By a young age, they can recall times when someone really took the time to hear them, or they spoke in a way that got others' attention. As they get older, students begin to explore how they are learning to communicate online, and times they felt unfairly attacked by a troll hiding behind a keyboard. They begin to discover what their own unique voice sounds like, what they want to say to the world, and how they want to say it.

As always, the circle requires an egalitarian shape, norms, and processes to ensure all students are invited to speak with differing levels of disclosure. Ask an initial question that allows each student to answer with one word, then ask a follow-up question that allows students to share more about their initial answer. For instance, begin by asking, "What one word describes how it feels when someone listens deeply to you?" and follow up by saying, "Describe a time when you felt truly heard by someone else." More questions to open the circle could include the following.

- What one word describes how it feels when someone isn't listening to you?
- Describe a time it felt like someone was trying not to hear you.
- What word describes how it feels to speak to a friend?
- What one word describes how it feels to speak to a peer you're not friends with?
- What one word describes how it feels to speak to a teacher?
- Describe a time you spoke where you felt powerful.
- Describe a time you spoke where you felt embarrassed.
- Describe a time you spoke where you felt proud.
- Describe a time someone else spoke where you felt inspired.
- What do you wish more people knew about you that you don't often say?
- Who is someone that inspires you? How are you like them?
- How does communicating through social media make you feel?
- Describe a time you felt more seen and connected through social media.
- Describe a time you felt hurt and isolated through social media.
- Describe a time you felt powerful communicating through social media.
- Have you ever had a viral post? What do you think drew people to it?
- Who is a content creator you can't get enough of? What makes them special? How are you like them?

An important caveat for a story circle focused on communication is to ensure the norm of not naming any particular people when telling a story of a time you were hurt so as to protect their identity in light of the fact that we can't hear their side of the story. Since participants may be disclosing vulnerable stories, it's also imperative to remind students that what is said in the circle stays in the circle. Teachers can invite students to return to the prompts repeatedly over time to share their experiences both inside and outside the classroom.

Improved Feedback Processes

To tell a better story of feedback, we need to shift our understanding of it from a monologue to a dialogue. This means we need to stop viewing feedback simply as a one-way transmission from teacher to student and instead see it as an opportunity for empathetic communication not only between teacher and student, but also between students and within each student themselves. In addition, we need to create the conditions for students to experience this shift firsthand so they can see the benefits to the quality of their work and themselves as a learner. Often, students come to tell the story of their learning through repeated experiences in school where they receive scores in the form of ratios, with "feedback" as the explanation for why they lost marks. When asked what it is, they can dutifully parrot that feedback helps them to improve, but they quickly associate it with negative feelings, leading them to avoid it. They see it as something that comes at the end of the learning process once work is completed rather than something they access to improve their work in progress. Without an intentional rewriting of this narrative, there is only one type of feedback students come to seek from their teachers during the creative process: "Am I done yet?"

The first step to rewriting this narrative is to update students' definition of feedback itself to include more nuance about what it is and isn't. We need to help them construct an understanding that moves closer to the description of the process and self-regulation levels of feedback as described by Hattie and Timperley (2007) where it involves more questions than answers. When Natalie was an instructional coach, she worked with a team of middle school mathematics teachers in an action research cycle to tackle this problem of practice. They were concerned with their students' learned helplessness, as their concept of feedback was asking the teacher whether they were correct. They wanted to see students *independently* seeking and providing higher-quality feedback to one another. To tackle this problem, Natalie designed a series of lessons, the first of which sought to help students inquire deeper into what feedback is. To do this, they filled in a Frayer Model map (a four-square graphic organizer that describes examples, nonexamples, facts, and a definition)

Craft Through Story

using different online sources of information, including Shari Harley's (2013) talk "Why Is Feedback Important?" and several examples and nonexamples from movie and TV clips on YouTube. Figure 9.2 depicts this lesson.

Definition	Facts
Feedback is information that lets us know if we need to shift our behavior to change or if we need to keep doing what we're doing.	Feedback tells you where you've been & where you are going It helps you improve Points out your strengths
FEEDBACK	
Listening and asking questions Conversation with honesty and trust Start by pointing out the positives Getting peer to come up with ideas	Ignoring the other person's reactions Advice meant to hurt Offering off-topic advice Appearing uninterested
Examples	Nonexamples

YouTube Feedback Examples	YouTube Feedback Nonexamples
"Best Coaching Conversation" by TheMattDr (2011) "4th Grade Peer Feedback on Problem Solving in Math" by the Core Collaborative (2018) "Teacher Provides Feedback During and After Instruction—Example 7" by EngageNY (2013)	"How NOT 2 to Give Negative Feedback" by How Not 2 Videos. Expert Incompetence (2015) "*Office Space* (1/5) Movie CLIP—Did You Get the Memo? (1999) HD" by Movieclips (2014) "*The Office*—Giving Feedback" by Dmitri Volov (2018)

FIGURE 9.2: A Frayer Model map, YouTube videos, and sample student responses from a lesson to improve feedback processes.

A week later, Natalie came back for the second lesson to ask the follow-up question, "Who can we get feedback from?" After revealing to students that not only are their teachers a source for feedback, but so are their peers and themselves, she led a brainstorm with the class about what questions they could ask each source of feedback, and more importantly, what questions they might ask when giving feedback. With their brainstormed questions on the board, students then engaged in a collaborative mathematics activity to see if they could demonstrate better feedback conversations. At the end of the lesson, their ability to seek and give feedback through targeted questioning was formatively assessed in the form of an exit ticket.

Over a month later, Natalie met with the middle school mathematics teachers again to see how they felt their students' behavior had changed. They were floored. They described a classroom that looked radically different from the one they began the year with. Students persisted longer in the face of challenge and saw their peers and teachers as partners in their learning rather than just the gatekeepers of task completion. To support sustainable implementation of the revised story of feedback, the teachers had created a checklist for each student, reminding them of the different sources of feedback and the types of questions to ask at each stage of task completion. Figure 9.3 is a template to create a similar checklist of your own.

The Creator's Commentary

As any movie fan in the early 2000s will remember, DVD rentals brought an exciting new development to the viewing experience: the option to watch the film with the director's commentary to better understand the mechanics of their craft. Of course, the idea of a creator's commentary predates DVDs. A book's acknowledgments section allows the author to list inspiring sources and influential people who offered feedback and support throughout their creative process. With the explosion of digital streaming services like Netflix, we have more access to the insights of creators than ever before. For instance, in a documentary (Segal, 2020) made about the creation of the popular Canadian Broadcast Corporation's series *Schitt's Creek*, the producers discuss the importance of representing a small rural town where there was zero bigotry or hatred toward the show's openly gay characters. They decided that presenting a version of the world as it could be—rather than as it too often is—was an important step toward creating a better future.

When we provide creative opportunities for our learners in the classroom, be it an interdisciplinary project or a digital story, gathering evidence of their craft as the creator is critical to assessing the quality of their process. In her book *Point-Less: An English Teacher's Guide to More Meaningful Grading*, high school AP English teacher Sarah M. Zerwin (2020) offers one means of this type of constructed-response assessment when she mandates that all written pieces must be accompanied by a reflection letter.

I'm struggling to start . . .	
Self	Break down the task into smaller steps.
	Review instructions or assignment criteria.
Peers	Ask a classmate to help clarify the task or brainstorm ideas together.
	Share initial thoughts and get feedback.
Teacher	Ask for clarification about the expectations of the task.
	Request guidance on how to begin.
I'm stuck and can't finish . . .	
Self	Look back at examples, rubrics, or past lessons for guidance.
	Take a short break and return with a fresh perspective.
Peers	Share what I've done so far and ask for feedback or suggestions.
	Collaborate on solutions for specific sticking points.
Teacher	Seek help in overcoming a specific challenge or question.
	Request an example or clarification to move forward.
I've done my best and want to make it better . . .	
Self	Review the work against the rubric or checklist.
	Check for spelling, grammar, or formatting errors.
Peers	Exchange work with a partner for peer feedback.
	Ask for constructive critique on specific sections.
Teacher	Confirm that the work aligns with the expectations.
	Inquire about opportunities for revision if needed.

FIGURE 9.3: A sample feedback checklist co-created between teacher and students.

*Visit **go.SolutionTree.com/assessment** for a free reproducible version of this figure.*

Questions to inspire reflection and insight into craft might include the following.

- Who would you like to acknowledge as an important contributor to your work? What did you learn from them?

- What changes did you make to your original plan?

- Where did you draw inspiration from for different aspects of your work?

- What was a specific aspect of your work that you feel especially proud of? Why?

- What is something you would have done differently if you had more time? Why?
- Was there a dark moment when you didn't know if completion was possible?
- Where did you take a risk in your work? Did it pay off?
- Were there any unexpected surprises you encountered throughout the process that you had to navigate?
- What did you learn from this work that you want to apply to your future work?

There are many formats teachers can offer students as a choice for their creator's commentary. They may complete a written reflection in the form of a letter, make a video through a platform like FlipGrid, or create a digital portfolio using Seesaw or SpacesEDU. Students could complete a voice-over if they created a media product. If they created a print product, the teacher could provide them a photocopy to annotate. There are endless possibilities to empower every student to tell their story of how they are developing their craft as a creator.

Summary

Though craft may at first appear elusive and conjure images of magic, it is anything but. Craft is when we develop experienced judgment in a particular domain so we might demonstrate refinement and finesse in the construction of beautiful work that captures deep learning. Not to be confused with the popular idea of "arts and crafts," it is akin to the deep cultural history of the hula dance when it is used as a form of storytelling rather than appropriated in North American depictions using grass skirts and bikini tops. Without this clear differentiation, hands-on projects in schools run the risk of becoming shallow, leading to inadequate evidence of deeper learning. When teachers embrace craft as enrichment within the learning progression, they give students the opportunity to refine their creative process as they build the critical competency of communication, seeking and offering better feedback to one another. In short, the development of craft requires that we update our view of feedback, treating it more as a dialogue than a monologue from the teacher.

Students are empowered to tell the story of their craft when we co-create with them the success criteria of the target competencies, provide mentor texts giving them language for the craft moves that might describe in their own work, and design projects grounded in digital storytelling so they can simultaneously deepen understanding of course content and cultivate their craft as a creator. Since craft is refined through feedback, and feedback is best achieved as a dialogue, inviting students to tell the story of how they are developing as a communicator becomes important. We must also support students to revise their narrative of feedback if they are to see the need for better communication in the first place. While clarity of competency-based learning goals and dialogic feedback are helpful throughout the process of learning and creating, offering opportunities for a creator's commentary following the completion of the beautiful work they create will pull all the pieces together, revealing craft through story.

Chapter 9 Discussion Questions for Learning Teams

Journal your response to the following prompts in the space provided. Share your thoughts during team discussion.

1. What quote or passage encapsulates your biggest takeaway from this chapter? What immediate action (small, medium, or large) will you take because of this takeaway? Explain both to your team.

2. In this chapter, we described craft as a level of refinement and finesse that often reflects the top level (advanced, sophisticated, extending, and so on) of a typical proficiency scale. What are you currently doing as a team to provide students instructional opportunities to develop in this area? Are these opportunities equally distributed to all students? Why or why not?

3. Are there any current projects that you undertake that you fear might be an example of a "Grecian urn," as described on page 218? How might you increase the cognitive rigor while still engaging students in the creation of beautiful work?

REPRODUCIBLE | 239

4. Are students currently invited to demonstrate their learning through a medium that blends the oral, visual, and written formats? What challenges are you running into in this medium?

5. How was your understanding of high-quality feedback affirmed in this chapter? What new ideas are stretching your understanding in new directions?

6. Do you believe a creative project is worth the time it takes if students are not invited to actively revise and verify their work through several feedback loops? Why or why not?

7. If students were to co-create the success criteria for a list of competencies your team is committed to developing, what would be a non-negotiable on that list? Would you have a shared list of competencies across your grade or department, or separate lists of discipline-specific competencies?

Page 2 of 2

Rehumanizing Assessment © 2025 Solution Tree Press • SolutionTree.com
Visit **go.SolutionTree.com/assessment** to download this free reproducible.

EPILOGUE

When students are the storytellers, the education story changes. For too long, education has reflected a period in our history when the media was a one-way transmission of information, often representing a limited and biased perspective of the world. Now, we need to meet the cultural moment and democratize storytelling just like social media has. If we fail to meet this cultural moment, we worry that we will see education become obsolete in our lifetime.

If we can imagine a classroom where students are invited to make deeper connections to course content through story and learn to embrace their conflicts and challenges as learning opportunities, then we can imagine a school where students can defend how they are developing the critical competencies needed in our world today and in the future. Then, we can imagine a society where each person is an active agent in their own life with the skills to learn quickly in the face of rapid change and find true mental health.

A story you might be telling yourself right now is, "Nothing I do will make any difference in a complex system like education." Likely, this story brings with it a feeling of futility. However, that is only *one* possible narrative. Allow us to offer you a different one. In the book *Presence: An Exploration of Profound Change*, renowned researcher of transformational change in organizations Peter Senge, along with coauthors C. Otto Scharmer, Joseph Jaworski, and Betty Sue Flowers (2005), writes, "When people who are actually *creating a system* start to see themselves as the source of their problems, they invariably discover a new capacity to create the *results they truly desire*" (p. 50). This quote offers us a different narrative, grounded in a lifetime of research, that the system isn't something *out there* that we must battle; *we are the system*. The system doesn't change and allow us to take the first step—we each take one step forward and the system starts to shift.

Take the First Step

Chapters 4 through 9 of this book are filled with practical assessment formats to support students to tell the story of *what* they are learning (curricular standards or outcomes) and *how* they are learning (metacognitive strategies). These practical formats are organized around big ideas that reflect the types of stories we tell as human beings across cultures, including conflict, harmony, reflection, perspective, imagination, and craft. If you were to implement one of this book's practical suggestions within each of these domains, you will experience a master class in culturally expansive assessment. Use the graphic organizer in figure E.1 to help you make an action plan. If you already use an assessment format that fits the domain, use this organizer to capture it. Or, flip back through the book to review the previous chapters to choose your favorite format.

How will I support my students to ...	Tell the story of **what** I'm learning?	Tell the story of **how** I'm learning?
Conflict Through Story (Chapter 4)	Format: (for example, struggle statements)	Format: (for example, conflict exit slips)
Harmony Through Story (Chapter 5)	Format:	Format:
Reflection Through Story (Chapter 6)	Format:	Format:
Perspective Through Story (Chapter 7)	Format:	Format:
Imagination Through Story (Chapter 8)	Format:	Format:
Craft Through Story (Chapter 9)	Format:	Format:

FIGURE E.1: Culturally expansive assessment action plan.

*Visit **go.SolutionTree.com/assessment** for a free reproducible version of this figure.*

As you fill out the template in figure E.1, notice whether you are consistently choosing either micro- or macrolevel formats. Microlevel assessment formats require only evidence from a single lesson (for example, conflict exit ticket). Macrolevel assessment formats require evidence from across an entire unit, project, semester, or even course (for example, grading conference). Ideally, you will have a balance of both micro- and macrolevel formats across the stories of what students are learning and how they are learning. That balance is likely going to be determined by the overarching goals of a discipline. For instance, it would be a good fit to embrace a macro story of perspective in history as any event has multiple viewpoints, whereas a macro story of imagination is best suited for science as innovation becomes an important concept.

Sustain the Journey

According to Learning Forward (n.d.), it takes three to five years for transformation through professional development to occur. When you take the first steps to implement student storytelling as a viable means of assessment, it's important to zoom out and recognize the full journey to transform your practice. As you implement the culturally expansive formats we offer in this book on both a micro- and a macrolevel, you will achieve the following outcomes in your assessment practice.

- Increased student hope of the likelihood of eventual success
- Increased student self-efficacy and motivation
- Increased achievement of grade-level standards for all students
- A shift from teacher-driven to student-driven assessment
- Future-focused competency development
- Enhanced community engagement

However, this doesn't happen all at once. Over the last thirteen years, we have collectively worked with thousands of schools and districts across twenty-five countries to expand their assessment literacy. We have witnessed the transformation journey countless times and noticed a pattern. As a teacher begins to add to their assessment repertoire, they naturally tend to wonder how they might further develop their students' critical competencies. As they start to witness the outcomes we listed, they eventually tackle the most emotionally charged assessment topic of all: grading. They want to share their many successes in the classroom with others, and grading is just the communication tool to do so. After all, what good is a 90 percent if a parent doesn't know how their child has become an innovative collaborator?

Whether you are reading this book as an individual teacher, a collaborative team, or a leader, use figure E.2 (page 244) to self-assess where you are on the culturally expansive assessment journey to better understand your next steps. Self-assess honestly and openly as this continuum is meant not to be evaluative, but rather to offer clarity about future learning.

Preinitiating	Assessment is entirely teacher driven, using a "teach-test-move on" approach heavily emphasizing individual written formats; students appear disinterested in authentic learning and attempt to harvest points.
Initiating	Students have few opportunities to tell the story of what they are learning and how they are learning, and those are in a traditional (individual and written) assessment paradigm; students may struggle to see the connection to their learning.
Developing	Students have frequent opportunities to tell the story of **what** they are learning and **how** they are learning, with oral and collective opportunities for assessment; student hope and motivation begin to noticeably improve.
Implementing	Critical competencies are identified within the curriculum of a discipline and all assessment opportunities are aligned to them; student achievement grows through repeated assessment opportunities of **what** and **how** they are learning.
Sustaining	Grading is aligned to curricular competencies and expressed qualitatively through fewer, more clearly distinguishable levels, also known as a rubric; students are empowered to gather evidence and partner with teachers in a grading conference. The school or district engages the parent community to develop a profile of a learner to align competency development across disciplines. Students publicly share learning stories aligned with the profile of a learner.

FIGURE E.2: Culturally expansive assessment practice continuum.

*Visit **go.SolutionTree.com/assessment** for a free reproducible version of this figure.*

In some cases of implementing culturally expansive assessment practices, we've witnessed schools or districts rushing into implementation before providing teachers the tools to change how they gather evidence of student learning. In these cases, what is a well-intentioned attempt to move toward a student-driven assessment model quickly becomes a case of forcing a square peg into a round hole. Many teachers will fail to see the connection to their assessment practices and use observations of students' "work ethic" and "effort" on traditional tasks as a proxy for their development of collaboration and critical thinking. Or, students will publicly defend their learning using test scores and percentage grades with little knowledge of their learning.

If you happen to find yourself in one of these contexts, the book is designed for you to go back and implement practical strategies to both teach and assess the critical competencies necessary for students to tell an authentic story of learning.

Will It Work?

Faced with the prospect of embarking on something new, it's natural to seek a guarantee. In education especially, we are typically risk averse. It makes sense. The job is incredibly demanding and we need to know that the metaphorical juice is worth the squeeze. With that in mind, here are two ways we can guarantee you will fail on your journey toward culturally expansive assessment practice:

1. Never starting
2. Quitting once you do

The truth is change doesn't happen overnight and we will never feel ready. However, only by *starting before we are ready* will we get to where we want to go. In other words, reaching the Holy Grail of student independence, motivation, and investment is only possible by taking the first step to change our assessment practices even though we feel too busy, too overwhelmed, too scared, and too unsure. Assessment can rob students of their voice, so let's use it as a tool to empower them instead. As we support students to tell their story, we must coach them to make better choices; to see them grow as learners, we must disrupt the narrative that school is a place where kids come to watch adults work.

You've read the book; now it's time to act: we learn by doing. Or, as Ganz (2020) offers, "Understanding does not precede action, it flows from it." All the questions still circling in your head will be answered as you trust your learners to tell their story and you accept your own call to adventure. We promise, you'll love the characters you discover along the way.

REFERENCES AND RESOURCES

Abrami, P. C., Bernard, R. M., Borokhovski, E., Waddington, D. I., Wade, C. A., & Persson, T. (2015). Strategies for teaching students to think critically: A meta-analysis. *Review of Educational Research, 85*(2), 275–314.

Alberta Health Services. (n.d.). *Patient & family storytelling.* Accessed at www.albertahealthservices.ca/info/Page17251.aspx on December 4, 2024.

Alberts, H. J. E. M. (2016). *The sailboat.* Positive Psychology Program. Accessed at https://s3.amazonaws.com/perspectiveinactiondownloads/The_Sailboat_Metaphor.pdf?utm_content=buffere343b&utm_medium=social&utm_source=plus.google.com&utm_campaign=buffer on August 27, 2024.

Aljarrah, A., & Towers, J. (2022). The emergence of collective mathematical creativity through students' productive struggle. *Canadian Journal of Science, Mathematics and Technology Education, 22*(4), 856–872.

Almeida, L. (2007). The journey toward effective assessment for English language learners. In D. B. Reeves (Ed.), *Ahead of the curve: The power of assessment to transform teaching and learning* (pp. 147–163). Solution Tree Press.

American Psychological Association. (2019, May 29). *Belief in learning styles myth may be detrimental* [Press release]. Accessed at www.apa.org/news/press/releases/2019/05/learning-styles-myth on August 30, 2024.

Aristotle. (2008). *Poetics* (S. Halliwell, Trans.). Harvard University Press. (Original work written ca. 335 BC)

Armstrong, P. B. (2020). *Stories and the brain: The neuroscience of narrative.* Johns Hopkins University Press.

Arstila, V., & Lloyd, D. (Eds.). (2014). *Subjective time: The philosophy, psychology, and neuroscience of temporality.* MIT Press.

AURA. (2020, April 9). *Iceberg identity exercise.* Accessed at www.auraforrefugees.org /index.php/sponsor-toolbox/resources-list/exercises-to-be-done-individually-or-in-a -group/iceberg-identity-exercise on August 27, 2024.

Azevedo, R. (2020). Reflections on the field of metacognition: Issues, challenges, and opportunities. *Metacognition and Learning, 15*(2), 91–98. https://doi.org/10.1007 /s11409-020-09231-x

Azgor, S. (2021, September 12). *The Rashomon effect: A well-known problem of eyewitness infidelity.* Medium. Accessed at https://medium.com/@samazgor/the-rashomon -effect-a-well-known-problem-of-eyewitness-infidelity-2db42c06753e on August 28, 2024.

Bailey, S. P. (2021, December 10). Tarot cards are having a moment with help from the pandemic. *The Washington Post.* Accessed at www.washingtonpost.com/religion /2021/12/10/tarot-cards-pandemic-trend/ on August 29, 2024.

Baker, L. (2010). Metacognition. In P. Peterson, E. Baker, & B. McGaw (Eds.), *International encyclopedia of education* (3rd ed., pp. 204–210). Elsevier.

Barbaro, M. (Host), & Tan, S. (Producer). (2023, June 28). Suspicion, cheating and bans: A.I. hits America's schools [Audio podcast episode]. In *The Daily.* Accessed at www.nytimes.com/2023/06/28/podcasts/the-daily/ai-chat-gpt-schools.html on January 17, 2025.

Battelle for Kids. (2019). *Framework for 21st century learning: Definitions.* Accessed at https://static.battelleforkids.org/documents/p21/P21_Framework_Definitions BFK.pdf on October 4, 2024.

Bellanca, J. A., Fogarty, R. J., & Pete, B. M. (2012). *How to teach thinking skills within the Common Core: 7 key student proficiencies of the new national standards.* Solution Tree Press.

Berger, R. (2003). *An ethic of excellence: Building a culture of craftsmanship with students.* Heinemann.

Bernabei, G., & Hall, D. (2012). *The story of my thinking: Expository writing activities for 13 teaching situations.* Heinemann.

Biography. (n.d.). *J. Robert Oppenheimer.* Accessed at https://www.biography.com /scientists/j-robert-oppenheimer on January 27, 2025.

Black, P. (2013). Formative and summative aspects of assessment: Theoretical and research foundations in the context of pedagogy. In J. H. McMillan (Ed.), *SAGE handbook of research on classroom assessment* (pp. 167–178). SAGE.

Black, P., & Wiliam, D. (1998). Inside the black box: Raising standards through classroom assessment. *Phi Delta Kappan, 80*(2), 139–148.

Bogliari, A. (2021). Four reasons why the creator economy is booming. *Forbes.* Accessed at www.forbes.com/councils/forbesagencycouncil/2021/11/18/four-reasons-why-the-creator-economy-is-booming on January 7, 2025.

Bong, J.-h. (Director). (2019). *Parasite* [Film]. Barunson E&A, CJ Entertainment.

BonJour, L. (1985). *The structure of empirical knowledge.* Harvard University Press.

Booker, C. (2004). *The seven basic plots: Why we tell stories.* Continuum.

Boyd, A. (2012, February 2). *Math wars.* University of Houston. Accessed at https://engines.egr.uh.edu/episode/2769 on January 10, 2025.

Brendtro, L. K., Brokenleg, M., & Van Bockern, S. (1990). *Reclaiming youth at risk: Our hope for the future.* National Educational Service.

Brown, B. (2012). *Daring greatly: How the courage to be vulnerable transforms the way we live, love, parent and lead.* Gotham Books.

Brown, B. (2015). *Rising strong: How the ability to reset transforms the way we live, love, parent, and lead.* Spiegel & Grau.

Brown, B. (2018). *Dare to lead: Brave work. Tough conversations. Whole hearts.* Random House.

Brown, B. (2021, December 5). *The practice of story stewardship.* Accessed at https://brenebrown.com/articles/2021/12/05/the-practice-of-story-stewardship on August 28, 2024.

Brown, G. T. L., & Harris, L. R. (2013). Student self-assessment. In J. H. McMillan (Ed.), *SAGE handbook of research on classroom assessment* (pp. 367–393). SAGE.

Bunting, J. (n.d.). *How to shape a story: The 6 types of story arcs for powerful narratives.* The Write Practice. Accessed at https://thewritepractice.com/story-arcs/ on August 26, 2024.

Burke, K. (1968). *Counter-statement* (2nd ed.). University of California Press.

Burns, E. C., Martin, A. J., & Collie, R. J. (2018). Understanding the role of goal setting in educational contexts: A review and synthesis of the research. *Educational Psychology Review, 30*(2), 431–465.

Burns, E. C., Martin, A. J., & Collie, R. J. (2019). Understanding the role of personal best (PB) goal setting in students' declining engagement: A latent growth model. *Journal of Educational Psychology, 111*(4), 557–572.

Butler, D. L., Schnellert, L., & Perry, N. E. (2016). *Developing self-regulating learners.* Pearson Canada.

Butler, R. (1998). Determinants of help seeking: Relations between perceived reasons for classroom help-avoidance and help-seeking behaviors in an experimental context. *Journal of Educational Psychology*, *90*(4), 630–644.

Butler, R. (2006). An achievement goal perspective on student help seeking and teacher help giving in the classroom: Theory, research, and educational implications. In S. A. Karabenick & R. S. Newman (Eds.), *Help seeking in academic setting: Goals, groups, and contexts* (pp. 15–44). Routledge.

Caldwell, J. H., Kobett, B., & Karp, K. (2014). *Putting essential understanding of addition and subtraction into practice, pre-K–2*. National Council of Teachers of Mathematics.

Campbell, J. (2008). *The hero with a thousand faces*. New World Library. (Original work published 1949)

Catmull, E., & Wallace, A. (2014). *Creativity inc.: Overcoming the unseen forces that stand in the way of true inspiration*. Random House.

Cavilla, D. (2017). The effects of student reflection on academic performance and motivation. *SAGE Open*, *7*(3). https://doi.org/10.1177/2158244017733790

Chappuis, J., & Stiggins, R. (2020). *Classroom assessment for student learning: Doing it right—Using it well*. Pearson.

Chung, G. K. W. K., Delacruz, G. C., Dionne, G. B., Baker, E. L., Lee, J. J., & Osmundson, E. (2016). *Towards individualized instruction with technology-enabled tools and methods: An exploratory study*. National Center for Research on Evaluation, Standards, and Student Testing & University of California, Los Angeles. Accessed at https://files.eric.ed.gov/fulltext/ED571793.pdf on January 31, 2025.

Clarke-Midura, J., & Dede, C. (2010). Assessment, technology, and change. *Journal of Research on Technology in Education*, *42*(3), 309–328.

Colley, B., Bilics, A., & Lerch, C. (2012). Reflection: A key component to thinking critically. *The Canadian Journal for the Scholarship of Teaching and Learning*, *3*, 1–19.

Collins, S. (2008). *The hunger games*. Scholastic Press.

Conflict. (n.d.). In *Britannica dictionary*. Accessed at www.britannica.com/dictionary/conflict on December 3, 2024.

ConnectEd. (2017). *New Media Academy: Video defense* [Video]. YouTube. Accessed at www.youtube.com/watch?v=vDUwcTPB3no&t=578s on August 30, 2024.

Core Collaborative. (2018, May 1). *4th grade peer feedback on problem solving in math* [Video]. YouTube. Accessed at www.youtube.com/watch?v=sTQNxz22tmU on January 13, 2025.

Craft. (n.d.). In *Merriam-Webster.com dictionary*. Accessed at www.merriam-webster.com /dictionary/craft on December 4, 2024.

Cronbach, L. J. (1971). Test validation. In R. L. Thorndike (Ed.); *Educational measurement* (2nd ed., pp. 443–507). American Council on Education.

Crowe, C. (Director). (2001). *Vanilla sky* [Film]. Cruise/Wagner Productions.

Culham, R., Blasingame, J., & Coutu, R. (2010). *Using mentor texts to teach writing with the traits: Middle school*. Scholastic.

Damasio, A. (1999). *The feeling of what happens: Body and emotion in the making of consciousness*. Mariner Books.

Darling-Hammond, L., & Friedlaender, D. (2008). Creating excellent and equitable schools. *Educational Leadership, 65*(8), 14–21.

David Comberg. (2004). *Kurt Vonnegut on the shapes of stories* [Video]. YouTube. Accessed at www.youtube.com/watch?v=oP3c1h8v2ZQ on January 13, 2025.

David, S. (2016). *Emotional agility: Get unstuck, embrace change, and thrive in work and life*. Avery.

Davis, A. (2020). Digital citizenship in Ontario education: A concept analysis. *In Education, 26*(1), 46–62. https://doi.org/10.37119/ojs2020.v26i1.467

Dear Math Project. (n.d.). *Dear Math Project* [Instagram post]. Accessed at www .instagram.com/dearmathproject on August 26, 2024.

Decety, J., & Lamm, C. (2009). Empathy versus personal distress: Recent evidence from social neuroscience. In J. Decety & W. Ickes (Eds.), *The social neuroscience of empathy* (pp. 199–213). MIT Press.

Deloitte. (2021). *The future of the creative economy*. Accessed at www2.deloitte.com/uk /en/pages/technology-media-and-telecommunications/articles/the-future-of-the -creative-economy.html on August 28, 2024.

Denke, J., Jarson, J., & Sinno, S. (2020). Making the invisible visible: Enhancing information literacy and metacognition with a constructivist activity. *International Journal for the Scholarship of Teaching and Learning, 14*(2). https://doi.org/10.20429 /ijsotl.2020.140207

Deutsch, M. (1973). *The resolution of conflict: Constructive and destructive processes*. Yale University Press.

Dewey, J. (1910). *How we think*. D. C. Heath and Company.

Dignan, A., & Evans, R. (Hosts). (2023, February 13). Help me help you: What if your coworkers came with instructions? (No. 159) [Audio podcast episode]. In *Brave New Work*. Accessed at www.theready.com/brave-new-work on August 28, 2024.

Dixon, T. L., Weeks, K. R., & Smith, M. A. (2019). Media constructions of culture, race, and ethnicity. *Oxford Research Encyclopedia of Communication*. https://doi.org/10.1093/acrefore/9780190228613.013.502

Dmitri Volov. (2018, December 30). The Office—*Giving feedback* [Video]. YouTube. Accessed at www.youtube.com/watch?v=PLaJq5Ec0rI on January 17, 2025.

Donaldson, R. (Director). (1997). *Dante's peak* [Film]. Universal Pictures.

Drew, C. (2023). *13 examples of metacognitive strategies*. Helpful Professor. Accessed at https://helpfulprofessor.com/metacognitive-strategies on August 28, 2024.

Durnová, A., & Karell, D. (2023). Emotions and the "truths" of contentious politics: Advances in research on emotions, knowledge and contemporary contentious politics. *Emotions and Society*, 5(3), 252–256. https://doi.org/10.1332/26316897Y2023D000000004

Dweck, C. S. (2006). *Mindset: The new psychology of success*. Random House.

Eldridge, E. (2012, April). *Why collaboration is an individual effort* [Video]. YouTube. Accessed at www.youtube.com/watch?v=DmGn2X9SETk&ab_channel=TEDxTalks on August 26, 2024.

EL Education. (n.d.). *Conflict by the numbers*. Accessed at https://modelsofexcellence.eleducation.org/projects/conflict-numbers on December 3, 2024.

EL Education. (2016, October 4). *Austin's butterfly: Models, critique and descriptive feedback* [Video]. YouTube. Accessed at www.youtube.com/watch?v=E_6PskE3zfQ&ab_channel=ELEducation on August 29, 2024.

EngageNY. (2013, December 20). *Teacher provides feedback during and after instruction—Example 7* [Video]. YouTube. Accessed at www.youtube.com/watch?v=I2Tdx-DeOLo on December 3, 2024.

Erkens, C., Schimmer, T., & Dimich, N. (2017). *Essential assessment: Six tenets for bringing hope, efficacy, and achievement to the classroom*. Solution Tree Press.

Erkens, C., Schimmer, T., & Dimich, N. (2019). *Growing tomorrow's citizens in today's classrooms: Assessing 7 critical competencies*. Solution Tree Press.

Evergreen School District. (n.d.). *Profile of a learner*. Accessed at www.eesd.org/departments/educational-services/general-programs-and-services/profile-of-a-learner on January 10, 2025.

Fey, C. [@mscynfey]. (2021, April 25). *TikTok is my university. Learned more about Black excellence, about toxic Whiteness, about culturally responsive teaching, about democratic classrooms* [X post]. X. Accessed at https://x.com/mscynfey/status/1386386965055029248 on January 31, 2025.

Filmmaking Lifestyle. (n.d.). *What is oneiric in film? Dream sequences that blur reality and imagination.* Accessed at https://filmlifestyle.com/what-is-oneiric on December 3, 2024.

Fincher, D. (Director). (2014). *Gone girl* [Film]. 20th Century Fox.

Fireman, G. D., McVay, T. E., & Flanagan, O. J. (Eds.). (2003). *Narrative and consciousness: Literature, psychology, and the brain.* Oxford University Press.

First Nations Education Steering Committee. (n.d.). *First Peoples principles of learning.* Accessed at www.fnesc.ca/first-peoples-principles-of-learning on August 30, 2024.

Fischer, C. S. (1992). *America calling: A social history of the telephone to 1940.* University of California Press.

Fisher, D., Frey, N., & Hattie, J. (2016). *Visible learning for literacy, grades K–12: Implementing the practices that work best to accelerate student learning.* Corwin.

Fleming, V., & Vidor, K. (Directors). (1939). *The wizard of Oz* [Film]. Metro-Goldwyn-Mayer.

Fleur, D. S., Bredeweg, B., & van den Bos, W. (2021). Metacognition: Ideas and insights from neuro- and educational sciences. *npj Science of Learning, 6*(13). https://doi.org/10.1038/s41539-021-00089-5

Forchheimer, S. (2022, June 28). *What exactly is futures thinking?* Accessed at https://www.iftf.org/insights/what-exactly-is-futures-thinking/ on January 28, 2025.

Foundationalism. (n.d.). In *Internet Encyclopedia of Philosophy.* Accessed at https://iep.utm.edu/foundationalism-in-epistemology on December 3, 2024.

Frey, N., Hattie, J., & Fisher, D. (2018). *Developing assessment-capable visible learners, grades K–12: Maximizing skill, will, and thrill.* Corwin.

Freytag, G. (1863). *Die Technik des Dramas [The technique of the drama].* Hirzel.

Frieden, J. E. [@SurthrivEDU]. (2021, April 25). *Okay, what about a TED Tok? Yep, that's how I'm finishing the year with my Sophomores. Thank you!* [X post]. X. Accessed at https://x.com/SurthrivEDU/status/1386339849473454084 on January 31, 2025.

Friedman, T. L. (2016). *Thank you for being late: An optimist's guide to thriving in the age of accelerations.* Farrar, Straus and Giroux.

Gallagher, K. (2011). *Write like this: Teaching real-world writing through modeling and mentor texts.* Routledge.

Gaman. (n.d.). In *Tibetan Buddhist Encyclopedia.* Accessed at https://tibetanbuddhistencyclopedia.com/en/index.php/Gaman on December 3, 2024.

Ganz, M. (Host). (2020, March 12). Community organizing and collective impact (No. 7) [Audio podcast episode]. In *Collective impact forum*. Apple Podcasts. Accessed at https://podcasts.apple.com/us/podcast/marshall-ganz-community-organizing-and-collective-impact/id1496436121?i=1000468108884 on August 29, 2024.

Garibaldi, A., Blanchard, L., & Brooks, S. (1996). Conflict resolution training, teacher effectiveness, and student suspension: The impact of a health and safety initiative in the New Orleans public schools. *The Journal of Negro Education*, *65*(4), 408–413.

Gilbert, E. (2015). *Big magic: Creative living beyond fear*. Riverhead Books.

Gillies, R. M. (2016). Cooperative learning: Review of research and practice. *Australian Journal of Teacher Education*, *41*(3), 39–54. https://doi.org/10.14221/ajte.2016v41n3.3

Gilligan, V. (Creator). (2008–2013). *Breaking bad* [TV series]. AMC.

Giroux, H. A. (2022, July 30). Resisting fascism and winning the education wars: How we can meet the challenge. *Salon*. Accessed at www.salon.com/2022/07/30/resisting-fascism-and-winning-the-education-wars-how-we-can-meet-the-challenge/ on August 29, 2024.

Glatch, S. (2024, May 31). *The 5 elements of dramatic structure: Understanding Freytag's Pyramid*. Writers.com. Accessed at https://writers.com/freytags-pyramid on January 27, 2025.

Gonzalez, J. (2016, October 30). *Is your lesson a Grecian urn?* Cult of Pedagogy. Accessed at www.cultofpedagogy.com/grecian-urn-lesson/ on August 29, 2024.

Government of British Columbia. (n.d.a). *BC's redesigned curriculum: An orientation guide*. Accessed at https://curriculum.gov.bc.ca/sites/curriculum.gov.bc.ca/files/pdf/supports/curriculum_brochure.pdf on August 30, 2024.

Government of British Columbia. (n.d.b). *Core competencies*. Accessed at https://curriculum.gov.bc.ca/competencies on August 26, 2024.

Government of British Columbia. (n.d.c). *Curriculum overview*. Accessed at https://curriculum.gov.bc.ca/curriculum/overview on January 10, 2025.

Grant, A. (2021). *Think again: The power of knowing what you don't know*. Viking.

Greenberg, S. (2021, November 10). The best way to master a new skill? Try this creative approach. *Harvard Business Review*. Accessed at https://hbr.org/2021/11/the-best-way-to-master-a-new-skill-try-this-creative-approach on January 10, 2025.

Greene, M. (2000). *Releasing the imagination: Essays on education, the arts, and social change*. Jossey-Bass.

Gregory, J., Cameron, D., & Kearney, J. (2011). The role of goal-setting in student motivation and achievement. *Journal of Educational Psychology*, *103*(3), 543–558.

Gregory, J. B., Beck, J. W., & Carr, A. E. (2011). Goals, feedback, and self-regulation: Control theory as a natural framework for executive coaching. *Consulting Psychology Journal: Practice and Research, 63*(1), 26–38.

Griffin, P., McGaw, B., & Care, E. (Eds.). (2012). *Assessment and teaching of 21st-century skills.* Springer. https://doi.org/10.1007/978-94-007-2324-5

Guber, P. (2007, December). The four truths of the storyteller. *Harvard Business Review.* Accessed at https://hbr.org/2007/12/the-four-truths-of-the-storyteller on August 29, 2024.

Guskey, T. R., & Brookhart, S. M. (Eds.). (2019). *What we know about grading: What works, what doesn't, and what's next.* ASCD.

Hammond, Z. L. (2015). *Culturally responsive teaching and the brain: Promoting authentic engagement and rigor among culturally and linguistically diverse students.* Corwin.

Harari, Y. N. (2018). *21 lessons for the 21st century.* Spiegel & Grau.

Hardcastle, V. G. (2003). The development of the self. In G. D. Fireman, T. E. McVay, & O. J. Flanagan (Eds.), *Narrative and consciousness: Literature, psychology, and the brain* (pp. 37–50). Oxford University Press.

Harley, S. (2013, March 5). *Why is feedback important?* [Video]. YouTube. Accessed at www.youtube.com/watch?v=udCqSrTzHSU on January 17, 2025.

Harmony. (n.d.). In *Cambridge English dictionary.* Accessed at https://dictionary .cambridge.org/dictionary/english/harmony on December 3, 2024.

Harris, K. R., Graham, S., Mason, L. H., & Saddler, B. (2002). Developing self-regulated writers. *Theory Into Practice, 41*(2), 110–115.

Hattie, J., & Donoghue, G. M. (2016). Learning strategies: A synthesis and conceptual model. *npj Science of Learning, 1,* 16013. Accessed at www.nature.com/articles /npjscilearn201613 on August 29, 2024.

Hattie, J., & Timperley, H. (2007). The power of feedback. *Review of Educational Research, 77*(1), 81–112.

Hein, G., & Singer, T. (2008). I feel how you feel but not always: The empathic brain and its modulation. *Current Opinion in Neurobiology, 18*(2),153–158.

Hiebert, J., & Grouws, D. A. (2007). The effects of classroom mathematics teaching on students' learning. In F. K. Lester Jr. (Ed.), *Second handbook of research on mathematics teaching and learning* (pp. 371–404). Information Age.

Hiroshima and Nagasaki. (n.d.). In *Encyclopaedia Britannica.* Accessed at www .britannica.com/event/World-War-II/Hiroshima-and-Nagasaki on December 3, 2024.

Hofstede, G., Hofstede, G. J., & Minkov, M. (2010). *Cultures and organizations: Software of the mind* (3rd ed.). McGraw-Hill.

How Not 2 Videos. Expert Incompetence. (2015, November 13). *How NOT 2 to give negative feedback* [Video]. YouTube. Accessed at www.youtube.com /watch?v=M9H8hWx0tg0 on December 4, 2024.

Huemer, W. (2004). *The constitution of consciousness: A study in analytic phenomenology.* Routledge.

Hutto, D. D. (2007). The narrative practice hypothesis: Origins and applications of folk psychology. *Royal Institute of Philosophy Supplement, 60*, 43–68. Accessed at www.researchgate.net/publication/30384463_The_Narrative_Practice_Hypothesis _Origins_and_Applications_of_Folk_Psychology on January 31, 2025.

International Astronomical Union. (n.d.). *Pluto and the developing landscape of our solar system.* Accessed at www.iau.org/public/themes/pluto/#n4 on December 8, 2024.

International Baccalaureate Organization. (n.d.). *The IB learner profile.* Accessed at www .ibo.org/benefits/learner-profile on January 10, 2025.

J. Robert Oppenheimer. (n.d.). In *Britannica.* Accessed at https://www.britannica.com /summary/J-Robert-Oppenheimer on January 31, 2025.

Jackson, Y. (2011). *The pedagogy of confidence: Inspiring high intellectual performance in urban schools.* Teachers College Press.

Jehn, K. A. (1995). A multimethod examination of the benefits and detriments of intragroup conflict. *Administrative Science Quarterly, 40*(2), 256–282.

Jehn, K. A., & Mannix, E. A. (2001). The dynamic nature of conflict: A longitudinal study of intragroup conflict and group performance. *The Academy of Management Journal, 44*(2), 238–251.

Johnson, D. W., & Johnson, R. T. (1995). *Creative controversy: Intellectual challenge in the classroom.* Interaction Book Company.

Johnson, D. W., & Johnson, R. T. (1996). Conflict resolution and peer mediation programs in elementary and secondary schools: A review of the research. *Review of Educational Research, 66*(4), 459–506.

Johnson, D. W., & Johnson, R. T. (2001). *Learning together and alone: Cooperative, competitive, and individualistic learning* (5th ed.). Allyn & Bacon.

Johnson, D. W., & Johnson, R. T. (2005). *Teaching students to be peacemakers* (4th ed.). Interaction Book Company.

Johnson, D. W., Johnson, R. T., Dudley, B., Ward, M., & Magnuson, D. (1995). The impact of peer mediation training on the management of school and home conflicts. *American Educational Research Journal, 32*(4), 829–844.

Karabenick, S. A. (Ed.). (1998). *Strategic help seeking: Implications for learning and teaching*. Erlbaum.

Karabenick, S. A. (2003). Seeking help in large college classes: A person-centered approach. *Contemporary Educational Psychology, 28*(1), 37–58.

Karabenick, S. A. (2004). Perceived achievement goal structure and college student help seeking. *Journal of Educational Psychology, 96*(3), 569–581.

Karabenick, S. A., & Berger, J.-L. (2013). Help seeking as a self-regulated learning strategy. In H. Bembenutty, T. J. Cleary, & A. Kitsantas (Eds.), *Applications of self-regulated learning across diverse disciplines: A tribute to Barry J. Zimmerman* (pp. 237–261). Information Age Publishing.

Karabenick, S. A., & Dembo, M. H. (2011). Understanding and facilitating self-regulated help seeking. *New Directions for Teaching and Learning, 126,* 33–43. Accessed at https://ssrlsig.org/wp-content/uploads/2018/01/karabenick-dembo -2011-understanding-and-facilitating-self-reg-help-seeking.pdf on January 27, 2025.

Karabenick, S. A., & Newman, R. S. (Eds.). (2006). *Help seeking in academic settings: Goals, groups, and contexts.* Erlbaum.

Kaufman, J. C., & Beghetto, R. A. (2009). Beyond big and little: The four C model of creativity. *Review of General Psychology, 13*(1), 1–12.

Khalifa, M. A., Gooden, M. A., & Davis, J. E. (2016). Culturally responsive school leadership: A synthesis of the literature. *Review of Educational Research, 86*(4), 1272–1311.

Kidd, D. C., & Castano, E. (2013). Reading literary fiction improves theory of mind. *Science, 342*(6156), 377–380.

Kind, A., & Kung, P. (Eds.). (2016). *Knowledge through imagination.* Oxford University Press.

Kirkpatrick, S. (2023, April 27). Understanding the rise of the creator economy. *Forbes.* Accessed at www.forbes.com/sites/quora/2023/04/27/understanding-the-rise-of-the -creator-economy/?sh=1f1e15287e16 on August 29, 2024.

Kittle, P. (2022). *Micro mentor texts: Using short passages from great books to teach writer's craft.* Scholastic.

Kluger, A., & DeNisi, A. (1996). The effects of feedback interventions on performance: A historical review, a meta-analysis, and a preliminary feedback intervention theory. *Psychological Bulletin, 119*(2), 254–284.

Kurosawa, A. (Director). (1950). *Rashomon* [Film]. Daiei Film.

Lambert, J. (2018). *Digital storytelling: Capturing lives, creating community* (5th ed.). Routledge.

Lane, S. (2013). Performance assessment. In J. H. McMillan (Ed.), *SAGE handbook of research on classroom assessment* (pp. 313–331). SAGE.

Lantieri, L., DeJong, W., & Dutrey, J. (1996). Waging peace in our schools: The Resolving Conflict Creatively Program. In A. Hoffman (Ed.), *Schools, violence, and society* (pp. 241–251). Praeger.

Larrazet, C., & Rigoni, I. (2014). Media and diversity: A century-long perspective on an enlarged and internationalized field of research. *InMedia, 5*. https://doi.org/10.4000/inmedia.747

Learning Forward. (n.d.). *Standards for professional learning*. Accessed at https://standards.learningforward.org/standards-for-professional-learning on July 11, 2024.

Liao, S.-y., & Gendler, T. S. (2020). Imagination. In E. N. Zalta (Ed.), *The Stanford encyclopedia of philosophy* (Fall 2020 ed.). Accessed at https://plato.stanford.edu/entries/imagination on January 10, 2025.

Lien, H. (2021, January 5). *Diversity plus: Diverse story forms and themes, not just diverse faces*. Science Fiction & Fantasy Writers Association. Accessed at www.sfwa.org/2021/01/05/diversity-plus-diverse-story-forms-and-themes-not-just-diverse-faces/ on August 29, 2024.

Liljedahl, P. (2021). *Building thinking classrooms in mathematics, grades K–12: 14 teaching practices for enhancing learning*. Corwin.

Linley, A. (2008). *Average to A+: Realising strengths in yourself and others*. CAPP Press.

Lipton, B. H. (2016). *The biology of belief: Unleashing the power of consciousness, matter & miracles* (10th anniversary ed.). Hay House.

Maier, S. F., & Seligman, M. E. P. (2016). Learned helplessness at fifty: Insights from neuroscience. *Psychological Review, 123*(4), 349–367. https://doi.org/10.1037/rev0000033

Main, P. (2022, January 4). *The learning pit: A guide for teachers*. Structural Learning. Accessed at www.structural-learning.com/post/the-learning-pit-a-guide-for-teachers on August 27, 2024.

Malick, T. (Director, writer). (2011). *The tree of life* [Film]. Cottonwood Pictures.

Marchetti, A., & O'Dell, R. (2021). *A teacher's guide to mentor texts, 6–12*. Heinemann.

McCabe, A. (1997). Cultural background and storytelling: A review and implications for schooling. *The Elementary School Journal, 97*(5), 453–473.

McCormick, C. B., Dimmitt, C. A., & Sullivan, F. R. (2013). Metacognition, learning, and instruction. In W. M. Reynolds, G. E. Miller, & I. B. Weiner (Eds.), *Handbook of psychology: Educational psychology* (2nd ed., pp. 69–97). Wiley.

McGonigal, J. (2022). *Imaginable: How to see the future coming and feel ready for anything—Even things that seem impossible today.* Spiegel & Grau.

Mentor Texts. (n.d.). *The New York Times.* Accessed at https://www.nytimes.com/column/learning-mentor-texts on February 3, 2025.

Millennium Ecosystem Assessment. (2005). *Ecosystems and human well-being: A report of the Millennium Ecosystem Assessment.* Island Press.

Mills, A. (2023, February 23). *Supporting successful curriculum reform in Kenya.* Girls' Education Challenge. Accessed at https://girlseducationchallenge.org/blogs/blog-article/supporting-successful-curriculum-reform-in-kenya on January 13, 2025.

Ministry of Education, Science and Technology. (2015). *National curriculum policy.* Accessed at https://kicd.ac.ke/curriculum-reform/curriculum-development-policy on January 19, 2025.

Ministry of Human Resource Development, Government of India. (2020). *National education policy 2020.* Accessed at www.education.gov.in/sites/upload_files/mhrd/files/NEP_Final_English_0.pdf on January 10, 2025.

Mitsuhashi, J. (2004). Entomophagy: Human consumption of insects. In J. L. Capinera (Ed.), *Encyclopedia of entomology* (pp. 786–787). Springer. https://doi.org/10.1007/0-306-48380-7_1433

Moore, D. S. (1995). The craft of teaching. *MAA Focus, 15*(2), 6–8.

Moore, G. E. (1965). Cramming more components onto integrated circuits. *Electronics Magazine, 38*, 114–117.

Movieclips. (2014, March 10). Office Space *(1/5) movie clip—Did you get the memo? (1999) HD* [Video]. YouTube. Accessed at www.youtube.com/watch?v=jsLUidiYm0w on January 13, 2025.

Neurath, O. (1973). Anti-Spengler. In M. Neurath & R. S. Cohen (Eds.), *Empiricism and sociology, Vol. 1* (pp. 158–213). D. Reidel Publishing. (Original work published 1921)

Neurath, O. (1983). Protocol statements. In R. S. Cohen & M. Neurath (Eds.), *Philosophical papers 1913–1946* (pp. 91–99). D. Reidel Publishing. (Original work published 1932)

Newkirk, T. (2014). *Minds made for stories: How we really read and write informational and persuasive texts.* Heinemann.

Newman, R. S. (2008). The motivational role of adaptive help seeking in self-regulated learning. In D. H. Schunk & B. J. Zimmerman (Eds.), *Motivation and self-regulated learning: Theory, research, and applications* (pp. 315–337). Erlbaum.

Ng, R. (2022, March 22). The surprising history of Hawai'i's hula tradition. *National Geographic*. Accessed at www.nationalgeographic.com/travel/article/the-surprising-history-of-hawaiis-hula-tradition on August 29, 2024.

Nickerson, C. (n.d.). *What is sociological imagination: Definition & examples*. Simply Psychology. Accessed at https://www.simplypsychology.org/sociological-imagination.html on January 28, 2025.

Nisbett, R. E., & Wilson, T. D. (1977). Telling more than we can know: Verbal reports on mental processes. *Psychological Review*, *84*(3), 231–259.

Norman, E., Pfuhl, G., Sæle, R. G., Svartdal, F., Låg, T., & Dahl, T. I. (2019). Metacognition in psychology. *Review of General Psychology*, *23*(4), 403–424. https://doi.org/10.1177/1089268019883821

Nottingham, J. (2024). *Teach brilliantly: Small shifts that lead to big gains in student learning*. Solution Tree Press.

Nunez, J. L. O. (2022, September 23). *A simple analysis of Ernest Hemingway's shortest story about baby shoes*. Medium. Accessed at https://writingcooperative.com/a-simple-analysis-of-ernest-hemingways-shortest-story-about-baby-shoes-1d7f5655372f on January 8, 2025.

Okri, B. (2009). *Tales of freedom*. Rider.

Okun, T. (2021). *White supremacy culture characteristics*. White Supremacy Culture. Accessed at www.whitesupremacyculture.info/characteristics.html on August 29, 2024.

Olivadese, M., & Dindo, M. L. (2023). Edible insects: A historical and cultural perspective on entomophagy with a focus on Western societies. *Insects*, *14*(8), 690. https://doi.org/10.3390/insects14080690

Organisation for Economic Co-operation and Development. (2017a). *The OECD handbook for innovative learning environments*. Accessed at www.oecd.org/education/the-oecd-handbook-for-innovative-learning-environments-9789264277274-en.htm on August 29, 2024.

Organisation for Economic Co-operation and Development. (2017b). *PISA 2015 assessment and analytical framework: Science, reading, mathematic, financial literacy and collaborative problem solving*. Accessed at www.oecd.org/en/publications/2017/08/pisa-2015-assessment-and-analytical-framework_g1g81b0f.html on January 13, 2025.

Organisation for Economic Co-operation and Development. (2017c). *Students' motivation and engagement: Insights from the OECD's PISA 2015 survey*. https://doi.org/10.1787/9789264285666-en

Organisation for Economic Co-operation and Development. (2018). *The future of education and skills: Education 2030.* Accessed at www.oecd.org/en/about/projects/future-of-education-and-skills-2030.html on January 13, 2025.

Organisation for Economic Co-operation and Development. (2019a). *OECD skills strategy 2019: Skills to shape a better future.* https://doi.org/10.1787/978926 4313835-en

Organisation for Economic Co-operation and Development. (2019b). *PISA 2018 assessment and analytical framework.* https://doi.org/10.1787/b25efab8-en

Panadero, E. (2017). A review of self-regulated learning: Six models and four directions for research. *Frontiers in Psychology, 8.* https://doi.org/10.3389/fpsyg.2017.00422

Papert, S. (1972). Teaching children thinking. *Programmed Learning and Educational Technology, 9*(5), 245–255.

Papert, S. (2005). Teaching children thinking. *Contemporary Issues in Technology and Teacher Education, 5*(3). Accessed at https://citejournal.org/volume-5/issue-3-05/seminal-articles/teaching-children-thinking on January 13, 2025.

Payne, K., Niemi, L., & Doris, J. M. (2018). How to think about "implicit bias." *Scientific American.* Accessed at www.scientificamerican.com/article/how-to-think-about-implicit-bias/ on August 29, 2024.

Pintrich, P. R., & Zusho, A. (2002). The development of academic self-regulation: The role of cognitive and motivational factors. In A. Wigfield & J. S. Eccles (Eds.), *Development of achievement motivation* (pp. 249–284). Academic Press.

Pronin, E. (2009). The introspection illusion. In M. P. Zanna (Ed.), *Advances in experimental social psychology, Vol. 41* (pp. 1–68). Elsevier. https://doi.org/10.1016/S0065-2601(08)00401-2

Propp, V. (1968). *Morphology of the folktale* (L. Scott, Trans.). University of Texas Press. (Original work published 1928)

Quine, W. V., & Ullian, J. S. (1970). *The web of belief.* Random House.

Quinn, D. M. (2021). How to reduce racial bias in grading: New research supports a simple, low-cost teaching tool. *Education Next, 21*(1). Accessed at www.educationnext.org/how-to-reduce-racial-bias-in-grading-research/ on January 20, 2025.

Revonsuo, A. (2000). The reinterpretation of dreams: An evolutionary hypothesis of the function of dreaming. *Behavioral and Brain Sciences, 23*(6), 877–901.

Ribble, M. (n.d.). *Nine elements: Nine themes of digital citizenship.* Digital Citizenship. Accessed at www.digitalcitizenship.net/nine-elements.html on January 13, 2025.

Ritchhart, R., Church, M., & Morrison, K. (2011). *Making thinking visible: How to promote engagement, understanding, and independence for all learners.* Jossey-Bass.

Ross, J. A. (2006). The reliability, validity, and utility of self-report measures of student goal setting. *Educational Assessment, Evaluation and Accountability, 18*(3), 253–270.

Rubin, D. C., & Greenberg, D. L. (2003). The role of narrative in recollection: A view from cognitive psychology and neuropsychology. In G. D. Fireman, T. E. McVay, & O. J. Flanagan (Eds.), *Narrative and consciousness: Literature, psychology, and the brain* (pp. 53–85). Oxford University Press.

Ruiz-Primo, M. A., & Li, M. (2013). Examining formative feedback in the classroom context: New research perspectives. In J. H. McMillan (Ed.), *SAGE handbook of research on classroom assessment* (pp. 215–232). SAGE.

Runco, M. A. (2007). *Creativity: Theories and themes—Research, development, and practice.* Elsevier.

Runco, M. A. (2014). *Creativity: Theories and themes—Research, development, and practice* (2nd ed.). Academic Press.

Rusche, S., & Jason, K. (2011). You have to absorb yourself in it: Using inquiry and reflection to promote student learning and self-knowledge. *Teaching Sociology, 39,* 338–353.

Ryan, A. M., Patrick, H., & Shim, S.-O. (2005). Differential profiles of students identified by their teacher as having avoidant, appropriate, or dependent help-seeking tendencies in the classroom. *Journal of Educational Psychology, 97*(2), 275–285.

Sadler, D. R. (1989). Formative assessment and the design of instructional systems. *Instructional Science, 18*(2), 119–144.

Safir, S., & Dugan, J. (2021). *Street data: A next-generation model for equity, pedagogy, and school transformation.* Corwin.

Sawyer, R. K. (2006). *Explaining creativity: The science of human innovation.* Oxford University Press.

Schunk, D. H., & Greene, J. A. (2018). Historical, contemporary, and future perspectives on self-regulated learning and performance. In D. H. Schunk & J. A. Greene (Eds.), *Handbook of self-regulation of learning and performance* (2nd ed., pp. 1–16). Routledge.

ScienceDirect. (n.d.). *Intersubjectivity.* Accessed at www.sciencedirect.com/topics/social-sciences/intersubjectivity on January 22, 2025.

Segal, A. (Director). (2020). *Best wishes, warmest regards: A* Schitt's Creek *farewell* [Film]. Canadian Broadcasting Corporation.

Senge, P. M., Scharmer, C. O., Jaworski, J., & Flowers, B. S. (2005). *Presence: An exploration of profound change in people, organizations, and society.* Currency.

Shklovsky, V. (1965). Art as technique. In L. T. Lemon & M. Reis (Eds.), *Russian formalist criticism: Four essays* (pp. 3–24). University of Nebraska Press. (Original work published 1917)

Shubitz, S. (2016). *Craft moves: Lesson sets for teaching writing with mentor texts.* Stenhouse.

Skinner, E. A. (2023). Four guideposts toward an integrated model of academic motivation. *Educational Psychology Review.* https://doi.org/10.1007/s10648-023-09790-w

Skinner, E. A., & Zimmer-Gembeck, M. J. (2007). The development of coping. *Annual Review of Clinical Psychology, 58,* 119–144.

Slavin, R. E., Hurley, E. A., & Chamberlain, A. (2003). Cooperative learning and achievement: Theory and research. In W. M. Reynolds & G. E. Miller (Eds.), *Handbook of psychology: Vol. 7. Educational psychology* (pp. 177–198). John Wiley & Sons.

Sosa, E. (1980). The raft and the pyramid: Coherence versus foundations in the theory of knowledge. *Midwest Studies in Philosophy, 5*(1), 3–26.

South Carolina Department of Education. (2011). *South Carolina social studies academic standards: Grade 6.* Accessed at https://ed.sc.gov/scdoe/assets/File/instruction/standards/Social%20Studies/2011%20Social%20Studies%20Support%20Documents/Grade%206.pdf on January 13, 2025.

Stahelski, C. (Director). (2014). *John Wick* [Film]. Summit Entertainment.

Steffen, W., Crutzen, P. J., & McNeill, J. R. (2007). The Anthropocene: Are humans now overwhelming the great forces of nature? *AMBIO: A Journal of the Human Environment, 36*(8), 614–621. https://doi.org/10.1579/0044-7447(2007)36[614:TAAHNO]2.0.CO;2

Storr, W. (2019). *The science of storytelling: Why stories make us human and how to tell them better.* William Collins.

Strong, S. (n.d.). *Activity sessions.* Accessed at https://teacher.desmos.com/activitybuilder/custom/6091f81192aec84ed6f5e51b on August 26, 2024.

Strong, S., & Butterfield, G. (2022). *Dear math: Why kids hate math and what teachers can do about it.* Times 10 Publications.

Suzuki, W. A., Feliú-Mójer, M. I., Hasson, U., Yehuda, R., & Zarate, J. M. (2018). Dialogues: The science and power of storytelling. *Journal of Neuroscience, 38*(44), 9468–9470.

Tarantino, Q. (Director). (1994). *Pulp fiction* [Film]. Miramax Films.

TED. (2011, January 3). *The power of vulnerability: Brené Brown* [Video]. YouTube. Accessed at www.youtube.com/watch?v=iCvmsMzlF7o on August 29, 2024.

TED. (2021, February 10). *Karen Eber: How your brain responds to stories—And why they are crucial for leaders* [Video]. YouTube. Accessed at www.youtube.com/watch?v =uJfGby1C3C4&ab_channel=TED on August 29, 2024.

TheMattDr. (2011, August 1). *Best coaching conversation* [Video]. YouTube. Accessed at www.youtube.com/watch?v=guclKsL-JbY on January 13, 2025.

Thornton, B. (2013, June 12). *A brief history of media bias.* Hoover Institution. Accessed at www.hoover.org/research/brief-history-media-bias on January 13, 2025.

Tuckman, B. W., & Jensen, M. A. C. (1977). Stages of small-group development revisited. *Group & Organization Management, 2*(4), 419–427. https://doi.org /10.1177/105960117700200404

Tuckman, B. W., & Jensen, M. A. C. (1977). Stages of small-group development revisited. *Group & Organization Management, 2*(4), 419–427. https://doi.org /10.1177/105960117700200404

UNESCO. (2015). *Transversal competencies in education policy and practice (Phase I): Regional synthesis report.* Accessed at https://unesdoc.unesco.org/ark:/48223 /pf0000234317 on January 13, 2025.

UNESCO. (2017). *Education for sustainable development goals: Learning objectives.* Accessed at https://unesdoc.unesco.org/ark:/48223/pf0000247444 on January 13, 2025.

UNESCO. (2021). *Reimagining our futures together: A new social contract for education.* Accessed at www.unesco.org/en/articles/reimagining-our-futures-together-new -social-contract-education on August 29, 2024.

Usher, A., & Kober, N. (2012a). *Can goals motivate students?* Center on Education Policy. Accessed at www.eric.ed.gov/?id=ED532668 on August 29, 2024.

Usher, A., & Kober, N. (2012b). *Student motivation: An overlooked piece of school reform.* Center on Education Policy.

van Knippenberg, D., Haslam, S. A., & Platow, M. J. (2007). Unity through diversity: Value-in-diversity beliefs, work group diversity, and group identification. *Group Dynamics: Theory, Research, and Practice, 11*(3), 207–222.

Vardabasso, N. [@natabasso]. (2021, April 24). *Fact: TikTok videos are only 60 seconds in length. Also fact: Explaining a complex concept accurately in 60 seconds shows* [X post]. X. Accessed at https://x.com/natabasso/status/1386201826609950721 on January 31, 2025.

Vardabasso, N. (Host). (2022, April 11). The story of street data (No. 66) [Audio podcast episode]. In *EduCrush.* Libsyn. Accessed at https://educrushpod.libsyn .com/66-the-story-of-street-data-w-shane-safir on January 13, 2025.

Vardabasso, N. (Host). (2023, November 27). What if students rewrote the narrative of school? (No. 76) [Audio podcast episode]. In *EduCrush*. Libsyn. Accessed at https://educrushpod.libsyn.com/76-what-if-students-rewrote-the-narrative-of-school-w-breana-jacques-shannon-finnegan on January 13, 2025.

Viereck, G. S. (1929, October 26). What life means to Einstein: An interview. *Saturday Evening Post, 202*(17), 110–117.

Voogt, J., & Pareja Roblin, N. (2010). *21st-century skills: Discussion paper.* University of Twente. Accessed at https://research.utwente.nl/en/publications/21st-century-skills-discussion-paper on January 13, 2025.

Waite, A. E. (Author), & Smith, P. C. (Illustrator). (n.d.). *Rider-Waite tarot deck.* U.S. Games Systems.

Wallas, G. (2014). *The art of thought* (Rev. ed.). Solis Press.

Warshauer, H. K. (2015). Productive struggle in middle school mathematics classrooms. *Journal of Mathematics Teacher Education, 18*(4), 375–399.

Weiner, B. (2010). The development of an attribution-based theory of motivation: A history of ideas. *Educational Psychologist, 45*(1), 28–36. https://doi.org/10.1080/00461520903433596

Wheatley, M. J. (2009). *Turning to one another: Simple conversations to restore hope to the future* (Expanded ed.). Berrett-Koehler.

White, K. (2021). *Student self-assessment: Data notebooks, portfolios, and other tools to advance learning.* Solution Tree Press.

White, V. (2003). *Children's stories of conflict at school: Exploring "realities" of resolution through narrative* [Master's thesis, University of British Columbia]. University of British Columbia Open Collections. Accessed at https://open.library.ubc.ca/soa/cIRcle/collections/ubctheses/831/items/1.0053835 on August 29, 2024.

Wiliam, D. (2011). *Embedded formative assessment.* Solution Tree Press.

Wiliam, D. (2018). Feedback: At the heart of—but definitely not all of—formative assessment. In A. A. Lipnevich & J. K. Smith (Eds.), *The Cambridge handbook of instructional feedback* (pp. 3–28). Cambridge University Press.

Wiliam, D. (2020). How to think about assessment. In S. Donarski (Ed.), *The researchED guide to assessment* (pp. 21–36). John Catt Educational Ltd.

Willingham, D. T. (2020). Ask the cognitive scientist: How can educators teach critical thinking? *American Educator, 44*(3), 41–51.

Wilson, K. G., & DuFrene, T. (2009). *Mindfulness for two: An acceptance and commitment therapy approach to mindfulness in psychotherapy.* New Harbinger Publications.

Wisniewski, B., Zierer, K., & Hattie, J. (2020). The power of feedback revisited: A meta-analysis of educational feedback research. *Frontiers in Psychology, 10*, Article 3087. https://doi.org/10.3389/fpsyg.2019.03087

Zeki, S. (2003). The disunity of consciousness. *Trends in Cognitive Sciences, 7*(5), 214–218.

Zerwin, S. M. (2020). *Point-less: An English teacher's guide to more meaningful grading*. Heinemann.

Zhao, Y. (2016). The danger of misguided outcomes: Lessons from Easter Island. In Y. Zhao (Ed.), *Counting what counts: Reframing education outcomes* (pp. 1–10). Solution Tree Press.

Zimmerman, B. J. (2000). Self-efficacy: An essential motive to learn. *Contemporary Educational Psychology, 25*(1), 82–91.

Zimmerman, B. J. (2011). Motivational sources and outcomes of self-regulated learning. In B. J. Zimmerman & D. H. Schunk (Eds.), *Handbook of self-regulation of learning and performance* (pp. 49–64). Routledge.

Zullow, H. M., Oettingen, G., Peterson, C., & Seligman, M. E. (1988). Pessimistic explanatory style in the historical record. *American Psychologist, 43*(9), 673–682.

Zumbrunn, S., Tadlock, J., & Roberts, E. D. (2011). *Encouraging self-regulated learning in the classroom: A review of the literature*. Accessed at https://www.researchgate.net/publication/325603134_Encouraging_self-regulated_learning_in_the_classroom_A_review_of_the_literature on August 29, 2024.

INDEX

A

Aboriginal perspectives and knowledge, 64
accurate interpretation, 11
achievement goals, 106. *See also* goals
active listening, 52, 169
active reading strategies, 52
adaptability and the age of acceleration, 58
adaptive expertise, 58
adaptive patterns, 104, 106
affordance, 87, 88
age of acceleration, 58
agility
    instructional, 11
    of assessment, 36, 46
Alberta Health Services, 228
Alberts, H., 130
all means all, 18
ambiguity, 189–190
amplifying stories of inspiration, 206
analogies, 197–198
analyzing, 45, 60, 146, 171
anchor charts, 227
architecture, 11, 36, 46
Armstrong, P., 13–14
artificial intelligence
    AI-assisted information, 7
    emergence of, 5, 46, 59
    introduces conflict, 86
asking questions to direct close reading, 227 *See also* questions
assessment
assessment tenets, 11
    the big idea, 35–40
    competency connection, 45–47
    cultural connection, 40–44
    defined, 5–6
    discussion questions for learning teams, 55–56

driving learning, 37–38
formative, 196–197
interpretation of assessment, 36, 46
    of the past, present, and future, 46–47
    performance, 43–44, 48
    reimagined, 6–7
    of self, 51–52, 54
    the story of how I'm learning, 49–53
    the story of what I'm learning, 47–49
    three cautions to consider, 52–53
    through story, 3–4, 35–56
attributional theory, 30–31
"Austin's Butterfly" (EL Education), 215
avoidant patterns, 104
Azgor, S., 166

B

balance, 153
behavior barriers, 206
Bellanca, J., 192–193
beyond the status quo, 2–3
bias, 3, 44, 111
the big ideas, 8
    assessment through story, 35–40
    conflict through story, 83–88
    craft through story, 211–215
    critical competencies through story, 57–60
    harmony through story, 109–112
    humanity through story, 13–16
    imagination through story, 183–187
    perspective through story, 161–165
    reflection through story, 139–143
Big Magic (Gilbert), 185
big-C level of creativity, 194
blind spots, 145
bottling, 93
brain as a storyteller, 13–14
British Columbia, 63–65, 74
Brown, B., 28, 129

C

Cambridge English Dictionary, 110
caring people, 153
Cavilla, D., 140–141
Chappuis, J., 3, 47
character, 23–24
ChatGPT, 25, 86, 216, 219. *See also* artificial
    intelligence
Classroom Assessment for Student Learning
    (Chappuis & Stiggins), 47
co-construction, 118–119, 225–226
cognition, defined, 90–91
cognitive complexity, 217–218
coherentism, 110
collaboration, 11, 60, 65–66
    assessment 45
    categories of, 116
    critical thinking about, 146–147
    defined, 115–116
    grading, 117 119
    grouping students randomly, 112
    problem solving, 117
    versus cooperation, 59
collaborative problem solving, 117
collaborative recalibration, 119–122
comedy, 23
communication, 11, 65–66, 68–69
    of assessment results, 36, 45–46
    story circle, 211, 230–232
communicators, 153, 223–225
competency connections, 8
    assessment through story, 45–47,
      76–77
    the big idea, 57–60
    collaboration defined, 115–116
    collaborative problem solving, 117
    communication, 68–69, 223–225
    conflict through story, 90–93
    craft through story, 219–225
    creativity and, 191–194
    critical competencies through story, 65–70
    critical thinking and, 146–147
    cultural connection, 60–65
    digital citizenship, 67–68
    discussion questions for learning teams,
      78–79
feedback and, 221–223
    grading collaboration, 117–119
    harmony through story, 115–119
    humanity through story, 19–22
    imagination through story, 191–194
    interpersonal and intrapersonal skills,
      92–93, 168–170
    leaders as storytellers, 20–21

    navigating the verification and
      implementation phases, 219–221
    perspective through story, 168–171
    reflection through story, 146–147
    self-regulation, 69–70, 90–92
    social competence, 92
    stories as a catalyst for change, 21–22
    the story of how I'm learning, 72–76
    the story of what I'm learning, 70–72
    storytelling as critical competency, 20
"Conflict by Numbers" (EL Education), 99
conflict exit tickets, 83, 99–101
conflict resolution, 7, 83, 99, 101–102
conflict, 23–24
    as productive struggle, 84–85
    the big idea, 83–88
    committing to work through, 118
    competency connection, 90–93
    cultural connection, 88–90
    discussion questions for learning teams,
      107–108
    external conflict, 85–86
    internal conflict, 86–88
    the story of how I'm learning, 99–106
    the story of what I'm learning, 93–99
    through story, 83
ConnectEd, 148
consensus building, 118
constructed response, 48
constructing beautiful work, 214–215
construction phase, 230
constructionism, 214–215
content as a means to an end, 59
contributing, 118
course letters, 95–98
COVID-19 pandemic, 4, 21
craft, 81
    the big idea, 211–215
    competency connection, 219–225
    constructing beautiful work, 214–215
    cultivating, 212–213
    cultural connection, 215–219
    defined, 211–212
    discussion questions for learning teams,
      238–239
    the story of how I'm learning, 230–236
    the story of what I'm learning, 225–230
    through story, 211, 236–237
creating meaning within, 190–191
creative fuel playlists, 183, 198, 203–206
creative thinking, 11, 45, 65–66
creativity
    as a process, 191–192
    as the new normal, 192–193

in the classroom context, 193–194
misconceptions about, 221
stages of, 191–192, 219–221
creator economy, 20
creator's commentary, 211, 234–236
credibility, assessing of a source, 45–46
critical competencies, 7, 11. *See also*
competency connection
are not silos, 70–71
assessment as, 45–46
storytelling as, 20
critical thinking, 11, 59–60, 65–66
about the collective, 146–147
about the self, 146
assessment, 45
defined, 91
within the collective, 147
critiquing, 146, 152, 171
cultivating craft, 212–213
cultural appropriation, 211, 215–217
cultural archetypes, 41–43, 115, 173
cultural awareness, 170
cultural bias, 3
cultural connections, 8, 16
assessment through story, 40–44
British Columbia, 63–65
conflict through story, 88–90
craft through story, 215–219
critical competencies through story, 60–65
cultural archetypes, 41–43, 115
culture as shared story, 16–17
ensuring cognitive complexity, 217–218
the entomophagy divide, 165–166
evolution of storytelling technology,
18–19
harmony through story, 112–115
honoring cultural authenticity, 216–217
imagination through story, 188–191
India, 62–63
inviting imperfection in school culture,
89–90
Kenya, 61
Kishōtenketsu, 112–114
perspective through story, 165–168
reflection through story, 143–145
surface, shallow, and deep culture, 114
values create storytelling styles, 17–18
cultural differences, 17–18
cultural harmony through inclusion, 111–112
culturally expansive assessment, 242, 244
Culturally Responsive Teaching and the Brain
(Hammond), 41
culture as shared story, 16–17
curiosity displaying

call for curiosity, 167–168
displaying, 118
curricular recalibration, 122–124
curricular standards, 242
cycle of recalibration, 113

D
Dator's Law, 196
David, S., 93
deep culture, 114
default mode network, 194
defaulting to being the knower, advice giver, or
problem solver, 27–28
defense of learning, 6, 147–149
Dembo, M., 106
dependent patterns, 104
describing a move and its impact, 227
design thinking, 47
developing communicators, 223–225
developing finesse, 221
dialogue, defined, 26
digital citizenship, 11, 45, 66–68
digital platforms, 175
digital storytelling, 228–230
digital wellness, 68
Dimich, N., 36
Dindo, M., 165
discussion questions for learning teams, 9
assessment through story, 55–56
conflict through story, 107–108
craft through story, 238–239
critical competencies through story, 78–79
harmony through story, 137–138
humanity through story, 33–34
imagination through story, 208–209
perspective through story, 181–182
reflection through story, 158–159
disimagination machines, 189
displaying curiosity, 118
diversity, learning about, 112
domain-generality, 50
domain-specificity, 50
dramatic questions, 229
Dweck, C., 91

E
ecology and the environment, 63
economy, 230
ecosystems documentary project, 124–128
efficacy, defined, 91
Einstein, A., 184
emotional agility, 93
emotional content, 229–230
emotional reactions, 2
emotions, 132–133

empathy, 14–16, 169, 224
end-beginning-middle structure, 139, 144, 150–151, 157
ensuring cognitive complexity, 217–218
entomophagy, 165–166
epistles, 26, 27
Erkens, C., 36, 65–67, 191
ethic of excellence, 215
evaluating, 45, 60
Evergreen School District (San Jose, Calif.), 153
evidence is evidence, 40–41
evolution of storytelling technology, 18–19
exemplars, 199
expansion, mental disharmony as, 109–111
explanatory style
    defined, 30
    explaining your quirks, 116
    self-awareness of, 30–32
external conflict, 85–86
extractive model, 174
extrospection illusion, 161, 164–165

F
fabula, 8, 157
    asynchronous relationship with *suyzhet*, 150
    defined, 144
fact versus fiction, 184
feedback, 24–25, 97–98
    effective, 37
    four levels, 222
    high-quality, 215
    improved processes, 211, 232–234
    providing, 221–223
    sample checklist, 235
    to demonstrate understanding, 169
Fey, C., 219
finding a natural fit, 71–72
First Build approach (GE Appliances), 193
First Nationals Education Steering Committee, 64–65, 153–154
first-lap reading, 227
fixed mindset, 30–31
flexible learning environments, 64
Flowers, B., 241
Fogarty, R., 192–193
forethought phase, 161, 176–177
formalism, defined, 143–144
formative assessment, 196–197
formative feedback loop, 98
foundationalism, 110
"four C" model, 193
four Cs, 65

Frayer Model map, 232–233
freedom, imagination as, 186–187
Freytag's Pyramid, 88–90

G
gaman, 122
Ganz, M., 245
Gendler, T., 194
gift of your voice, 230
Gilbert, E., 185
Giroux, H., 187, 189
goals, 131, 133
    achievement, 106
    focusing on, 118
    imagining, 183, 198–200
    performance, 106
    setting, 201
Gonzalez, J., 217–218
Google Sites, 135
grading collaboration, 117–119
grading conferences, 149–152
graphic organizers, 52, 242
    for resolving conflict and seeking help, 105
    Kishōtenketsu, 121, 123, 125–126
Great Acceleration, 58
Greenberg, S., 154
Greene, M., 199
grind culture, 145–146
grouping students randomly, 112
groupthink, 167
Growing Tomorrow's Citizens in Today's Classroom (Erkens et al.), 65–67, 191
growth mindset, 30–31, 91

H
habits, 53
hamartia, 88
Hammond, Z., 41–42
Harari, Y., 192
harmony
    the big idea, 109–112
    competency connection, 115–119
    cultural connection, 112–115
cultural harmony through inclusion, 111–112
    defined, 110
    discussion questions for learning teams, 137–138
    mental disharmony as expansion, 110–111
    the story of how I'm learning, 128–136
    the story of what I'm learning, 119–128
    through adaptation, 110
    through story, 109
Hawaiian hula, 215–217, 236
help seeking 102–106

Index

Hemingway, E., 26
higher-order thinking, 3
highlighting possibilities and pitfalls, 134
historical wrongs, 63
history, 122
honoring cultural authenticity, 216–217
hope
  defined, 91
  increasing, 206
humanity through story, 13
  the big idea, 13–16
  competency connection, 19–22
  cultural connection, 16–19
  discussion questions for learning teams,
    33–34
  the story of how I'm learning, 27–32
  the story of what I'm learning, 22–27
humanized course content, 48–49
hypotheses, 60

I

iceberg metaphor, 187
illusion of objectivity, 161–163
Imaginable (McGonigal), 196
imagination, 81
  as freedom, 186–187
  as inspiration, 185
  the big idea, 183–187
  competency connection, 191–194
  cultural connection, 188–191
  defined, 194
  discussion questions for learning teams,
    208–209
imagination and knowledge, 184
  instructive versus transcendent, 186
  knowledge and, 184
  the story of how I'm learning, 198–206
  the story of what I'm learning, 194–198
  through story, 183, 206–207
implicit bias, 44
including criteria, 227
inclusion, 111–112
incorporating oral and visual expressions of
    learning, 218–219
independence, 134
India, 62–63
individual versus collective cultures, 41,
    114–115
individualism, 223–225
informational literacy, 140
innovation, 192–193
inquirers, 153
instant clarity, 189–190
instructional agility, 11

integration of learning, 140
intentionality, 142–143
intercultural competence, 28
interdisciplinary projects, 98–99
internal conflict, 86–88
International Astronomical Union (IAU), 162
International Baccalaureate (IB) program, 153
interpersonal social competence
  defined, 92
skills, 92–93, 169–170
intersubjectivity, 15
intrapersonal social competence
  defined, 93
  skills, 92–93, 168–169
introspection illusion, 53, 141, 161, 163–164
inviting imperfection in school culture, 83,
    89–90

J

Jaworski, J., 241
Joon-ho, B., 113
Journal of Neuroscience, 21

K

Kamohoali, K., 217
Karabenick, S., 106
Kenya, 61
Kishōtenketsu, 8, 81, 109, 112–114, 122, 136
  four acts, 112–113
  four-part design, 127–128
  graphic organizers, 121, 123, 125–126
knowing what to do when you don't know, 118
Knowledge Society, The (TKS), 117
knowledge, skills, and attitudes, 59–60
knowledgeable people, 153

L

Lane, S., 43
leaders as storytellers, 20–21
learned helplessness, 30
learning journey map, 139, 152, 154–155
learning pit story, the, 83, 99, 102–106
learning
  as a social process, 140
  conflict through story, 83–108
  continuous, active, and experiential, 140
  craft through story, 211–238
  harmony through story, 109–138
  imagination through story, 183–209
  integration of, 140
  personalized, 63–64
  perspective through story, 161–182
  reflection through story, 139–159
styles, awareness of, 51–53
  through story, 81
Liao, S., 194

Lien, H., 114
like-attracts-like cognitive bias, 111
list storytelling, 26
listening, 118
    active, 52, 169
    attentive, 224
    coupling with visual curation, 206
    empathetic, 224–225
    ignoring, 224
    individualism and, 223–225
    pretending, 224
    proficiency scale, 224–225
    selective, 224
literacy, assessing, 37
little-c level of creativity, 194
looking back to look forward, 11
    critical competencies through story, 57–79
    essential assessment through story, 35–56
    humanity through story, 13–34
loose prompts, 142

M

macrolevel assessment, 242–2432
"Man in a Hole" (Vonnegut), 102–103
math wars, 168
McGonigal, J., 196
meaning
creating within, 190–191
making meaning of story without structure, 188–189
means and *ends* switching places, 58–59
mediation, 85
meditation, 51
mental disharmony as expansion, 110–111
mental fire drills, 188
mentor texts, 200, 226–228
mentors, 87–88
Merriam-Webster online dictionary, 212
metacognition, 50
    defined, 91
    domain-generality and domain-specificity, 50
    essential skill, 140–141
metaphors, 197–198
method versus format, 48
micro fiction, defined, 26
microlevel assessment, 242–243
Millennium Ecosystem Assessment (WHO), 124
mini-c level of creativity, 193
mirror neurons, 15
Mitsuhashi, J., 165
mnemonic aids, 52
modeling using the moves, 227

modern insistence on instant clarity, 189–190
Moore, D., 212
Moore's Law, 58
motivational self-talk, 176
moving toward refinement and finesse, 213–214
multiple perspectives, 170–171
music, resources for, 230

N

naming the move, 227
narrative takeover, 28
narrative tap-outs, 28
navigating blind spots, 145
navigating the verification and implementation phases, 219–221
Neurath, O., 110
Newkirk, T., 13, 174
ninety-day letter, 18, 183, 198, 200–203
non-negotiable prompts, 135

O

objectivity, illusion of, 162–163
observable versus nonobservable facets of identity, 187
observing, 118
Olivadese, M., 165
oneiric style, 188–189
one-on-one conferences, 205–206
open-ended questions, 86, 107
open-mindedness, 153, 169
oral expressions of learning, 218–219
oral format, 25, 27
oral tradition, 28–30, 41–42
Organisation for Economic Co-operation and Development (OECD), 69
other people, 132–133
otherizing, 54
overcoming the monster stories, 24

P

pacing, 230
Papert, S., 214
Parasite (Joon-ho), 113
peacemaking, 85
percentage-based grades, 162–163
performance assessments, 43–44, 48
performance goals, 106
performance phase, 161, 176–178
personal awareness, 64
personal feedback, 222
personalized learning, 63–64
perspective, 81
    the big idea, 161–165
    choosing, 172
    competency connection, 168–171

cultural connection, 165–168
defined, 151
discussion questions for learning teams, 181–182
multiple perspectives, 170–171
sharing, 174–175
the story of how I'm learning, 175–179
the story of what I'm learning, 171–175
taking, 173–174
telling, 171–173
through story, 161–171, 179–180
Peter, B., 192–193
physical education, 124
physical environment, 131, 133
planning ahead, 52
plot, 23–24
"plussing" practice, 193, 221
point of view (POV), 26, 229
positive psychology, 130
possibilities outside the actual, 195
the potential for empathy, 14–16
practicing digital storytelling, 228–230
predictable routines, 200
predicting, 60, 146
Presence (Stenge et al.), 241
principled people, 153
probing questions, 87–88
problem solving, collaborative, 117
pro-c level of creativity, 194
process feedback, 222
productive struggle, 81, 84–85
professional judgment, 212
profile of a learner, 6, 139, 152–154
prompts
intentionality, 142–143
loose, 142–143
ninety-day letter, 201–202
non-negotiable, 135
story, 53, 97, 102
student choice, 135
tight, 142–143
Pronin, E., 163
providing effective feedback, 221–223
public narrative, 21–22
purpose, 11
of assessment, 36, 46
purposeful goal setting, 176

Q

quest stories, 23
questions. *See also* discussion questions for
learning teams
about craft, 235–236
asking questions to direct close reading, 227

creative fuel playlist, 204
encouraging, 152
examining perspective, 169
navigating the verification and
implementation phases, 220
open-ended, 86, 107
performance phase, 177–178
probing, 87–88
to open a story circle, 231
Quinn, D., 44
quirks, explaining your, 116

R

rags to riches stories, 23
Rashomon effect, 166–168
real-time reflections, 139, 152, 155–156
rebirth stories, 24
recalibration, 109
collaborative, 119–122
curricular, 122–124
the truth, 171
reconciliation, 109
refinement and finesse, 213–214
reflection, 51, 81
the big idea, 139–143
competency connection, 146–147
cultural connection, 143–145
discussion questions for learning teams, 158–159
in real time, 155–156
is challenging, 141–142
is necessary, 140–141
requires specificity, 142–143
the story of how I'm learning, 152–156
the story of what I'm learning, 147–152
through story, 139, 157
reflective people, 153
regulation checklists, 52
reordering the story, 143–145
respect, 169
Rising Strong (Brown), 129
risk-takers, 153
rubrics, 43–44
rumbles, 129

S

Safir, S., 14–15
sailboard metaphor, 109–110, 130–134, 136
samples, 199
Sawyer, R., 221
scaffolding, 24, 94
Scharmer, C., 241
school culture, 215
science, 122–124
second-lap reading, 227

second-person storytelling, 26, 27
seeing your tragic flaw, 83, 88
selected response, 48
self-assessment, 54
self-awareness, 169–170
    how a student's style impacts mindset and
        behavior, 31
    of explanatory style, 30–32, 1334
self-questioning, 51
self-reflection phase, 161, 176, 178–179
self-regulated feedback, 222
self-regulated learning strategies, 200, 201
self-regulation, 90–92, 169
    defined, 66, 69–70, 90
    the learning pit story, 102
    of learning, 11, 38–40, 45
    symbiotic relationship with assessment,
        36, 53–54
    three-step models, 38–39
Senge, P., 241
setting, 23–24
shallow culture, 114
simulation theory, 15
skill of learning, 90–92
social competence, 11, 67, 92
social media, 16–17, 167, 241
society polarization, 5
soft skills, 92
solipsism, 15
soundtracks, 230
sourcing, 118
specificity, 142–143
starting before we are ready, 245
stereotypes, 19, 44
Stiggins, R., 3, 47
stories as a catalyst for change, 21–22
stormy first draft (SFD), 109, 128–130, 136
story, five essential elements of, 23–24
story circles, 28–30
    communication, 211, 230–232
    conflict resolution, 83, 99, 101–102
    prompts, 29–30
the story of how I'm learning, 9
    assessment through story, 49–53
    conflict through story, 99–106
    craft through story, 230–236
    critical competencies through story, 72–76
    harmony through story, 128–136
    humanity through story, 27–32
    imagination through story, 198–206
    metacognition, 50
    perspective through story, 175–179
    reflection through story, 152–156
story of now, 21–22

story of self, 21
story of us, 21–22
the story of what I'm learning, 8
    assessment through story, 47–49
    conflict through story, 93–99
    craft through story, 225–230
    critical competencies through story, 70–72
    harmony through story, 119–128
    humanity through story, 22–27
    imagination through story, 194–198
    perspective through story, 165–168,
        171–175
    reflection through story, 147–152
story prompts, 53, 97, 102
story stewardship, 27–28
storytelling
    as critical competency, 20
    cultural differences, 17–18
    digital, 228–230
    humanity through, 13–34
    is innately human, 7
    micro moments and macro moments,
        22, 32
    outcomes, 243
    self-sabotage, 1–2
    to elicit evidence of learning, 7
    via cultural archetypes, 42
strengths, 132–133
awareness of 51
    focusing on, 118
structure and predictability, 72–75
end-beginning-middle structure, 139, 144,
        150–151, 157
    making meaning of story without
        structure, 188–189
    single-point rubrics for creative thinking,
        72–73
struggle statements, 93–95
student agency, 69–70
student autonomy, 134
student choice prompts, 135
student efficacy, 8
student investment, 11, 36
    assessment, 46–47, 53
student ownership, 200
student voice, 3
summative assessments, rejection of, 215
surface culture, 114
synthesizing, 45, 60, 118, 146, 171
systemic racism, 4–5
syuzhet, 8, 157
    asynchronous relationship with
        fabula, 150
    defined, 144

Index

T

taking a perspective, 173–174
target-match method, 3, 47–48
tarot cards, 190–191
task conflict, 84
task feedback, 222
teachers as role models, 75–76
Teaching Children Thinking (Papert), 214
technology
    assessment and, 40–41
    democratizes storytelling, 16
    digital platforms, 175
    disruption, 192–193
    evolution of storytelling, 18–19
    the telephone, 111
telling a perspective, 171–173
theme, 23–24
theory of mind, 15
thinkers, 153
thinking aloud, 52
thinking backward, 139
thinking nontraditionally, 175
three assessment methods, 48
three assessment questions (Sadler), 38–39
three cautions to consider in assessment, 52–53
three phases of self-regulations (Zimmerman),
        38–39
tight prompts, 142–143
time for change, 4–6
times outside the present, 195–197
traditional assessment, 2–3, 4–6
tragedy, 23
transfer, 197
Truth with a capital T, 170
21 Lessons for the 21st Century (Harari), 192
21st century competencies, 5
    British Columbia, 63–65, 74
    India, 62–63
    Kenya, 61

U

uncontrollable circumstances, 132–133
understanding and articulating your unique
        perspective, 116
unproductive struggle, 84
unusual point of view (POV), 26
user manual, 109, 134–136
using mentor texts, 226–228

V

values, 131, 133
    create storytelling styles, 17–18
    defined, 17
Vardabasso, N., 2, 14–15, 218, 233
verification stage of creativity, 192

    defined, 220
    navigating, 219–221
Vidor, K., 103
vignette, defined, 25–26
visual curation coupled with listening, 206
visual expressions of learning, 218–219
visual format, 25
vocabulary, 227
voyage and return stories, 23–24
vulnerability
    embracing, 83, 89
    learned skills, 15

W

we are the system, 241
weaknesses, 51, 131–133
Wheatley, M., 84–85
White, K., 199
White, V., 86
Wiliam, D., 43
will of learning, 91–92
willingness to be disturbed, 85
willingness to talk about struggles, 89
The Wizard of Oz (Fleming & Vidor), 103
World Health Organization (WHO), 124
writing down your thinking, 52
writing phase, 229–230
written format, 25, 27
written tradition, 41–42

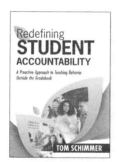

Redefining Student Accountability
Tom Schimmer
The time has come to separate academic achievement from student behavior. Learn a three-tiered framework, as well as trauma-informed, restorative, and schoolwide approaches to teaching responsibility, nurturing student accountability, and addressing student behavior to support student ownership in the classroom.
BKG002

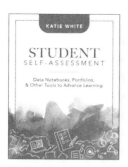

Student Self-Assessment
Katie White
Increase the achievement of every learner with *Student Self-Assessment*. In this practical guide, author Katie White outlines how to plan and implement various self-assessment strategies to ensure student growth at all grade levels. She covers every stage of the process—from setup to goal setting to celebrating.
BKG038

Concise Answers to Frequently Asked Questions About Assessment and Grading
Nicole Dimich, Cassandra Erkens, Jadi Miller, Tom Schimmer, and Katie White
Get answers to your most challenging questions about implementing effective assessment and grading practices. Each chapter contains answers to dozens of questions covering key tenets of assessment and grading, making it easy to build strong practices quickly.
BKG051

Assessment as a Catalyst for Learning
Garnet Hillman and Mandy Stalets
Embrace a fresh mindset where the assessment process is a gift to students and propels meaningful learning for all. With this resource as your guide, you'll learn how to work individually or collaboratively to intentionally identify and unwrap priority standards, develop learning progressions, design assessments, and plan daily instruction.
BKG007

Solution Tree | Press

Visit SolutionTree.com or call 800.733.6786 to order.

We don't just help schools make a change, we help them *be* the change

REAL IMPACT. RELEVANT SOLUTIONS. RESULTS-DRIVEN APPROACH.

From funding to faculty retention, the evolving demands schools face can be overwhelming. That's where we come in. With professional development rooted in decades of research and delivered by many of the educators who literally wrote the book on it, we empower schools to achieve meaningful change with real, sustainable results.

The change starts here. We can make it happen together.

See how we can get real results for your school or district.

Scan the code or visit:

SolutionTree.com/Results-Driven

 Solution Tree

LET'S SEE WHAT **WE CAN** DO TOGETHER